George K.

Healing the Body Politic

Bahá'í Perspectives on Peace and Conflict Resolution

Other titles in the *George Ronald Bahá'í Studies Series*

Sacred Acts, Sacred Space, Sacred Time (Walbridge, 1996)
Unveiling the Hidden Words (Malouf, 1997)
Spirit and Revelation (ed. Momen, 1997)
Making the Crooked Straight (ed. Schaefer, Towfigh, Gollmer, 2000)
Bahá'í Lore (Piff, 2000)
Re-Thinking, Re-Visioning, Re-Placing (Cope, 2001)
Processes of the Lesser Peace (eds. Bahador and Ghanea, 2002)

Other titles edited by Charles Lerche in the *New World Order Series* (Bahá'í Publishing Trust, United Kingdom)

Emergence: Dimensions of a New World Order (1991)
Towards the Most Great Justice: Elements of Justice in the New World Order (1996)

George Ronald Bahá'í Studies Series

Healing the Body Politic

Bahá'í Perspectives on Peace and Conflict Resolution

edited by
Charles O. Lerche

GR

George Ronald
Oxford

George Ronald, *Publisher*
Oxford

A catalogue record for this book is available from the British Library

ISBN 0–85398–476–X

The publisher is grateful to the *International Journal of Peace Studies* for permission to reprint part of Dr Hossain Danesh's article 'Has Conflict Resolution Grown Up?: Towards a Developmental Model of Conflict Resolution and Decision Making', published in its Spring/Summer 2002 edition, vol. 7, no. 1.

Contents

Introduction

Unto the emblems of justice and exponents of equity it is indubitably clear and evident that this Wronged One, strengthened by the transcendent power of the Kingdom, is seeking to efface from among the peoples and kindreds of the earth every evidence of disorder, discord, dissension, differences or divisions; and it is for no other reason but this great, this momentous object that He hath again and again been cast into prison and many a day and a night hath been subjected to chains and fetters. Bahá'u'lláh[1]

That all nations should become one in faith and all men as brothers; that the bonds of affection and unity between the sons of men should be strengthened; that diversity of religion should cease, and differences of race be annulled – what harm is there in this? . . . Yet so it shall be; these fruitless strifes, these ruinous wars shall pass away, and the 'Most Great Peace' shall come . . . These strifes and this bloodshed and discord must cease, and all men be as one kindred and one family . . . Let not a man glory in this, that he loves his country; let him rather glory in this, that he loves his kind . . .

Bahá'u'lláh[2]

Everyone is aware of and concerned about conflict. We hear constantly of terrorism, ethnic disturbances, trade wars, political partisanship, labour disputes and family breakdown. From the interpersonal to the international levels, mutually incompatible ends and ineffective and destructive means characterize human relations. As the new millennium opens, the agenda of complex and contentious issues continues to lengthen, overwhelming in many cases existing social institutions. However, the very fact that many conflicts have proved resistant to traditional methods of containment and resolution has stimulated the search for more innovative, more comprehensive and more fully human approaches to dealing with conflict. This volume of the *George Ronald Bahá'í Studies Series* reflects an effort by a group of scholars from around the world, united by common convictions, to contribute to this search.

Peace and Conflict Resolution Studies (PCR) are rooted in the ancient quest for peace. However PCR emerged as a distinct field in the wake of World War Two. Though the field resists precise definition it can be described as:

> . . . an interdisciplinary academic field that analyses the causes of war, violence, and systemic oppression, and explores processes by which conflict and change can be managed so as to maximize justice while minimizing violence. It encompasses the study of economic, political, and social systems at the local, national, and global levels, and ideology, culture, and technology as they relate to conflict and change.[3]

Thus PCR studies the whole continuum of violent versus peaceful activity (from the individual to the group to the globe as a whole) and encompasses the past, the present and the future. Finally, PCR is both value explicit and policy-oriented: it favours peace (non-violent conflict resolution) over violence and war, includes social and economic justice and environmental balance as desired social goals and does not hesitate to promote these preferred values.

Conflict,[4] the primary focus of PCR, occurs at all levels of society and is neither the opposite of order nor the same as chaos. There is debate as to whether conflict itself is deviant or pathological *per se*: some argue it may be a healthy reaction to injustice or an indicator of strains in the social system that demand attention. In many instances, the origins of conflict are in the non-fulfilment or blockage of fundamental human needs. Conventionally, conflict may be defined as 'the opposition and divergence of interests, ideas, beliefs and/or values between two or more parties with the potential of manifesting negative, destructive behaviour'. Struggle over identity, values, power and scarce resources are at the heart of all social conflict. In summary, the literature suggests that a conflict may be said to be *resolved* when all the parties involved freely accept a solution that has some of the following characteristics:

- The solution satisfies the interests and needs underlying the conflict
- The solution does not sacrifice any party's important values
- The parties will not wish to repudiate the solution even if they are in a position to do so later
- The solution meets the standards of justice and fairness
- The solution is sufficiently advantageous to all parties that it becomes self-supporting or self-enforcing

A conflict resolution approach to disputes focuses, therefore, on the process of moving conflict presentation and escalation to resolution and on the processes or behaviour used by third parties to assist in this transformation. Basically, there are two approaches to conflict resolution: 1) the pro-active prevention, or 'provention'[5] of conflict, in its early stages, that has not yet manifested itself in a negative, destructive manner and/or 2) the management (i.e. peacemaking and peacekeeping) and resolution (i.e. peace building and implementation of the first process) of conflict that has outwardly expressed itself in a negative, destructive manner.

Over the last two decades several important contributions to conflict analysis and resolution have been made. Among the major areas of concern have been: the causes of war at the international level; the origins of civil strife within states; the dynamics of negotiation; the impact of human needs and 'structural violence' on conflict processes; the complementary role of unofficial, informal interaction among members of adversary groups in conflict resolution (now widely known as 'track two' diplomacy); the emergence of an international mediation capability to assist conflict parties in 'getting to the table' to deal with their problems; and, most recently, the development of the 'problem-solving workshop' to promote reconciliation and personal transformation among adversaries. Additionally, the field of 'alternative dispute resolution' (ADR) has evolved as an alternative to adversarial/legal approaches to disputes, which are expensive, time-consuming and, seemingly at times, never-ending.

This brief survey demonstrates that current efforts at conflict resolution and peacemaking constitute a step forward in addressing many of the dilemmas that afflict world society. However, work in this area has just begun. Consider, for instance, this assessment by the Carnegie Commission on Preventing Violent Conflict:

> In our world of unprecedented levels of destructive weaponry and increased geographic and social proximity, competition between groups has become extremely dangerous. In the century to come, human survival may well depend on our ability to learn a new form of adaptation, one in which intergroup competition is largely replaced by mutual understanding and human cooperation. Curiously, a vital part of human experience – learning to live together – has been badly neglected throughout the world.[6]

The Bahá'í Faith, whose literature is the primary source of insight and inspiration for the articles in this volume, has from its inception in the 19th century been directly concerned with these issues. Its teachings emphasize the need for a new world order based on unity and justice, supported by a personal vision that is global in scope. It declares that humanity has come of age, that world civilization is dawning and that we are currently in an age of transition when old values and institutions are crumbling and new ones are struggling to be born. It is against the background of these dramatic and far-reaching historical processes that the problem of burgeoning social conflict should be seen. Also, as argued in several of the essays, widespread conflict should be understood as fundamentally a spiritual problem: as one indicator of a need for spiritual renewal, for a regeneration of humanity's connection with its Creator and a rededication to His purpose for the human race. Thus, the subject of this book is both timely and compelling.

The Essays

Peace and Conflict Resolution Studies is too broad a field to be covered fully in one volume of essays. However, the articles that follow do deal with a number of different though related areas of contemporary concern. Each one also points a direction for further inquiry and provides an example, both in substance and method, for future efforts to understand and explore solutions to social problems from that 'world-embracing' perspective characteristic of the Revelation of Bahá'u'lláh.

In 'Perspectives on Peace Building: An Overview and Some Insights from the Bahá'í Writings', Cheshmak Farhoumand-Sims and Charles O. Lerche provide a summary of contemporary conflict resolution theory and specifically that dimension of it which deals with peace building and reconciliation. They explain how these concepts figure in the Bahá'í teachings and what new insights a Bahá'í perspective provides on the broader problem of rebuilding war-torn societies.

Hossain B. Danesh and Roshan Danesh's paper, 'Bahá'í Consultation: Worldview or Process?', explores the relationship between Bahá'í consultation and popular methods of conflict resolution. A developmental model of conflict resolution known as 'Conflict-free Conflict Resolution' is presented as a framework for analysing consultation in light of the contemporary conflict resolution movement.

Principles from the Bahá'í teachings relating generally to government and politics are explored in Graham Hassall's 'Contemporary Governance and Conflict Resolution: A Bahá'í Reading'. Dr Hassall considers several of the shortcomings commonly associated with the institutions and processes of modern political life, both at the conceptual and practical levels, and assesses them in light of a Bahá'í vision of world order.

In 'Beyond Linguistic Conflict: Spiritual Foundations of a Universal Auxiliary Language', Jeffrey Gruber identifies spiritual principles relevant to the selection, adoption and development of a universal auxiliary language. He argues that these principles are essential both to resolving contemporary linguistic conflicts and to fostering peace, unity and that degree of collaboration necessary for the establishment and continuing development of a new world order.

The problem of human rights, and specifically minority rights, is the main concern of Nazila Ghanea's 'International Human Rights: A Common Code in Resolving Intra-state and Inter-state Conflicts?' She shows that the rights of minorities, as witnessed by contemporary events, remain one of the most significant causes of conflict. She draws on passages from the Bahá'í writings and from recent Bahá'í International Community statements to develop a paradigm of peaceful and just conflict resolution for minority issues.

'Reforming the United Nations: Issues and Options' by Olivia Lopez critically assesses the need for reform of the world organization. Her assessment highlights the extent to which the UN, while a great step forward at the time of its creation, is not capable of responding effectively to the lengthening list of demands being made upon it.

Ariane Sabet in 'Bahá'u'lláh's Concept of Collective Security in Historical and Theoretical Perspective' looks specifically at collective security as a method of preventing and resolving international conflicts. She compares the model of collective security found in the Bahá'í writings to earlier, contemporary and more modern approaches to the subject.

'Conflict and Harmony Among Nations: The Case of International Trade' by Shahruz Mohtadi is an analysis of the current world trading system as both a cause of conflict and a force for integration among countries and peoples. He demonstrates that the application of those spiritual principles central to a Bahá'í conception of world order could enhance the integrative effects of trade and contribute significantly to world peace and stability.

This volume's final paper, 'Globalization and Its Conflicts' by Charles O. Lerche, looks at the negative consequences of increasing interdependence in all areas of life. The paper traces the new 'fault lines' that have appeared as a global economy has emerged and peoples and cultures have been thrown together with unprecedented frequency and intensity. The Bahá'í Faith is presented as an important source of positive and creative globalist vision for anyone seeking solutions for the planetary problems of the 21st century.

The Contributors

Dr H.B. Danesh is a founder and director of the International Education for Peace Institute, Switzerland. He is an author, international lecturer and consultant, with more than 30 years of academic and clinical experience as a psychiatrist. Dr Danesh's areas of research and expertise include the causes and prevention of violence, marriage and family therapy, death and dying, consultation and conflict resolution, ethics, spiritual psychology, and world order and peace studies. Dr Danesh is the author and creator of the internationally acclaimed Education for Peace Program, first piloted in Bosnia and Herzegovina. In addition to several scientific papers in his areas of speciality, Dr Danesh is author of *The Violence-Free Society: A Gift for Our Children* (1979), *Unity: The Creative Foundation of Peace* (1986), *The Psychology of Spirituality* (1994) and *The Violence-Free Family: The Building Block of a Peaceful Civilization* (1995).

Roshan Danesh is a lawyer and conflict resolution specialist specializing in Conflict-free Conflict Resolution (CFCR), the relationships between religion, law and conflict, and comparative constitutional law. He recently completed his Doctor of Juridical Science (SJD) at Harvard Law School and also holds degrees from McGill University and the University of Victoria. He served as the Chair of the Department of Conflict Resolution at LIU from 1999 to 2001 and taught for the Akitsiraq Law Programme, Nunavut, in 2002.

Cheshmak Farhoumand-Sims has a BA in Peace and Conflict Studies, an MSc in Conflict Analysis and Resolution and is currently working on her PhD in International Relations at York University in Toronto. Her dissertation focuses on women's human rights and peace building in Afghanistan. She is a lecturer at the Centre for the Study of Peace and Conflict at the University of Toronto, the Department of Political Science, University of Western Ontario and the Centre for Peace and Conflict Studies at McMaster University. She also regularly provides human rights, conflict resolution and peace education training.

Nazila Ghanea is the Course Convenor for the MA in Understanding and Securing Human Rights at the University of London, Institute of Commonwealth Studies and a lecturer in international law and human rights. A graduate of the University of Leeds and Keele University, her publications and doctoral research have addressed religious minorities in Iran, Islam and human rights, religious liberty and the UN human rights machinery. Her recent publications include the monograph *Human Rights, the UN and the Bahá'ís in Iran* (Oxford: George Ronald and The Hague: Kluwer Law, 2002); the edited collection (with Babak Bahador) *Processes of the Lesser Peace* (Oxford: George Ronald, 2002); the edited collection *The Challenge of Religious Discrimination at the Dawn of the New Millennium* (Leiden: Martinus Nijhoff, 2003) and a forthcoming journal article with *Human Rights Quarterly*, 'Convergences and disparities between the human rights of religious minorities and of women in the Middle East'.

Jeffrey Gruber attended Massachusetts Institute of Technology, receiving an SB in Life Sciences in 1962 and a PhD in Linguistics in 1965. His work in linguistic theory led to the publication in 1976 of a book, *Lexical Structures in Syntax and Semantics*, that became widely known. He has done linguistic field research in Botswana and has held appointments as Professor and Head of Department of Linguistics in two Nigerian universities. From 1992 to the present he has been engaged in linguistic research, until 1997 based at the University of Quebec at Montreal and presently as visitor at the Massachusetts Institute of Technology, developing theoretical work that has appeared in various journals and books, most notably his contribution in *A Handbook of Contemporary Syntactic Theory* (Blackwell, 2000).

Previous work on the universal auxiliary language appeared in *World Order* magazine in 1967, 'On the Selection of an International Auxiliary Language'; in 1998, 'Language as Justice in the New World Order'; and in 2002, 'The movement toward a world language: Indigenization and Universalization'. Jeffrey Gruber also paints in oils and acrylics <www.JeffreyGruber.com> in a visionary style, often meditating on Bahá'í writings.

Graham Hassall is Professor of Governance at the University of the South Pacific. He obtained his PhD from the Australian National University in 1990. He has previously taught at the University of Melbourne, the University of Papua New Guinea and Landegg International University. He is interested in contemporary issues in governance and conflict, both within the Bahá'í community and in contemporary political societies. His book *Asia Pacific Constitutional Systems* was published by Cambridge University Press in 2002.

Charles O. Lerche teaches in two graduate programmes in International Relations in the United States (Norwich University and Troy State University). His research interests include international relations, the politics of the Global South, world order and peace and conflict studies. He has co-authored *Concepts of International Politics in Global Perspective*, edited two volumes of essays on world order studies and published articles in several academic journals, including *The Journal of African Studies*, *The Journal of Asian and African Studies*, *Peace and Conflict Studies*, *The International Journal of Peace Studies* and *International Politics*.

Olivia Lopez is a graduate of the London School of Economics and Georgetown University, where she studied International Politics, spending an academic year at the Sorbonne in Paris. Her personal and academic experience encompasses a broad spectrum of interests which include literature, languages and the performing arts. Having resided in Russia, Chile, Europe, the United States and Japan, Olivia's research interests relate to particular aspects of comparative political sociology and philosophy.

Shahruz Mohtadi is an Associate Professor of Economics and Director of the Graduate Program at Suffolk University in Boston and an Adjunct Faculty member at Babson College. His areas of teaching and research are international trade, international monetary economics, money and banking and the political economy of international economic relations. He has published articles in professional journals dealing with exchange rates and the reform of the international monetary systems and papers in edited volumes dealing with economic justice and conflict resolution. His current research is in the area of the ethical, moral and religious perspectives on the global economy.

Ariane Sabet received an MA in International Relations from the University of Geneva and the Graduate Institute of International Studies, with additional study at Columbia and Harvard Universities, and a PhD in Political Science from the University of St Gallen, Switzerland. She worked as a researcher in the Department of Political Science at the University of St Gallen, for the Commission of Swiss Diplomatic Documents in Berne, co-editing *Documents Diplomatiques Suisses,* and as a lecturer at the KS Graduate Business School, St Gallen. She was appointed Head of the Department of Global Governance at Landegg in 2002. Her research interests include political ethics, security and peace studies.

Bibliography

Bahá'u'lláh. *Tablets of Bahá'u'lláh.* Wilmette, IL: Bahá'í Publishing Trust, 1988.

Burton, J. W. *Conflict: Resolution and Provention.* New York: St Martin's Press, 1990.

Carnegie Commission on Preventing Deadly Conflict. *Preventing Deadly Conflict: Final Report.* New York: Carnegie Publications.

Esslemont, J. E. *Bahá'u'lláh and the New Era.* London: Bahá'í Publishing Trust, 1974.

Harris, Ian M. 'Peace Studies in the United States at the University and College Levels', in Ake Bjerstedt (ed.). *Peace, Environment and*

Education. Malmö, Sweden: Peace Education Commission, International Peace Research Association, Spring 1992.

Notes

1. Bahá'u'lláh, *Tablets*, p. 260.
2. Quoted in Esslemont, *Bahá'u'lláh and the New Era*, p. 37.
3. D. C. Thomas quoted in Harris, 'Peace Studies in the United States at the University and College Levels', p. 5.
4. The author is grateful to Dwight Bashir and Shahram Ahmedzadegan for bringing this material about conflict resolution to his attention.
5. The term 'provention' has been introduced to signify taking steps to remove sources of conflict and more positively to promote conditions in which collaborative and valued relationships control behaviours. See Burton, *Conflict*.
6. Carnegie Commission on Preventing Deadly Conflict. *Preventing Deadly Conflict*, ch. 7, 'Toward a Culture of Prevention'.

I

Perspectives on Peace Building

An Overview and Some Insights from the Bahá'í Writings

Cheshmak A. Farhoumand-Sims and Charles O. Lerche

Rest thou assured that in this era of the spirit,
the Kingdom of Peace will raise up its tabernacle
on the summits of the world . . .
'Abdu'l-Bahá[1]

People cannot live apart and in agony forever.
Johan Galtung[2]

Almost a decade and a half have passed since the extraordinary events that prompted the end of the cold war and ushered in a new world order distinguished by significant changes in the international community. For many people, these unexpected events renewed hope for a more peaceful world. However, these hopes have not been realized. The years since the end of the cold war have been characterized by a plethora of violent conflicts sparked by festering ethnic and tribal tensions and resulting in hundreds of thousands of civilian deaths and casualties and millions of displaced individuals. Traditional methods of diplomacy have proved ineffective in preventing and resolving these hostilities. And while peace initiatives on behalf of the international community have inspired efforts towards peace, these efforts have more often than not failed to provide long-term solutions to the problems underlying them. As Lederach suggests,

> . . . contemporary conflicts necessitate peace-building approaches that respond to the realities of their very nature . . . and thus demand innovation, and the development of ideas and practices that go beyond substantive interests and issues, probing into the realm of the subjective, emotionally deep-rooted, and generationally accumulated fear and hatred.[3]

Clearly, new mechanisms are needed to address and eliminate the root causes of violent conflict and allow for renewed relationships based on trust, justice and peace.

The field of peace and conflict studies developed as a critical response to the traditional realist approach to international relations theory and practice focusing on power and interest as the motivator of state action. The premise of this new discipline was to apply a multi-disciplinary, holistic approach to the understanding of peace and security issues. Such an approach would address not only structural factors such as the role of the state and its institutions in international conflict but also consider other important elements – such as psychology, history, anthropology and others that contribute to the development, escalation and resolution of war and other types of conflicts. In recent years, this more comprehensive and sensitive approach to the study of international relations has attracted increased attention in academic circles for its ability to explain and address the new trends in international relations. As a result, peace and conflict literature has grown not only in volume but in scope and depth. Some of the most important and interesting literature focuses on the theory and practice of 'reconciliation'. The concept of reconciliation is deeply rooted in the literature of the world's great religions and usually coupled with the notion of forgiveness. The academic literature on reconciliation applies this spiritual principle to international relations to demonstrate that without reconciliation, true and lasting peace is not possible.

In this paper the concept of peace building is explained and a selection of the conceptual and practical problems associated with it discussed. It is argued that effective peace building should be pro-active in nature and should be informed, both in theory and practice, by both a model of civilization and a conception of human nature that provides for the fulfilment of emotional, psychological and spiritual as well as physical needs. The Bahá'í teachings are discussed as one important source of insight into and guidance for finding solutions to the contemporary problems of peace building and specifically in regard to the challenging question of reconciliation.

Peace Building: The Concept and Its Context

Peace and conflict literature offers various definitions of conflict, each highlighting a different element of conflict. Some definitions focus on the psychological factors such as perception, while others emphasize the outcome of conflict as defined by behaviour. However, most definitions will identify the components of a conflict as issues, parties, perceptions and behaviours. The simplest definition describes conflict as a situation in which two or more human beings pursue incompatible goals. A more detailed definition is offered by Sandole who refers to conflict as an 'aggressive manifest conflict process' in which

> . . . at least two actors, or their representatives, try to pursue their perceptions of mutually incompatible goals by physically damaging or destroying the property and high value symbols of one another, and/or psychologically or physically injuring, destroying or otherwise forcibly eliminating one another.[4]

These and other definitions of conflict emphasize the role of perception and behaviours in the dynamics of conflict.

There are a variety of theories that seek to analyse and explain conflict processes and their potentially violent manifestations. These theories have developed across various disciplines and highlight the multi-faceted nature of conflict, offering insight into the fundamental psychological, structural and cultural sources of conflict and proposing ways in which they can be addressed, thereby contributing to the resolution of the conflict. Each conflict situation is unique. However, they share certain elements that allow for the application of theories of conflict and conflict resolution. These theories can have preventive value by noting the presence of particular conditions and elements that may lead to the outburst of potential conflict. Furthermore, in post-conflict situations, they can offer insights into the factors that led to conflict that need to be addressed in order for resolution to occur.

Conflict resolution is one of the ways in which conflict termination is achieved. It is an attempt to deal with the underlying issues that separate parties and provoke violence. It implies the development of a new and acceptable relationship between former adversaries.[5] Conflict resolution is a deep-rooted therapy which offers parties a long-term solution to the issues that separate them. Mitchell characterizes conflict resolution as a solution which is complete, acceptable, self-supporting, satisfactory, uncompromising, innovative and uncoerced.[6]

At first glance, 'conflict', 'war' and 'peace' might seem straightforward: peace is what we want and war and conflict are what we want to avoid or stop. Regrettably, however, several decades of analysis have shown that they are anything but straightforward and, more importantly perhaps, they are used by different people for different purposes. Consider the following passage from Johan Galtung, a leading peace theorist and practitioner:

> The word peace is used both by the naïve who confuse absence of direct violence with peace and do not understand that the work to make and build peace is now just about to start, and by the less naïve who know this and do not want that work to get started. Thus the word 'peace' becomes a very effective peace-blocker.[7]

This helps us to better understand peace building, since it is now clearly not enough just to stop a given conflict. If 'conflict resolution' only involves what Galtung calls the 'one mistake which is no longer pardonable: the single-shot "table at the top", the high table, for the "leaders"',[8] then there is every likelihood that the same conflict, one very much like it or some other forms of violence, will occur. There are a number of reasons for this. First, mainstream approaches like this have had little or no impact on societies characterized by cycles of violence. Lumsden has observed, for instance, that 'the worst atrocities in Bosnia in the 1990s were exactly in the areas most affected by the World War II massacres' and that 'Two of the Bosnian Serb generals involved were themselves child survivors of World War II massacres in which their whole villages and families had been wiped out'.[9]

Second, what are known as intractable conflicts all have two dimensions: the 'real' conflict over tangible stakes and the 'meta-conflict', a 'conflict that comes out of, or after, the root conflict, the over layer'.[10] The meta-conflict has its own dynamics and can become deeply embedded in a group's culture, perpetrating militarism, the 'glory' of killing the 'other' and the legitimacy of violence as a means for dealing with conflict. Mainstream, elite to elite, negotiation approaches to conflict resolution may address the stakes but do nothing about the meta-conflict. They also tend to only address overt, direct violence but largely ignore those social inequalities, now frequently called 'structural' violence, from which overt violence springs. Thus the conventional approach promotes *negative* peace (stop the fighting and its direct consequences) but has been slow to acknowledge the need to promote *positive* peace (creating social structures that are creative and nonviolent).

Third, violent conflict breeds other forms of social violence and these are not addressed through conventional approaches. Simpson describes, in this regard, 'the prevalence of well-organized criminal activity, very often associated with high levels of violence, in societies going through major transition' and says that in South Africa 'there has been a tendency to blur the dividing lines between political and criminal violence'.[11] In effect, the violence associated with a specific conflict system may only be displaced rather than eliminated. Furthermore, in most societies experiencing violent social conflict, women have suffered most. However, conventional conflict resolution has been very slow to acknowledge and address this fact, thus leaving several of the root causes of social violence and victimization unacknowledged.

These factors, and many more, have led to a widespread dissatisfaction with traditional power and interest approaches to conflict which have not dealt effectively with the new realities of the post-cold war era and re-thinking of what is necessary to truly move a given society away from cycles of violent conflict towards a better condition called, conventionally, peace. This requires, as indicated above, moving beyond conflict resolution to *peace building*, understood to include: 1) efforts to increase cooperation among former parties to conflict through fostering positive attitudes and allaying distrust through reconciliation initiatives; and 2) building or strengthening the institutions and processes through which the former enemies interact. What is perceived as most innovative here is including the *subjective*: true peace building involves both outward and inward reconstruction and renewal. Galtung writes, for instance, that what he calls the 'three Rs' – resolution, reconstruction and reconciliation – are all essential to stabilization and progress in post-conflict situations and omitting any one will undermine efforts to achieve the other two.[12] In a similar vein, Øberg describes post-conflict 'reconstruction' as involving the reconstruction of '1) human beings, soul and bodies, 2) social structure, 3) culture, 4) environment, and 5) a peace culture of reconciliation, repentance, forgiveness, respect . . . and simultaneously moving toward a vision of peaceful coexistence'.[13] Clements suggests that the keys to 'development of more stable peaceful relationships between people lie in a deepening awareness of the key psychological, social and political processes which generate trusting communities within which individuals can realize their deepest sense of self'.[14] These are important insights: it is increasingly obvious that the real long run goal in most countries which have experienced prolonged violent conflict is to build a society which is truly participatory and fulfilling for all groups. Otherwise, fissures giving rise to alienation and deep-seated conflict will emerge in the new order as they did in the old, eventually necessitating further efforts at conflict resolution – efforts which would certainly be greeted with more cynicism than enthusiasm.

The writers mentioned so far all emphasize the need to 'transform' or 'transcend' the social context which produced violent conflict. This is an important point, since a more conservative approach would see peace building initiatives as intended to repair and restore a previously existing status quo. Consider in this regard, the following statement by Fisher about reconciliation as a peace building initiative: 'Reconciliation involves *re-establishing* harmony and cooperation between antagonists who have inflicted harm in either a one-sided or reciprocal manner.'[15] Though plausible at first glance, this formulation does not reflect conditions in any society currently attempting post-conflict peace building. In how many cases – whether South Africa, Chile, Guatemala or Argentina – is it realistic to suggest that 'harmony and cooperation' ever truly existed among the groups concerned and that what is needed is to *re*create it? This is not just a semantic point since it raises the issue of how much reform is necessary in a transitional society. If there was a past when the state and the social arrangements it ordered were 'all right' until communal conflict (somehow) upset them, then peace building may indeed be about re-establishing something that existed previously. If, however, it is acknowledged that the type of intergroup relations envisioned as the goal of peace building has *never* existed in a given society, then peace building is equivalent to not just conflict transformation but, in fact, social, political and economic transformation on an unprecedented scale.

To pursue the point further, following Keohane's well-known analysis, *harmony* signifies a condition in which there is an inherent compatibility of groups' needs and interests requiring no adjustment or coordination among them and is not very relevant to peace building – at least in its earlier stages. Whereas, *cooperation*, defined by Keohane as a process which requires 'actions of separate individuals or organizations – which are not in pre-existent harmony – be brought into conformity with one another through a process of negotiation'[16] is a more reasonable goal for post-conflict transitions. At the best of times, most contemporary societies are characterized by multiple *cleavages*, defined by Lane as 'a division on the basis of some criteria of individuals, groups or organizations among whom conflict may arise'.[17] Race, caste, ideology or religion are important bases for social cleavage, and groups divided along these lines compete, one way or another, for resources. How this core political process is handled is fundamental to the quality of social life in any society:

> Whatever the size of the amount of resources to be allocated, the distribution of utilities in societies raises vital moral questions about equity, equality and justice. Such matters activate interests, which define groups and motivate individuals or collectivities to move against each other.[18]

Thus some level of conflict among groups' interests is really politics as usual but when it takes an overtly violent form it indicates the political system can no longer contain this inevitable competition for material and non-material stakes. We should not, therefore, expect relations between any politically significant cleavage groups to be definitively transformed into a state of harmony. Rather, the groups involved need to acquire what Galtung calls 'the capacity to handle conflict creatively and non-violently'.[19] This is, in fact, what Galtung defines as peace. It is also close to Keohane's notion of cooperation and represents a goal for peace building compatible with the politics of a pluralistic society.

Simply put, the kind of deeply-rooted, and often prolonged, violent conflicts that seem so common today are indicative of tragically dysfunctional institutions and cultures, both within the societies where they occur and at the regional and global levels where the means to prevent or diffuse them either do not exist or are not used in time – or with enough commitment. This is a crucial point, since, as Clark has argued, only when social values and institutions are required to give account of themselves, when their fundamental assumptions are thoroughly questioned, is there any hope of creating a political culture which fulfils rather than frustrates human needs.[20] The Carnegie Commission on Preventing Deadly Conflict goes even further with this theme, suggesting that finding and implementing such a new model of pro-active peace building represents a critical evolutionary threshold for our species:

> In our world of unprecedented levels of destructive weaponry and increased geographic and social proximity, competition between groups has become extremely dangerous. In the century to come, human survival may well depend on our ability to learn a new form of adaptation, one in which intergroup competition is largely replaced by mutual understanding and human cooperation. Curiously, a vital part of human experience – learning to live together – has been badly neglected throughout the world.[21]

Posing the problem of peace in this way has, in fact, led to some very creative work on the fundamental question of human needs and John Burton's approach, in particular, provides a useful benchmark against which plans for peace building can be measured. Burton starts from the premise 'that there are limits to the extent to which the human person, acting separately or within a wider ethnic or national community, can be socialized or manipulated' and 'that there are human development needs that must be satisfied and catered for by institutions, if these institutions are to be stable, and if societies are to be significantly free of conflict'.[22] While acknowledging that this is still a new and contested area of research, Burton presents a plausible list of needs. First, human beings require a sense of *security* and of *identity*. Second, since people have a generic drive to learn, they require a 'consistent response from the environment, without which learning is impossible'. Third, from their social context people require both *recognition* and *valued relationships*, or *bonding*. Finally, and perhaps most importantly, individuals require (some) *control* over their environments in order to insure that their needs are fulfilled.[23] This approach has important implications for social institutions. If, on balance, needs are being met within an institution, the institution receives support and is consolidated and perpetuated. If, however, needs are not met, the institution loses support and legitimacy and confronts increasing opposition. In the latter case, authorities tend to react with repression and coercion but if an institution is 'de-legitimated' for enough people, conflict cannot be resolved this way. Rather, the institutional structures have to evolve, sooner or later, to more fully accommodate the needs of the people they affect.

To Burton, legitimacy is a dynamic, rather than a static, condition which 'stresses the reciprocal nature of relations with authorities, the support given because of the services they render, and respect for legal norms when these are legitimized norms'.[24] He contrasts this with a static notion of *legality* which 'has associated with it . . . loyalty to a sovereign or formal leader right or wrong, elitism, the common good and the national interest as interpreted by elites'.[25] From this perspective, peace building would not be complete until the social and political order was popularly perceived as legitimate: until there was a general correspondence between the outer structure and process of institutions and inner needs of people. Though such legitimacy is currently considered to inhere in liberal democratic institutions, Burton has recently argued that conventional representative democracy is only effective in a society with 'relative ethnic homogeneity, classlessness and equality'; and this model alone is not able to guarantee institutional legitimacy 'in a society that contains major income differences, and in which minorities are unrepresented but must observe the norms of a majority'[26] – conditions characteristic of many transitional countries. In summary, Burton's work indicates that social reform which goes further than conventional western models of governance to meet human needs is necessary if the deep-seated conflicts of war-torn societies are ever to be transformed into peaceful and creative relations among the groups concerned.

There is, in fact, a widening consensus among human needs theorists, human rights advocates, international organizations concerned with development and peace researchers about the requisite qualities of such a new social order. Consider the United Nations Development Programme's (UNDP) 'five aspects of sustainable development':[27]

> *Empowerment*: The expansion of men and women's capabilities and choices increases their ability to exercise those choices free of hunger, want and deprivation. It also increases their opportunity to participate in, or endorse, decision-making affecting their lives.
>
> *Cooperation*: With a sense of belonging important for personal

fulfilment, well-being and a sense of purpose and meaning, human development is concerned with the ways in which people work together and interact.

Equity: The expansion of capabilities and opportunities means more than income – it also means equity, such as an educational system to which everybody should have access.

Sustainability: The needs of this generation must be met without compromising the right of future generations to be free of poverty and deprivation and to exercise their basic capabilities.

Security: Particularly the security of livelihood. People need to be freed from threats, such as disease or repression and from sudden harmful disruption in their lives.[28]

These characteristics closely resemble Burton's needs. In a similar vein, the UNDP goes on to outline the elements of a governance system which would promote sustainable development, suggesting that sustainable development can only be realized through political institutions which function according to similar principles.[29]

The convergence evident here parallels recent advances in the theory and practice of human rights. The cold war division between the capitalist camp's emphasis on civil and political rights and the socialist/Third World preference for social, economic and cultural rights has now been recognized as unhelpful and unacceptable. All five major areas of human rights have been acknowledged by the international community (however grudgingly in some cases) as an indivisible whole. However, as indicated above, rights and the improved quality of individual and collective life they represent cannot simply be legislated into existence, an understanding reflected in the emphasis by many activists and organizations on a 'cultural' approach to the problem. Consider the following sample of such initiatives:

- The United Nations Educational, Cultural and Scientific Organization (UNESCO) and others are promoting a 'Culture of Peace' defined as 'a set of values, attitudes and behaviours which reflect and inspire participatory democracy, social interaction, sharing, tolerance, gender equity, solidarity, human rights, the rejection of violence and conflict prevention through dialogue'.[30]

- A group of Nobel Laureates is promoting a 'Culture of Non-Violence', which would encompass love, justice, harmony; reject oppression; and embrace social diversity, nonviolence and personal transformation.[31]

- A former United Nations Secretary General promoted the creation of a 'universal culture of human rights'.[32]

- The Institute for Democracy and Electoral Assistance promotes a 'Culture of Democracy', which highlights nonviolent conflict resolution, open decision-making, the role of civil society, transparency and participation.[33]

Finally, the World Commission on Culture and Development draws some far-reaching conclusions from this burgeoning consensus. They believe it provides strong evidence that there is a discernible 'global civic culture' from which important elements of global ethics can be derived.[34] These 'global ethics' are:

> . . . general principles denoting the fundamental moral concern that in a social and political community ought to find adequate reflection . . . the basic moral concern – *to protect the integrity and to respect the vulnerability of human beings* – is universal in its appeal and can be shown to be part of all major traditions of moral teaching . . .[35]

In their own formulation, they put forth five principles that should form the core of global ethics:

- Human rights and responsibilities
- Democracy and the development of civil society
- Protection of minorities
- Peaceful conflict resolution
- Equity within and between generations

These principles, like those cited earlier, reject elitism and give priority to participation in all institutions and social programmes. Furthermore, they argue that states, though historically the worst violators of these principles, are now under increasing pressure from global civil society and international organizations to conform to standards of global ethics both domestically and in international relations. Only then can the dominant pattern of conflict and power politics be replaced by something else.[36]

Sometimes, however, conflicts are so deep-rooted that they are seemingly intractable. These conflicts are usually those which have a long history of animosity involving perceived incompatibilities of values and needs. In these situations, conflict resolution often does not offer a long-term solution but a temporary one. Many theorists suggest that these intractable conflicts are more amenable to resolution if efforts at what they call 'reconciliation' are incorporated into the conflict resolution process.

Reconciliation is a familiar word and concept to most people. For many, it has a religious connotation relating to Christian theology; for others it relates to legal debates pertaining to victim–offender reconciliation. The word itself comes from *conciliatus* which means to come together, to assemble and to walk together. Webster's Dictionary defines 'reconciliation' as an effort 'to make friendly again after an estrangement; to settle (a quarrel); to harmonize; to make compatible; to show compatibility of, by argument or in practice'.

In conflict resolution terms, reconciliation is a more well-developed concept, referring to the human dimension of peace building and peacemaking which focuses on relational transformation. Reconciliation is the act by which people who have been separated by conflict come together to restore a broken relationship and begin anew. It is a process of healing and restoring social relations among people, or peoples, recently involved in deep-seated conflict.

At its deepest level, reconciliation is the process that initiates psychological and spiritual transformation, allowing parties to recognize the humanity in the other, overcome past hurts and rebuild a relationship based on new understandings of oneself and the other. Reconciliation goes beyond traditional attempts to address relational and substantive issues, goals and interests. It is a transformative process which links the past to the present and the future. By addressing painful past events, reconciliation allows parties to mourn and heal. This is shown to change the relationship between adversaries and allow for a cooperative visioning and action towards a different future. Thus reconciliation represents a *shift* from an antagonistic to an accommodating relationship. Reconciliation, therefore, is an effort to provide parties with an opportunity to try and come to terms with a history of pain and transform the relational, structural and moral foundations that created and supported the systems that allowed for such a history.

Although reconciliation is an important concept with significant implications for international relations and conflict resolution, it has received relatively little attention in the literature of these fields. Rather, most work on the subject comes from psychological and sociological literature concerned with interpersonal reconciliation and aspects of this research have been applied to politics in the international realm.

A conceptual and empirical framework for reconciliation is offered by a number of respected academics, including Jean-Paul Lederach and Joseph Montville. The central components of these frameworks are the same, focusing on the concepts of truth, mercy, justice and peace. As Lederach explains:

> *Truth* is longing for acknowledgement of wrong and the validation of painful losses and experiences, but it is coupled with *Mercy* which articulates the need for acceptance, letting go and a new start. *Justice* represents the search for individual and group rights, restructuring and restitution, but is linked with *Peace* which underscores the need for interdependence, well-being and security.[37]

Montville is convinced that 'healing and reconciliation in violent ethnic and religious conflicts depend on a process of transactional contrition and forgiveness between aggressors and victims which is indispensable to the establishment of a new relationship based on mutual acceptance and reasonable trust'.[38] He suggests that this process depends on the ability of parties to jointly analyse the history of their conflict, recognize injustices and resulting historic wounds, and accept moral responsibility where it is due.[39] Engaging in this process allows parties to understand and appreciate the depth of the pain, fear and hatred that a history of unatoned violence creates and reflect on how their experiences have contributed to the formation of a victimhood identity[40] that exacerbates the psychological response to the conflict.

In his work, Montville highlights the importance of psychological healing by mourning individuals and collective psychological traumas resulting from traumatic historical memories and experiences. Mourning is a 'naturally occurring, predictable and unfolding process whereby individuals react to real or threatened loss or change in their life'. Volkan explains that,

> When changes are not mourned, the inability to mourn and its psychological effects carry on from one generation to the next, like other grievances; children and grandchildren want to recreate aspects of what is lost, and of events pertaining to the loss in order to complete the mourning. This is potentially harmful, stimulating an unconscious thrust toward political action, a kind of persistent group compulsion toward mastering shared hurts.[41]

'Acknowledgment', 'contrition' and 'forgiveness' represent the three conceptual elements of Joseph Montville's reconciliation framework. He suggests that each of these has significant psychological and emotional impact on both the victim and victimizer. When followed in a linear fashion, they allow for members of two communities to move towards reconciliation and a renewed relationship.

Montville proposes that the critical first step towards reconciliation is acknowledgment. 'Acknowledgment' can be defined as 'the act of explicitly describing and accepting moral responsibility for the violent acts or events which caused traumatic losses to the victims'.[42] By having the offensive act explicitly described and acknowledged, the victim is assured that none of the violations are overlooked.[43] This acknowledgment serves to address the victim's fear that the oppressor will strike again. Acknowledgment therefore provides psychological relief and release to the victim. This relief begins the internal healing process which is then extended in the next two stages of contrition and forgiveness, the 'ultimate aim of the healing process' upon which the psychological foundations for genuine reconciliation are built.[44] In international relations, acknowledgment should be offered by the aggressor group/nation or its successors, even if the current leaders are not directly responsible for the unjust actions of their predecessors. Even years, or generations, later acknowledgment offers assurance that the oppressor is attentive and regretful of past injustices. Acknowledgment requires courage and integrity. It is a symbolic gesture which has practical consequences of promoting empathy and trust.

Similar pleas for acknowledgement have been expressed in other workshops involving communities in conflict. Acknowledgment and recognition of injuries and losses experienced are therefore a fundamental aspect of reconciliation. Failure to provide these promote anger and frustration and contribute to the escalation of the conflict.

The second component of reconciliation is contrition. Contrition signifies an expression of regret for past feelings or actions and involves an explicit request for forgiveness. Contrition, or the offer of an apology, is an important component in psychological healing in reconciliation. This may be due to several factors. An act of contrition symbolizes the taking of responsibility for one's actions and therefore implies that it will not be repeated. Also, apologies have a humanizing and civilizing potential by demonstrating that the offender is only human and liable to make mistakes. Finally, such an admission warrants courage and elicits gratitude.

One of the most difficult tasks in the psychodynamic approach to international conflict resolution is to 'persuade victimizers or their descendants to offer a meaningful, unambiguous and unqualified apology to the victimized group or nation'.[45] Such action, however, requires political will and moral leadership. One example of such courage was provided by Franz Vranitsky, Chancellor of Austria, who delivered an unexpected and powerful speech on live television in 1991. In his presentation, Vranitsky publicly accepted Austria's complicity in the Holocaust.[46] He cited new information arising from research conducted by an Austrian historian of archived documents which unequivocally confirmed the complicity of numerous Austrian officials, businesses, NGOs and individuals in the Nazi persecution of the Jewish community in the late 1930s. While there are no empirical studies to analyse and discuss the impact and consequence of this admission, it can be said that Vranitsky's morally responsible and dignified act did indeed serve to end an illusion and forced people to re-examine their nation's past history. In effect, Vranitsky ended decades of denial on the part of Austria's government and population regarding Austria's complicity in the horrors of the Holocaust. By devaluing the perception that Austria was one of Hitler's victims, Vranitsky took away a powerful platform from Austria's neo-Nazi and fascist groups.

The reconciliation process is incomplete unless accompanied by forgiveness. Ideally, expressions of acknowledgment and regret on the part of the oppressor encourage acts of mercy and forgiveness on the part of the victimized. Forgiveness is central and customarily included in reconciliation literature. This may be related to the fact that both these notions find their theoretical roots in religious literature and are usually linked one to the other. According to Webster's Third Edition, forgiveness is 'to cease to feel resentment against on accord of wrong committed [sic], to give up claim to requital from or retribution upon an offender'. A more comprehensive definition is offered by North who suggests that forgiveness is,

> . . . the overcoming of negative affect and judgement toward the offender, not by denying ourselves the right to such affect and judgement, but by endeavouring to view the offender with compassion, benevolence and love while recognizing that he or she has abandoned the right to them.[47]

Forgiveness, therefore, is a voluntary act whereby an offended individual makes a decision about how to deal with an offence and an offender. Among these choices, he/she may decide to try to judge and measure the offence and decide to even things out by giving an equal amount of retribution to the offender; *or* choose to forgive and absolve the wrong committed by the other. Forgiveness is 'an important, and perhaps the core element in the therapeutic process' and 'a key part of the psychological healing process'.[48] It signals a change in cognition, perception and judgement and seems to induce healing from psychological injuries and wounds that result from a sense of being wronged. Forgiveness is facilitated by psychological transformation and involves a change of perceptions.[49]

For many who suffer pain at the hand of another, sometimes the only perceived choice is to focus on anger and hatred and respond with revenge. Lewes Smedes suggests that for some people, the only way to deal with unfair pain is to 'want the abuser to suffer what we suffered'.[50] If anger is not recognized and released, it can be misdirected onto others and result in new enemies and increased frustration. This notion is supported by studies that look at the long-term consequences of abuse on victims.[51] These studies suggest that victims of abuse are more likely to become abusive later in life. The same has been suggested about nations: victims of historical injustice are more likely to victimize others, whether or not the others were those who victimized them. Addressing the issues that perpetuate violence and revenge is one of the factors that can contribute to breaking this cycle of victimization.

Van der Merwe and Johnson posit that forgiveness is a requirement for a stable, just and peaceful society.[52] They argue that in many deep-rooted conflicts 'there is no possibility that the hurt of the past can be undone or the injuries inflicted can be truly compensated. For that reason, no reconciliation and healing can take place without forgiveness.'[53] Many people, however, confuse forgiving with forgetting. Forgiveness does not imply forgetting or condoning the behaviour of the offender. Rather, it implies that the victim absorb the full impact of the injustice while not losing sight of the perpetrator's humanity[54] and involves a choice to change one's perceptions and offer compassion. The result can be a very powerful transformation in both the victim and the victimizer. This transformation involves owning our pain and taking responsibility for our thoughts and beliefs by cutting through our psychological defences so that we can choose to change our perceptions.[55]

Forgiveness, however necessary and important to reconciliation, is not a sufficient component. While forgiveness provides psychological release from past pains, it does not give assurance that past injustices will not recur. Hence, the importance of linking forgiveness with justice as the foundation for peace and reconciliation. The coupling of forgiveness and justice is further discussed and incorporated in Lederach and Kriesberg's reconciliation framework. Lederach's framework is founded on three main premises. First, it places relationship as the source of conflict as well as its resolution. Second, to engage one another assumes an encounter which involves people in several different and highly interdependent streams of activity. Finally, reconciliation requires a paradigm shift, looking outside the mainstay of international political traditions, discourse and operational modalities to find a creative, innovative and durable solution.[56]

The Role of Religion

Attempts to promote peace cannot ignore religion. Religion is a potent force which influences perceptions and impacts behaviours among both individuals and collectives. It provides a lens through which one sees and interprets one's environment and rationalizes one's conduct. Religion is particularly relevant in conflict resolution and reconciliation when those in conflict profess religious convictions and use these to justify their actions. Furthermore, spiritual principles that transcend any particular culture, religion and nationality can have a transforming effect on individuals if they are effectively incorporated into conflict resolution and reconciliation processes. Introducing the authority of religion into the equation may influence the attitudes and decisions of parties to conflict.

In conflict, especially those conflicts involving deep-rooted hatred, parties often focus on the negative behaviour of the other and fail to consider the ways in which their own behaviour may have contributed to escalating the situation. Reminding people of religious and spiritual values may prompt them to reflect on their own convictions and to have the moral courage to look within and consider how their own attitudes and behaviours may be contributing to escalation. H. Assefa agrees with this notion:

> . . . there is no doubt that a peacemaking process which enables the parties to reflect on the spiritual implications of their behaviour, especially their hatred, contempt, callousness, or self-centredness, and their destructive actions in general, is likely to lead to a more conducive atmosphere for the quest of just and lasting solutions to their disputes. Bringing the spiritual dimension into the peacemaking process can give access to the more deep-seated, affective base of the parties' behaviour enabling them to examine critically their own attitudes and actions.[57]

Including religion and spirituality in reconciliation efforts, then, serves to shift the focus away from a rational, cognitive process that is concerned with cost/benefit calculations to include emotional and affective considerations.

Religion is a powerful force in human society and for many people plays an important function in their everyday life. Religion has a spiritual and a secular function. Spiritually, it provides a sense of sacred meaning and inner growth and development. Its binding function facilitates community relationships that foster a sense of belonging, which is regarded as an essential need for human development.[58] Despite doctrinal differences and social practices, the diverse religions of the world share a number of spiritual principles which can serve as the basis for dialogue and understanding in reconciliation. A study of religious scriptures illustrates that at the core of each faith there is a commitment to social order and peace. This is evident in the articulation of teachings such as:

> . . . compassion, love of strangers, the suppression of unbridled ego and acquisitiveness, commitment to laws governing property and the rights of the individual, unilateral gestures of forgiveness, humility, the acceptance of responsibility for past errors, the drive

for social justice, the capacity to change through repentance, and even the capacity to feel love for an enemy.[59]

The concept of reconciliation is deeply embedded in the literature of the world's religions and is discussed in terms of the responsibility of the offender to repent and the victim to forgive. This stems strongly from the notion that being forgiven by God requires that we offer the same to others. In fact, in many religions, forgiveness is a religious duty.[60] Therefore, introducing and incorporating spiritual principles into the reconciliation process can make a powerful impact on individual and conflict transformation.

In Christian biblical texts there are four dimensions to the concept of reconciliation.[61] The first is reconciliation with God which involves repentance and rectitude of action in order to create a harmonious relationship with the Creator. The second is reconciliation with the self, which refers to overcoming the guilty feelings after repentance and rectitude. The third dimension calls for reconciliation with one's neighbour and the human community at large. This is related to reconciliation with God in that 'the privilege of being forgiven and reconciled with God creates the obligation to forgive and be reconciled with others'.[62] The final form of reconciliation can be called reconciliation with nature whereby respect and love of God is extended to all His creation.

In Islam, Allah is a forgiving Creator who bestows forgiveness upon those who seek it. The Qur'án admonishes, 'the recompense for an injury is an injury equal thereto (in degree): but if a person forgives and makes reconciliation, his reward is due from God'.[63] Another sura advises believers to 'hold to forgiveness',[64] 'even when angry'.[65]

Elements of a New Paradigm

The discussion so far highlights the point that peace building is really more about changing attitudes and feelings than it is about finding acceptable ways to divide the material stakes of conflicts. In that sense it must be pro-active. To move from a world of confrontation to a world of cooperation, an approach to peace is required that would assist parties, in the words of Galtung, to transcend – literally to 'go beyond' – the limited perspective defined by their incompatible goals and past negative experience.[66] Furthermore, in our rapidly globalizing era, relevant models of peace building must envision humanity as a collective whole rather than contending parts, be based on global ethics as described above and more fully incorporate the inward, spiritual dimensions of human experience – that internal source of inspiration where we find the strength to confront the dark side of our own and others' character. Peace building means, therefore, building new societies which are both more integrated internally (both esoterically and exoterically) and more integrated among themselves; or, to put the matter more simply, to be sustainable, peace requires a new world order.

The Bahá'í Faith has much to contribute to meeting this world-embracing challenge. Its literature provides a valuable and timely application of the pacific principles found in all world religions to the problems and challenges of an emerging global civilization. A Bahá'í view of peace, whether at the individual, national or international level, is grounded in a conception of the spiritual reality of human nature and a conviction that the significance of this reality must be properly understood and integrated into any effective long-term approach to social change. The Bahá'í teachings explain that human nature has two aspects, the material and the spiritual. If material concerns dominate individual and collective consciousness, the result is selfishness, injustice and cruelty, all of which aggravate conflict; while humankind's spiritual nature is characterized by qualities such as love, mercy, kindness, generosity and reciprocity – qualities which are conducive to resolution and reconciliation among conflicting parties. To train human character in such wise that the latter dominates the former is one of the fundamental purposes of religion as portrayed in Bahá'í literature.

From this perspective, religion is seen as central to human life and history and as always having been a powerful force for personal transformation and social integration. In the west, for instance, Christianity was able to reconcile and unite Jews and Gentiles in a new community while Islam brought together diverse peoples in Arabia, South Asia, Africa and elsewhere.

Furthermore, most ethical and moral values originate, directly or indirectly, from religious traditions. In our era, a new infusion of this same transcendent integrating power is required to establish a basis for cooperation and, eventually, integration among the various elements of world society. Commenting on this need for spiritual renewal, Shoghi Effendi, Guardian of the Bahá'í Faith, wrote over 60 years ago that the contemporary world:

> . . . contracted and transformed into a single highly complex organism by the marvellous progress achieved in the realm of physical science, by the world-wide expansion of commerce and industry, and struggling, under the pressure of world economic forces, amidst the pitfalls of a materialistic civilization, stands in dire need of a restatement of the Truth underlying all the Revelations of the past in a language suited to its essential requirements.[67]

More recently, the Universal House of Justice explained that:

> No serious attempt to set human affairs aright, to achieve world peace, can ignore religion. Man's perception and practice of it are largely the stuff of history. An eminent historian described religion as a 'faculty of human nature'. That the perversion of this faculty has contributed to much of the confusion in society and the conflicts in and between individuals can hardly be denied. But neither can any fair-minded observer discount the preponderating influence exerted by religion on the vital expressions of civilization. Furthermore, its indispensability to social order has repeatedly been demonstrated by its direct effect on laws and morality.[68]

Writing of religion as a social force, Bahá'u'lláh said, 'Religion is the greatest of all means for the establishment of order in the world and for the peaceful contentment of all that dwell therein.'[69]

When 'as a result of human perversity' this 'greatest of all means' is neglected, 'a deplorable decline in the fortunes of humanity immediately sets in'.[70] This decline brings with it widespread moral decay and political and economic disintegration.

Elaborating on this theme, Shoghi Effendi described the world of the late 1930s as offering 'the sad and pitiful spectacle of a vast, an enfeebled, and moribund organism' which was 'being torn politically and strangulated economically by forces it has ceased to either control or comprehend'.[71] These passages, and many more in Bahá'í literature, indicate that increasing intractable and violent conflict is one aspect of a wider process of social disruption, a process which is itself a reflection and necessary consequence of the declining influence of spiritual values on human behaviour. By implication, only a renewed acceptance and dedication to such values, and their creative application to the multidimensional challenges of our time, can offer any prospect of reversing the decline.

In the Bahá'í Faith the 'light' of religion is specifically focused on unity and peace. Bahá'u'lláh Himself, the Prophet-Founder, referred to this theme many times. In the Kitáb-i-Aqdas, His book of laws, He declares categorically that 'Ye have been forbidden in the Book of God to engage in contention and conflict';[72] and in the Kitáb-i-'Ahd, His Will and Testament, He again affirms that 'Conflict and contention are categorically forbidden in His Book. This is a decree of God in this Most Great Revelation. It is divinely preserved from annulment and is invested by Him with the splendour of His confirmation.'[73] Elsewhere He states that 'Strife and contention befit the beasts of the wild'[74] but 'To act like the beasts of the field is unworthy of man.'[75] 'Abdu'l-Bahá, Bahá'u'lláh's eldest son and the authorized interpreter of His teachings, elaborated on these themes in some depth during His travels in North America in 1912 – a voyage He said was dedicated to 'the establishment of universal peace and the oneness of mankind'.[76] He frequently spoke about the connections between religion, unity and peace, and one can extract from His various talks a number of principles which convey the essence of a Bahá'í approach to peace and peace building.

Unity of religion

> The central purpose of the divine religions is the establishment of peace and unity among mankind . . . There is but one light of the

material sun, one ocean, one rain, one atmosphere. Similarly, in the spiritual world there is one divine reality forming the centre and altruistic basis for peace and reconciliation among various and conflicting nations and peoples.[77]

True religion fosters peace

. . . the divine teachings are intended to create a bond of unity in the human world and establish the foundations of love and fellowship among mankind. Divine religion is not a cause for discord and disagreement. If religion becomes the source of antagonism and strife, the absence of religion is to be preferred. Religion is meant to be the quickening life of the body politic; if it be the cause of death to humanity, its nonexistence would be a blessing and benefit to man.[78]

Human conflict is caused by selfishness and prejudice

Wolves, lions, tigers are ferocious because it is their natural and necessary means for obtaining food. Man has no need of such ferocity . . . it is evident that warfare, cruelty and bloodshed in the kingdom of man are caused by human greed, hatred and selfishness.[79]

Most of the wars have been caused by religious prejudice, fanaticism and sectarian hatred.[80]

The earth is one earth, and the same atmosphere surrounds it. No difference or preference has been made by God for its human inhabitants; but man has laid the foundation of prejudice, hatred and discord with his fellowman by considering nationalities separate in importance and races different in rights and privileges.[81]

Peace and unity bring healing to the 'body politic'

The body politic may be likened to the human organism. As long as the various members and parts of that organism are coordinated and cooperating in harmony, we have as a result the expression of life in its fullest degree. When these members lack coordination and harmony, we have the reverse, which in the human organism is disease, dissolution, death. Similarly, in the body politic of humanity dissension, discord and warfare are always destructive and inevitably fatal. All created beings are dependent upon peace and coordination, for every contingent and phenomenal being is a composition of distinct elements. As long as there is affinity and cohesion among these constituent elements, strength and life are manifest; but when dissension and repulsion arise among them, disintegration follows.[82]

Need for international arbitration and disarmament

Bahá'u'lláh declared the Most Great Peace and international arbitration. He voiced these principles in numerous Epistles which were circulated broadcast throughout the East. He wrote to all the kings and rulers, encouraging, advising and admonishing them in regard to the establishment of peace, making it evident by conclusive proofs that the happiness and glory of humanity can only be assured through disarmament and arbitration.[83]

In explicating these themes, Shoghi Effendi, the Guardian of the Faith, further emphasized the need for global institutions of sufficient scope and power to guarantee justice and order:

Some form of a world super-state must needs be evolved, in whose favour all the nations of the world will have willingly ceded every claim to make war, certain rights to impose taxation and all rights to maintain armaments, except for purposes of maintaining internal order within their respective dominions. Such a state will have to include within its orbit an international executive adequate to enforce supreme and unchallengeable authority on every recalcitrant member of the commonwealth; a world parliament whose members shall be elected by the people in their respective countries and whose election shall be confirmed by their respective governments; and a supreme

> tribunal whose judgement will have a binding effect even in such cases where the parties concerned did not voluntarily agree to submit their case to its consideration.[84]

The Bahá'í International Community (BIC) has in recent years applied these and other Bahá'í principles to the contemporary global *problematique*. It argues, in a vein similar to the peace theorists cited earlier, the need for a long-term pro-active approach to the problem of peace, rather than one which gives priority only to short-term problem-solving. Thus the only approach to conflict resolution that promises *lasting* results requires reconstructing our planet's collective life in accord with, and to promote the fulfilment of, the basic needs of all humanity. This process, which it describes as 'laying the groundwork for global civilization'

> . . . calls for the creation of laws and institutions that are universal in both character and authority. The effort can begin only when the concept of the oneness of humanity has been wholeheartedly embraced by those in whose hands the responsibility for decision making rests, and when the related principles are propagated through both educational systems and the media of mass communication. Once this threshold is crossed, a process will have been set in motion through which the peoples of the world can be drawn into the task of formulating common goals and committing themselves to their attainment. Only so fundamental a reorientation can protect them, too, from the age-old demons of ethnic and religious strife. *Only through the dawning consciousness that they constitute a single people will the inhabitants of the planet be enabled to turn away from the patterns of conflict that have dominated social organization in the past and begin to learn the ways of collaboration and conciliation.*[85]

Going further, the BIC analyses several dimensions of structural violence in contemporary society and points out directions for moderating or eliminating them. For instance, in discussing human rights – the deprivation of which is one of the most prominent causes of violent conflict – the BIC introduces the globalist principle of 'collective trusteeship' as a basis for analysing social obligation:

> Since the body of humankind is one and indivisible, each member of the race is born into the world as a trust of the whole. This trusteeship constitutes the moral foundation of most of the other rights – principally economic and social – which the instruments of the United Nations are attempting similarly to define.[86]

This trusteeship involves a number of obligations of society towards its members, among which are 'employment, mental and physical healthcare, social security, fair wages, rest and recreation'.[87] Then, in a passage bearing directly on issues underlying contemporary 'identity' conflicts, it explains that:

> The principle of collective trusteeship creates also the right of every person to expect that those cultural conditions essential to his or her identity enjoy the protection of national and international law. Much like the role played by the gene pool in the biological life of humankind and its environment, the immense wealth of cultural diversity achieved over thousands of years is vital to the social and economic development of a human race experiencing its collective coming of age. It represents a heritage that must be permitted to bear its fruit in a global civilization. On the one hand, cultural expressions need to be protected from suffocation by the materialistic influences currently holding sway. On the other, cultures must be enabled to interact with one another in ever-changing patterns of civilization, free of manipulation for partisan political ends.[88]

Furthermore, if taken seriously as a basis for new policies, principles such as these require a new paradigm which involves 'a fundamental rethinking of economic issues'.[89] In this regard the BIC declares that:

> The classical economic models of impersonal markets in which human beings act as autonomous makers of self-regarding choices will not serve the needs of a world motivated by ideals of unity and justice. Society will find itself increasingly challenged to develop new economic models shaped by insights that arise from a sympathetic understanding of shared experience, from viewing

human beings in relation to others, and from a recognition of the centrality to social well-being of the role of the family and the community.[90]

Reconciliation: A Bahá'í Framework

The Bahá'í writings are rich with guidance on various concepts and themes that are essential to reconciliation. Study of these writings provide insight into a Bahá'í framework for reconciliation. This framework confirms the centrality of unity, suggests that forgiveness and justice together are the twin pillars of reconciliation and encourages the use of the consultative process in the search for truth. Bahá'u'lláh, in one of His Tablets, writes, 'Say: no man can attain his true station except through his justice. No power can exist except through unity. No welfare and no well-being can be attained except through consultation.'[91] All this guidance provides the foundation for a Bahá'í approach to reconciliation.

Unity and the Nobility of the Human Spirit

For centuries, large segments of humanity have believed in the sinful nature of human beings. This opinion is rooted in the Judaeo-Christian notion of original sin and has implications for the development of concepts of self and other. Negative views of the human reality therefore strongly influence relationships in conflict.[92] Focusing on the imperfections of humanity facilitates negative feelings and attitudes and psychological processes such as enemy imaging. Highlighting and appreciating the potential for perfection in humanity shifts these attitudes to positive ones that focus on potentialities in other people and in one's relationship with them.

Danesh suggests that it is necessary to review the processes and events which frame this negative view of human nature[93] and cogently presents an alternate perspective:

> . . . the blows dealt to man's identity as a unique and noble being (by the Copernicans, Darwinians, and Freudian revolution) were

> accompanied by painful insights as to the tremendous destructive properties and potential of science and technology when used by man in a misguided manner, as demonstrated during the First and Second World Wars. An interesting aspect of all these observations is that they focus solely on the biological and psychosocial aspects of human reality, as well as on the physical habitat of man. They fail to see poetry in the universe, and they ignore love found in the lives of men and women, husbands and wives, parents and children, friends and countrymen, and God. They fail to see that the most exciting aspect of a human being is his humanity, rising like a phoenix out of the ashes of his animal dimension.[94]

This perspective acknowledges that humans are capable of violence but can also be gentle and loving beings, capable of charity and sympathy.

The Bahá'í Faith affirms the nobility of the human spirit and teaches that the reality of the human being is his soul, a reflection of God. This teaching of the nobility of humanity is eloquently articulated in the writings of Bahá'u'lláh. In the Hidden Words, He writes,

> O Son of Being! Thou art My lamp and My light is in thee. Get thou from it thy radiance and seek none other than Me. For I have created thee rich and have bountifully shed My favour upon thee.[95]

And again He writes,

> O Son of Spirit! I created thee rich, why dost thou bring thyself down to poverty? Noble I made thee, wherewith dost thou abase thyself? Out of the essence of knowledge I gave thee being, why seekest thou enlightenment from anyone beside Me? Out of the clay of love I moulded thee, how dost thou busy thyself with another? Turn thy sight unto thyself, that thou mayest find Me standing within thee, mighty, powerful and self-subsisting.[96]

In another Hidden Word, He writes:

> O Son of Spirit! Noble have I created thee, yet thou hast abased thyself. Rise then unto that for which thou wast created.[97]

These and other verses from the Bahá'í writings can serve as inspiration for a reconciliation framework that incorporates the principle of nobility.

Emphasizing the inherent goodness in all humans can have a significant impact on the breakdown of negative perceptions and attitudes. Adam Curle, a Quaker conflict resolution practitioner, agrees and argues that the religiously-based spiritual principle of 'God in everyone' facilitates the psychological process of changing perceptions, reducing fear and improving communication.[98] Curle and others who incorporate this principle into their reconciliation efforts have found that encouraging and enabling parties to recognize the potential for goodness in their adversary also promotes empathy and a willingness to consider working with the adversary towards reaching an agreement.

Related to the notion of the God (good) in all humans is the belief in many faiths that the 'divine spark' connects humanity. This principle is one of the pivotal teachings of the Bahá'í Revelation and is presented as both the purpose and the eventual result of it. Bahá'u'lláh articulates this principle in many of His writings, referring to humanity as the 'fruits of one tree, and the leaves of one branch'.[99] In the Hidden Words, Bahá'u'lláh also expresses the following:

> O Children of Men! Know ye not why We created you all from the same dust? That no one should exalt himself over the other. Ponder at all times in your hearts how ye were created. Since We have created you all from one same substance it is incumbent on you to be even as one soul, to walk with the same feet, eat with the same mouth and dwell in the same land, that from your inmost being, by your deeds and actions, the signs of oneness and the essence of detachment may be made manifest. Such is My counsel to you, O concourse of light! Heed ye this counsel that ye may obtain the fruit of holiness from the tree of wondrous glory.[100]

In these and other writings Bahá'u'lláh proclaims the oneness of humankind, stating that we are all children of the same God, created from the same 'dust'. Moreover, this spiritual truth implies that we are all one in essence and any kind of prejudice or hatred based on difference is not only unfounded but unacceptable in the sight of our Creator.

The Power of Prayer and Consultation

Prayer and meditation serve as essential tools for reconciliation. They allow for detachment from one's feelings and emotions and provide clear thought before action. Prayer puts the individual in touch with the source of her being and prepares one spiritually and mentally for the task of reconciliation by providing a link between the individual and the Source. Viewed from a spiritual perspective, those engaged in reconciliation processes are instruments of the divine purpose ('Blessed are the peacemakers') and their effectiveness can be enhanced through awareness of His desire and will – one of the main purposes of prayer and meditation in most religious traditions. In the Bahá'í Faith, the spiritual connection between prayer and listening is made explicit in the process of consultation. With its emphasis on a prayerful attitude and open and frank discussion, Bahá'í consultation provides a structural framework for dialogue and understanding.

According to the Bahá'í writings, the object of consultation is the investigation of truth. Bahá'u'lláh says,

> Consultation bestoweth greater awareness and transmuteth conjecture into certitude. It is a shining light which, in a dark world, leadeth the way and guideth. For everything there is and will continue to be a station of perfection and maturity. The maturity of the gift of understanding is made manifest through consultation.[101]

Elsewhere He says, 'The heaven of divine wisdom is illumined with the two luminaries of consultation and compassion. Take ye counsel together in all matters, inasmuch as consultation is the lamp of guidance which leadeth the way, and is the bestower of understanding.'[102] 'Abdu'l-Bahá writes that 'The question of consultation is of utmost importance, and is one of the most potent instruments conducive to the tranquillity and felicity of the people.'[103] The main objective of consultation is the investigation of truth and from the inevitable clash of opinions, this light of truth is made manifest.[104]

Bahá'í consultation is a unique process designed to facilitate decision-making and conflict resolution. When properly used and spiritually infused, consultation acts as a pro-active exercise leading to unity and preventing alienation and conflict from occurring and escalating. Introducing the consultative process in reconciliation efforts would allow parties to comfortably express their views, thoughts and feelings in an open and frank manner without fear of repercussion. Such open dialogue would not only provide the necessary information for determining the causes and solutions of the conflict but would also contribute to the creation of new relationships based on mutual respect and trust, unity, forgiveness and justice. In fact, spiritually informed consultation can be said to represent an institutionalized process of conciliation, which makes efforts at *re*conciliation less often necessary.

Forgiveness and Justice as the Twin Pillars of Reconciliation

In the Bahá'í Faith, forgiveness and reconciliation are religious duties derived from the principle of unity. The writings counsel against judgement and instruct Bahá'ís to overlook the faults of others and strive to maintain unity through prayer, meditation, fellowship and consultation. This emphasis on unity mandates a decree to forgive and seek reconciliation. However, the Bahá'í notion of reconciliation is also based on justice, a central principle underlying Bahá'í theology. From a Bahá'í perspective, justice and forgiveness together provide the twin pillars for reconciliation. Without justice, social order and cohesion are not possible, as confirmed by the fact that the quest for justice is frequently the underlying cause of conflict and violence. As Bahá'u'lláh says in the fifth Ṭaráz,

> In these days truthfulness and sincerity are sorely afflicted in the clutches of falsehood, and justice is tormented by the scourge of injustice. The smoke of corruption hath enveloped the whole world in such wise that naught can be seen in any direction save regiments of soldiers and nothing is heard from any land but the clashing of swords. We beseech God, the True One, to strengthen the wielders of His power in that which will rehabilitate the world and bring tranquillity to the nations.[105]

And speaking directly about reconciliation, Bahá'u'lláh says,

> At present the light of reconciliation is dimmed in most countries and its radiance extinguished while the fire of strife and disorder hath been kindled and is blazing fiercely . . . Be ye warned, O men of understanding. It ill beseemeth the station of man to commit tyranny; rather it behoveth him to observe equity and be attired with the raiment of justice under all conditions.[106]

Hence, it is clear from Bahá'u'lláh's writings that the absence of justice is the principal source of social upheaval and unrest. His writings respond to this with an emphasis on the need to establish and exercise justice.

In one of His most cited verses, Bahá'u'lláh eloquently referred to justice in the following way:

> O Son of Spirit! The best beloved of all things in My sight is Justice; turn not away therefrom if thou desirest Me, and neglect it not that I may confide in thee. By its aid thou shalt see with thine own eyes and not through the eyes of others, and shalt know of thine own knowledge and not through the knowledge of thy neighbour. Ponder this in thy heart; how it behoveth thee to be. Verily justice is My gift to thee and the sign of My loving-kindness. Set it then before thine eyes.[107]

Bahá'u'lláh refers extensively to various aspects of justice in the Lawḥ-i-Maqṣúd. In this Tablet He writes:

> Take heed, O concourse of the rulers of the world! There is no

> force on earth that can equal in its conquering power the force of justice and wisdom. I, verily, affirm that there is not, and hath never been, a host more mighty than that of justice and wisdom.[108]

Moreover, He advises that,

> It behoveth every ruler to weigh his own being every day in the balance of equity and justice and then to judge between men and counsel them to do that which would direct their steps unto the path of wisdom and understanding.[109]

Moreover, in the Kalimát-i-Firdawsíyyih, Bahá'u'lláh refers to justice as 'the light of men' and urges us to 'Quench it not with the contrary winds of oppression and tyranny. The purpose of justice is the appearance of unity among men.'[110] He admonishes that 'It ill beseemeth the station of man to commit tyranny; rather it behoveth him to observe equity and be attired with the raiment of justice under all conditions.'[111]

All of these writings point to the importance of justice to peace and tranquillity. 'Abdu'l-Bahá further develops this theme and its relevance to reconciliation in *Some Answered Questions*. His words can be said to provide the framework for the Bahá'í notion of reconciliation. When asked about punishment and justice, 'Abdu'l-Bahá said:

> As forgiveness is one of the attributes of the Merciful One, so also justice is one of the attributes of the Lord. The tent of existence is upheld upon the pillar of justice and not upon forgiveness. The continuance of mankind depends upon justice and not upon forgiveness. So if, at present, the law of pardon were practised in all countries, in a short time the world would be disordered, and the foundations of human life would crumble . . . the constitution of the communities depends upon justice, not upon forgiveness.[112]

In the same talk, 'Abdu'l-Bahá suggests that while the twin pillars of justice are reward and punishment, justice would more quickly permeate society through a concentrated effort to educate both academically and spiritually than to focus the energies of society on punishment. This inner transformation, the ability to distinguish right from wrong and the application of the Golden Rule of doing unto others as you would have them do unto you, represents the personal, individual level of transformation necessary to reconciliation and the development of a culture of peace. The second and equally important dimension is the creation of social institutions that would be responsible for the promotion and exercise of justice at all levels of society, at the community level as well as the international one.

These institutions are to promote 'an ever-advancing civilization'[113] through spiritual education and the development of the necessary agencies for a world commonwealth characterized by principles of equality, justice, unity and peace.

The cornerstone of this commonwealth and the institution responsible for its unfoldment is the Universal House of Justice. Bahá'u'lláh refers to the members of the Universal House of Justice as the 'Trustees of God among His servants and the daysprings of authority in His countries' and charges them with 'the affairs of the people'.[114] The scope and influence envisioned for this institution are reflected in the various roles and responsibilities summarized in its constitution. They extend to a wide range of duties, including these which are most directly relevant to our theme:

> . . . to usher in the World Order of Bahá'u'lláh . . . to do its utmost for the realization of greater cordiality and comity amongst the nations and for the attainment of universal peace; and to foster that which is conducive to the enlightenment and illumination of the souls of men and the advancement and betterment of the world;
>
> . . . to deliberate upon all problems which have caused difference . . . to safeguard the personal rights, freedom and initiatives of individuals; and to give attention to the preservation of human honour, to the development of countries and the stability of states;
>
> . . . to be the exponent and guardian of that Divine Justice which can alone ensure the security of, and establish the reign of law and order in, the world.[115]

Conclusion

Peace building should not be a subject reserved to specialist scholars and practitioners. Peace should be considered a right and means to 'building' peace at all levels of world society should be considered among the most basic skills to be imparted, through both formal and informal education, to each new generation. The crises of our times will serve to promote and spread these ideas and generate an openness to new social models which can contribute to their implementation. The worldwide Bahá'í community provides one such model, since, as the Universal House of Justice wrote 15 years ago:

> It is a single social organism, representative of the diversity of the human family, conducting its affairs through a system of commonly accepted consultative principles . . . Its existence is yet another convincing proof of the practicality of its Founder's vision of a united world, another evidence that humanity can live as one global society . . .[116]

Finally, Bahá'í literature states unequivocally that the human race will ultimately acquire the capacity for conciliation and collaboration essential to building the first planetary civilization. However, such knowledge seems often to come only after suffering and disruption. Therefore, the immediate future will be shaped by the pace at which people and institutions overcome those 'ingrained habits of mind that breed conflict'[117] and integrate the kinds of attitudes, skills and principles which alone can serve as the foundation for long-term positive peace.

The Bahá'í framework for reconciliation is comprehensive and complex. It encompasses both personal and societal transformation and emphasizes both the capacity of the individual to offer forgiveness and the right of society to exercise justice. The principle of the oneness of humanity and a belief in the nobility of the human spirit provide the foundation for unity and dialogue. Consultation offers a structured approach to this dialogue which allows for open and frank expression of thoughts and feelings, fears and frustrations. The exercise of justice provides victims with a sense of relief and possible assurance that past offences will not recur. On the societal level, the Bahá'í writings argue that institutions must promote reconciliation and exercise justice in order for tyranny and oppression to become historical memories replaced by peace and equality. The worldwide Bahá'í community can already serve as a model for the principles articulated in this paper and stands ready to share its approach to conflict and conflict resolution with all the peoples of the world as a gift of peace.

Bibliography

'Abdu'l-Bahá. *The Promulgation of Universal Peace.* Wilmette, IL: Bahá'í Publishing Trust, 1982.

— *Selections from the Writings of 'Abdu'l-Bahá.* Haifa: Bahá'í World Centre, 1978.

— *Some Answered Questions.* Wilmette, IL: Bahá'í Publishing Trust, 1981.

Assefa, H. *Peace and Reconciliation as a Paradigm.* Nairobi: Majestic Printing Works Ltd., 1993.

Bahá'í International Community. *The Prosperity of Humankind.* London: Bahá'í Publishing Trust, 1995.

— *Who is Writing the Future? Reflections on the Twentieth Century.* London: Bahá'í Publishing Trust, 1999.

Bahá'u'lláh. *Gleanings from the Writings of Bahá'u'lláh.* Wilmette, IL: Bahá'í Publishing Trust, 1983.

— *The Hidden Words.* Wilmette, IL: Bahá'í Publishing Trust, 1990.

— 'Kitáb-i-'Ahd', in *Tablets of Bahá'u'lláh.* Wilmette, IL: Bahá'í Publishing Trust, 1988.

— *The Kitáb-i-Aqdas.* Haifa: Bahá'í World Centre, 1992.

— *Tablets of Bahá'u'lláh revealed after the Kitáb-i-Aqdas.* Haifa: Bahá'í World Centre, 1978.

Balyuzi, H. M. *'Abdu'l-Bahá.* Oxford: George Ronald, 1971.

Baures, M. 'Letting Go of Bitterness and Hate'. *Journal of Humanistic Psychology,* vol. 36, no. 1, 1996.

Burton, John. *Conflict: Resolution and Provention.* New York: St Martin's Press, 1990.

— 'Conflict Resolution: The Human Dimension'. *International Journal of Peace Studies*, vol. 3, no. 1, January 1998.

Carnegie Commission on Preventing Deadly Conflict. *Preventing Deadly Conflict: Final Report.* Ch. 7: 'Toward a Culture of Prevention'. New York: Carnegie Publications, 1997. <http://www.ccpdc.org/pubs/rept97/zip/7.zip>

Clark, M. 'Meaningful Social Bonding as a Universal Human Need', in J. Burton (ed.), *Conflict: Human Needs Theory.* New York: St Martin's Press, 1990.

Clark, Mary E. 'Symptoms of Cultural Pathologies: A Hypothesis', in Dennis J. D. Sandole and Hugo van der Merwe, *Conflict Resolution Theory and Practice: Integration and Application.* New York: Manchester University Press, 1993.

Clements, Kevin P. 'Peace Building and Conflict Transformation'. *Peace and Conflict Studies*, vol. 4, no.1, July 1997. <http://www.gmu.edu/academic/pcs/clements.htm>

The Compilation of Compilations. Prepared by the Universal House of Justice 1963–1990. 2 vols. [Sydney]: Bahá'í Publications Australia, 1991.

Danesh, H. *Unity: The Creative Foundation of Peace.* Ottawa: Bahá'í Studies Publications, 1986.

Decade for a Culture of Non-Violence. 'For the Children of the World: The Appeal of the Nobel Peace Prize Laureates', 1998. <http://www.buddhanetz.net/actuell/appeal.htm>

Fisher, Ronald J. 'Social-Psychological Processes in Interactive Conflict Analysis and Reconciliation', in Howon Jeong (ed.), *The New Agenda for Peace Research.* Aldershot: Ashgate, 1999.

Galtung, Johan. 'After Violence: 3R, Reconstruction, Reconciliation, Resolution: Coping with Visible and Invisible Effects of War and Violence'. *Transcend: A Peace and Development Network*, July 1998. <http://www.transcend.org/TRRECBAS.HTM>

— 'Conflict Transformation by Peaceful Means (the TRANSCEND Method): A Manual Prepared for the United Nations Disaster Management Training Program', 1998. <http://www.transcend.org/trmanpar.htm>

— 'Peace and Conflict Research in the Age of the Cholera: Ten Pointers to the Future of Peace Studies'. *Peace and Conflict Studies*,

vol. 4, no. 1, July 1995.
<http://www.trenton.edu/~psm/pcs>

Gopin, M. *Religion and Conflict Resolution: A Proposal*. Unpublished manuscript, 1995.

Hamlin, B. 'Moral Re-Armament and Forgiveness in International Affairs', in *Forgiveness in International Affairs*. London: Grosvenor Books, 1992.

Hope, D. 'The Healing Paradox of Forgiveness'. *Psychotherapy*, vol. 24, no. 2, 1987.

International Institute for Democracy and Electoral Assistance Democracy Forum. 'A Culture of Democracy: The Issues', 1998. <http://www.int_idea.se/97df/df98/df3.html>

Keohane, Robert O. *After Hegemony: Cooperation and Discord in the World Political Economy*. Princeton: Princeton University Press, 1984.

Lane, Jan-Erik. *Politics and Society in Western Europe*. London: Sage, 1994.

Lauritzen, P. 'Forgiveness: Moral Prerogative or Religious Duty?' *Journal of Religious Ethics*, vol. 15, no. 2, Fall 1987.

Lederach, John Paul. *Building Peace: Sustainable Reconciliation in Divided Societies*. Washington DC: United States Institute of Peace, 1994.

Lumsden, Malvern. 'Breaking the Cycle of Violence: Three Zones of Social Reconstruction', in Howon Jeong (ed.), *The New Agenda for Peace Research*. Aldershot: Ashgate, 1999.

Mitchell, C. *The Structure of International Conflict*. London: Macmillan, 2nd edn. 1994.

Montville, J. 'The Healing Function in Political Conflict Resolution', in Dennis J. D. Sandole and Hugo van der Merwe (eds.), *Conflict Resolution Theory and Practice: Integration and Application*. New York: Manchester University Press, 1993.

—*The Psychological Burdens of History*. Unpublished manuscript, 1995.

North, J. 'Wrongdoing and Forgiveness'. *Philosophy*, vol. 62, 1987.

Øberg, Jan. 'Conflict Mitigation in Reconstruction and Development'. *Peace and Conflict Studies*, vol. 3, no. 2, December 1996. <http://www.gmu.edu/academic/pcs/oberg.htm>

Sampson, C. 'To Make Real the Bond Between Us All: Quaker Conciliation During the Nigerian Civil War', in D. Johnson and C. Sampson (eds.), *Religion: The Missing Dimension of Statecraft*. New York: Oxford University Press, 1994.

Sandole, Dennis J. D. and Hugo van der Merwe. *Conflict Resolution Theory and Practice: Integration and Application*. New York: Manchester University Press, 1993.

Shoghi Effendi. *The World Order of Bahá'u'lláh*. Wilmette, IL: Bahá'í Publishing Trust, 1991.

Simpson, G. 'Reconstruction and Reconciliation: Emerging from Transition'. *Development in Practice*, vol. 7, no. 4, 1997. <http://www.csvr.org.za/papers/papr&rgs.htm>

United Nations Development Programme. 'Governance for Sustainable Development: A UNDP Policy Document', 1997. <http://magnet.undp.org/policy>

United Nations Educational, Scientific and Cultural Organization. *Culture of Peace Newsletter*, 1996. <http://www.unesco.org/cpp/uk/newsletter>

United Nations Secretary General. 'Secretary General's Report to the Forty-fifth session of the Commission on Human Rights' (document E/CN.4/1989/210), 1989.

The Universal House of Justice. *The Constitution of the Universal House of Justice*. Haifa: Bahá'í World Centre, 1972.

— *The Promise of World Peace*. London: Bahá'í Publishing Trust, 1985.

van der Merwe, H. and T. Johnson. 'Restitution After Apartheid: From Revenge to Forgiveness'. *Cambridge Review of International Affairs*, vol. 8, no. 2 and vol. 9, no. 1, 1994/95.

Volkan, V. 'Psychological Concepts Useful in the Building of Political Foundations'. *Journal of the American Psychoanalytic Association*, vol. 35, 1987.

Woodall, J. *Collective Identity and Collective Security*. Unpublished manuscript. Programme on International Affairs and Conflict Resolution. University of California – Irvine, Department of Psychiatry, 1995.

World Commission on Culture and Development. *Our Creative Diversity: Report of the World Commission on Culture and Development*, 1996. <http://www.kit.nl/kvc/boekteksten/intro.html>

Notes

1. 'Abdu'l-Bahá, *Selections*, p. 246.
2. Galtung, 'After Violence', p. 14.
3. Lederach, *Building Peace*, p. 94.
4. Sandole and van der Merwe, *Conflict Resolution Theory and Practice*, p. 7.
5. Mitchell, *Structure of International Conflict*, p. 151.
6. ibid. pp. 150–1.
7. Galtung, 'After Violence', p. 3.
8. Galtung, 'Peace and Conflict Research in the Age of the Cholera', p. 12.
9. Lumsden, 'Breaking the Cycle of Violence', p. 1.
10. Galtung, 'After Violence', p. 3.
11. Simpson, 'Reconstruction and Reconciliation'.
12. Galtung, 'After Violence'.
13. Øberg, 'Conflict Mitigation in Reconstruction and Development'.
14. Clements, 'Peace Building and Conflict Transformation'.
15. Fisher, 'Social-Psychological Processes in Interactive Conflict Analysis and Reconciliation', p. 83. Emphasis added.
16. Keohane, *After Hegemony*, p. 51.
17. Lane, *Politics and Society in Western Europe*, p. 53.
18. ibid.
19. Galtung, 'Conflict Transformation by Peaceful Means (the TRANSCEND Method)'.
20. Clark, 'Symptoms of Cultural Pathologies: A Hypothesis', p. 51.
21. Carnegie Commission on Preventing Deadly Conflict, *Preventing Deadly Conflict*.
22. Burton, *Conflict: Resolution and Provention*, p. 23.
23. ibid. pp. 47 and 95.
24. ibid. p. 127.
25. ibid.
26. Burton, 'Conflict Resolution: The Human Dimension', p. 4.
27. The UNDP defines sustainable development as 'expanding the choices for all people in society. This means that men and women – particularly the poor and vulnerable – are at the centre of the development process. It also means "protection of the life opportunities of future generations . . . and . . . the natural systems on which all life depends".' (UNDP, *Human Development Report 1996*) This makes the central purpose of

development the creation of an enabling environment in which all can enjoy long, healthy and creative lives.' United Nations Development Programme, 'Governance for Sustainable Development: A UNDP Policy Document'.

28. United Nations Development Programme, 'Governance for Sustainable Development: A UNDP Policy Document'.
29. The entire list of characteristics includes:

Participation: All men and women should have a voice in decision-making, either directly or through legitimate intermediate institutions that represent their interests. Such broad participation is built on freedom of association and speech, as well as capacities to participate constructively.

Rule of law: Legal frameworks should be fair and enforced impartially, particularly the laws on human rights.

Transparency: Transparency is built on the free flow of information. Processes, institutions and information are directly accessible to those concerned with them, and enough information is provided to understand and monitor them.

Responsiveness: Institutions and processes try to serve all stakeholders.

Consensus orientation: Good governance mediates differing interests to reach a broad consensus on what is in the best interests of the group and, where possible, on policies and procedures.

Equity: All men and women have opportunities to improve or maintain their well-being.

Effectiveness and efficiency: Processes and institutions produce results that meet needs while making the best use of resources.

Accountability: Decision-makers in government, the private sector and civil society organizations are accountable to the public, as well as to institutional stakeholders. This accountability differs depending on the organization and whether the decision is internal or external to an organization.

Strategic vision: Leaders and the public have a broad and long-term perspective on good governance and human development, along with a sense of what is needed for such development. There is also an understanding of the historical, cultural and social complexities in which that perspective is grounded.

30. United Nations Educational, Scientific and Cultural Organization, *Culture of Peace Newsletter*.
31. Decade for a Culture of Non-Violence, 'For the Children of the World: The Appeal of the Nobel Peace Prize Laureates'.
32. United Nations Secretary General. 'Secretary General's Report to the Forty-fifth session of the Commission on Human Rights' (document E/CN.4/1989/210).
33. International Institute for Democracy and Electoral Assistance Democracy Forum, 'A Culture of Democracy: The Issues'.
34. World Commission on Culture and Development, *Our Creative Diversity*.
35. ibid.
36. ibid.
37. Lederach, *Building Peace*, p. 100.
38. Montville, 'The Healing Function in Political Conflict Resolution', p. 112.
39. ibid.
40. ibid. p. 113.
41. Volkan, 'Psychological Concepts Useful in the Building of Political Foundations', p. 925.
42. Montville, *Psychological Burdens of History*, p. 4.
43. ibid.
44. ibid.
45. ibid. p. 14.
46. ibid. p. 5.
47. North, 'Wrongdoing and Forgiveness', p. 502.
48. Hope, 'The Healing Paradox of Forgiveness', p. 5.
49. Hamlin, 'Moral Re-Armament and Forgiveness in International Affairs', p. 8.
50. Quoted in ibid. p. 77.
51. Baures, 'Letting Go of Bitterness and Hate'; Hope, 'The Healing Paradox of Forgiveness'; Montville, 'The Healing Function in Political Conflict Resolution'.
52. van der Merwe and Johnson, 'Restitution After Apartheid:

From Revenge to Forgiveness', p. 10.

53. ibid. p. 11.
54. ibid. p. 78.
55. ibid. p. 8.
56. Lederach, *Building Peace*, pp. 94–6.
57. Assefa, *Peace and Reconciliation as a Paradigm*, p. 18.
58. Clark, 'Meaningful Social Bonding as a Universal Human Need', pp. 49–51.
59. Gopin, *Religion and Conflict Resolution*, p. 2.
60. Lauritzen, 'Forgiveness: Moral Prerogative or Religious Duty?'
61. Assefa, *Peace and Reconciliation as a Paradigm*, p. 10.
62. ibid. p. 11.
63. Qur'án 42:40
64. Qur'án 7:199
65. Qur'án 42:37
66. Galtung, 'Conflict Transformation by Peaceful Means (the TRANSCEND Method).
67. Shoghi Effendi, *World Order*, p. 47.
68. The Universal House of Justice, *Promise of World Peace*, para. 13.
69. Bahá'u'lláh, quoted in the Universal House of Justice, *Promise of World Peace*, para. 14.
70. Shoghi Effendi, *World Order*, p. 187.
71. ibid. p. 188.
72. Bahá'u'lláh, *Kitáb-i-Aqdas*, para. 148.
73. Bahá'u'lláh, *Tablets*, p. 221.
74. ibid. p. 85.
75. Bahá'u'lláh, *Gleanings*, p. 215.
76. Balyuzi, *'Abdu'l-Bahá*, p. 172.
77. 'Abdu'l-Bahá, *Promulgation*, p. 98.
78. ibid. p. 117.
79. ibid. p. 119.
80. ibid. p. 266.
81. ibid. p. 232.
82. ibid. pp. 98–9.
83. ibid. p. 120.
84. Shoghi Effendi, *World Order*, pp. 40–1.
85. Bahá'í International Community, *Prosperity of Humankind*, p. 8. Emphasis added.
86. ibid. p. 12.
87. ibid.
88. ibid. pp. 12–13.

89. ibid. p. 26.
90. ibid. pp. 26–7.
91. Bahá'u'lláh, in *Compilation*, vol. 1, p. 93, no. 167.
92. Danesh, *Unity*; Woodall, *Collective Identity and Collective Security*.
93. Danesh, *Unity*, p. 65.
94. ibid. p. 66.
95. Bahá'u'lláh, *Hidden Words*, Arabic no. 11.
96. ibid. Arabic no. 13.
97. ibid. Arabic no. 22.
98. Sampson, 'To Make Real the Bond Between Us All: Quaker Conciliation During the Nigerian Civil War', p. 95.
99. Bahá'u'lláh, *Gleanings*, p. 288.
100. Bahá'u'lláh, *Hidden Words*, Arabic no. 68.
101. Bahá'u'lláh, in *Compilation*, vol. 1, p. 93, no. 168.
102. Bahá'u'lláh, *Tablets*, p. 168.
103. 'Abdu'l-Bahá, in *Compilation*, vol. 1, p. 96, no. 179.
104. 'Abdu'l-Bahá, *Selections*, p. 87.
105. Bahá'u'lláh, *Tablets*, p. 39.
106. ibid. p. 170.
107. Bahá'u'lláh, *Hidden Words*, Arabic no. 2.
108. Bahá'u'lláh, *Tablets*, p. 164.
109. ibid. pp. 166–7.
110. ibid. p. 67.
111. ibid. p. 170.
112. 'Abdu'l-Bahá, *Some Answered Questions*, p. 270.
113. Bahá'u'lláh, *Gleanings*, p. 215.
114. Bahá'u'lláh, *Tablets*, pp. 26–7.
115. The Universal House of Justice, *Constitution*, pp. 5–6.
116. The Universal House of Justice, *Promise of World Peace*, para 52.
117. Bahá'í International Community, *Who is Writing the Future?*, p. 7.

2

Bahá'í Consultation: Worldview or Process?[1]

Hossain B. Danesh and Roshan Danesh[2]

Consultation has an exalted place in the Bahá'í writings. It is spoken of as an unambiguous individual and social good. 'Consultation bestoweth greater awareness and transmuteth conjecture into certitude'[3] and as such is a means for individual confirmation, transformation and understanding. Further, 'no welfare and no well-being can be attained except through consultation'.[4] There also appear to be no limitations to the contexts in which consultation should be employed. As 'Abdu'l-Bahá writes, 'Man must consult on all matters, whether major or minor, so that he may become cognizant of what is good.'[5]

Because the Bahá'í writings stress consultation to such a degree, consultation is central to the individual and collective life of the popular Bahá'í religion. It is employed in the individual lives of Bahá'ís, utilized as the central mechanism for public decision-making and positioned as a tool that mediates the demand for unity in contexts of diversity. Bahá'ís also extensively use the language and rhetoric of consultation. Community members frequently state that decisions have been made 'after consultation', that the 'consultative portion' of community meetings is of utmost importance, and when faced with conflicts or difficult decisions individual Bahá'ís often seek out opportunities for consultation.[6]

Yet while the language of consultation is embedded within Bahá'í culture, it has been noted that there is a gap between consultation 'talk' and consultation 'practice' – raising the question of whether there is anything different or distinctive about the practice of Bahá'í consultation.[7] Anecdotal evidence abounds with instances of individuals commenting that 'we did not consult properly' or 'two or three members of the community make all the decisions'.[8]

The issue of the distinctiveness of consultation is highlighted by typical answers offered to questions such as 'What is Bahá'í consultation?' In asking this question over the past six years to members of the Bahá'í community, graduate and undergraduate students and individuals who hold Bahá'í administrative posts, a strikingly consistent set of answers has been offered. Typically there has been a description of the process of consultation, an emphasis on the place of unity in the process, a recounting of 'Abdu'l-Bahá's conditions for consultation[9] and perhaps talk about some of the contexts in which the community uses it. In other words, the most common answers stress process, skills and attitudes.

But is that what consultation is? Does speaking about process, skills and attitudes distinguish Bahá'í consultation from social and ordering practices in other communities? And, importantly, does stressing process, skills and attitudes support Bahá'u'lláh's claims concerning the universal and unlimited potential benefits of consultation?

This article argues that the focus on process, skills and attitudes in Bahá'í culture as a way of defining and describing Bahá'í consultation is a problematic minimalist account of consultation. Through an analysis of consultation as a process of conflict resolution, it is argued that the distinctive elements of consultation, if any, can only be identified through an analysis of the worldview which informs it. This article advocates thinking of consultation as a worldview prior to conceiving of it as a process. Such a focus may allow for a better understanding of the place of consultation within the Bahá'í Faith, the ways in which it can be used and the method through which its potential may be reached. It also assists in reconciling the centrality of consultation and the idealized claims found in the Bahá'í writings with the current state of the Bahá'í practice of consultation. In other words, closing the gap between Bahá'í 'consultation-talk' and 'consultation-practice' may be effected by a shift away from a process-based definition of consultation.

Practical Dissonance: Consultation as a Process of Conflict Resolution

Since the second world war and more intensely since the 1960s there has been an exponential growth in the popular use of conflict resolution processes. Mediation, negotiation and arbitration have become commonplace in North America, used in a variety of settings from the schoolyard to the justice system. There has been similar growth in the academic study of conflict resolution, even while the parameters and foci of the field remain a subject of widespread debate.[10]

It is not uncommon for Bahá'ís to try to position consultation within the parameters of the contemporary conflict resolution movement, particularly within the American and Canadian Bahá'í communities. At most large conferences of peacemaking and conflict resolution practitioners, consultation is typically presented as the subject of training workshops and skills sessions, just like other processes and techniques such as mediation and negotiation.[11] This tendency is also reflected in some recent scholarship. In one of the first substantive scholarly attempts to discuss Bahá'í consultation in the light of the contemporary conflict resolution movement, Steven Gonzales notes the 'parallelism between the growth of conflict resolution and the fundamental Bahá'í principles of arbitration, consultation, and unity being preferred over the existing adversarial systems'.[12] Further, he writes that 'the conflict resolution movement . . . arising parallel with Bahá'í consultation, is the early dawn of the principle of consultation among the masses, working its way through humanity and transforming outdated systems designed to cope with conflict in a more brutish age'.[13]

Leaving Gonzales's specific thesis of historical convergence, which appears to resonate with recent statements of the Universal House of Justice concerning conflict resolution,[14] the broader question we are interested in is the tension in thinking about consultation as a process of conflict resolution within the contemporary parameters of how conflict resolution is defined and understood. As we will argue, there exist some fundamental asymmetries between conflict resolution processes such as mediation and consultation. This raises questions about the coherence of thinking of consultation in primarily process terms.

Structure and Role Definition

Predominant asymmetries between consultation and conflict resolution processes exist at the level of structure. The dominant processes of the contemporary conflict resolution movement each have certain inalienable structural features which distinguish them from each other. Mediation involves intervention by a third party neutral without decision-making authority. Arbitration can be distinguished by the power of the third party neutral to impose an outcome. Negotiation by definition does not include intervention between the parties. If there is intervention in a negotiation by a third party who assists in reaching a resolution then that negotiation has become a mediation. Similarly, if a third party intervenes in a negotiation to impose an outcome, that negotiation has become an arbitration.

Mapping and comparing processes according to the architecture of intervention does not provide a useful way of talking about consultation. Consultation is distinct from any particular structure and it is clear that consultation is something which can be used within any particular architecture of intervention. For example, the term 'arbitration' appears in a number of places in the writings of 'Abdu'l-Bahá in reference to the settlement of international disputes. Shoghi Effendi also used the term 'adjudication' when referring to international processes. Bahá'í Assemblies[15] have also operated according to the principle that they may act as a 'board of arbitration'[16] when settling private disputes, such as a divorce. There are pitfalls, however, in associating the use of this terminology with the connotations typically attached by the contemporary conflict resolution movement. The reference to an Assembly as a 'board of arbitration' could be interpreted broadly, implying that an Assembly should function according to the dynamics and procedures which are usually seen in arbitration as a form of private litigation. On the other hand, a narrow rendering would suggest that all that is implied is the power to make a binding decision. The process through which the Assembly makes that decision, however, would deviate from contemporary notions of arbitration. The expectation would be that the Assembly would use Bahá'í consultation to decide on the outcome.

Further, consider more broadly the role of Assemblies during divorce proceedings under Bahá'í law. In the Bahá'í Faith divorce is permitted after one year of separation. During this 'year of patience' the couple is encouraged to seek out any possible avenues of reconciliation. The Assembly has no control over the final decision whether to divorce, except to indicate the completion of the year of patience. An outside observer might conclude that the Assembly is positioned as a mediator during this year of patience – intervening in the dispute to attempt to reconcile the parties. The Assembly has no inherent jurisdiction to force an outcome concerning whether or not to divorce or to impose a resolution concerning issues during the year of separation. The Assembly may be called upon to impose settlement terms, as noted above, but this is typically as a result of referral of the dispute by the couple and not an act of inherent jurisdiction. Yet, while the Assembly in this context could be defined as a mediator (or as a mediator-arbitrator), the dominant practices and role of the Assembly are not captured by this description. Consultation ideally dominates and is the foci of the process. The Assembly will devise a strategy and make decisions through consultation, it will attempt to engage the separated couple in consultation and will often stress education in the practice of consultation as part of the year of separation process.

The further implication of these examples is that, depending upon context, consultation as a process of conflict resolution can look radically different. For example, suppose two individuals were in a conflict with one another. Both being aware of consultation, they may choose to try to consult with one another to reach a resolution. Alternatively, they may accept the authority of a third party – most likely an Assembly that would then consult and impose an outcome. Finally, there may be situations where individuals in conflict wish to consult but are having trouble doing so. In such situations they may ask a third party to intervene, not to impose an outcome but to assist the parties to consult. In the eyes of the contemporary conflict resolution movement these examples would simply be termed forms of negotiation, arbitration and mediation, respectively.

The significance of this structural asymmetry can also be seen by looking at certain debates within political theory which animate the self-perception of the contemporary conflict resolution movement. Conflict resolution literature is replete with allegations that the movement has been co-opted by the legal profession. A by-product of this co-option is seen as a shift of the movement to emphasize liberal values of proceduralism. This is opposed to a competing view of the movement as a part of a rejuvenation of community life with important potential impacts on the substantive quality of human relationships and the values which inform them. The very fact that a focus on process, structure and role definition is a predominant axis through which the movement is defined and debated reflects the context liberalism provides for thinking about conflict resolution.

Bahá'í political thought, a complex and largely understudied subject, is easily classified as distant from contemporary liberalism and its resultant proceduralism.[17] Consultation, as such, is potentially distorted and misunderstood not only by attempts to place it on contemporary conflict resolution spectrums which emphasize structural features but also by the preliminary choice of viewing 'conflict resolution' or the 'contemporary conflict resolution movement' as a criterion for comparison. To the degree that the discourse surrounding contemporary processes is embedded within liberal political philosophy, Bahá'í consultation can only engage in the terms of the movement by adopting a foreign frame of reference. This divorces consultation from the theory and context which underlie it and leaves it exposed to co-option and redefinition by foreign standards and assumptions.

Values

The co-option concern raised by the dissonance between liberalism and Bahá'í political thought is reiterated in an examination of the asymmetrical values which inform the contemporary conflict resolution movement and Bahá'í consultation. In addition to structure and role definition, the contemporary conflict resolution movement defines itself around the values of autonomy, flexibility and accommodation and the valuing of the public/private distinction. These values all fit comfortably within liberal thought but arguably are not treated the same way in Bahá'í thought as it is currently understood.

The autonomy continuum is a prevalent value in conflict resolution literature – often discussed as decision-making power. Preference is expressed for processes which maximize the amount of decision-making power that remains vested in the disputants. The oft-cited 'Continuum of Conflict Management and Resolution Approaches' diagrams movement from processes where the disputants retain decision-making authority (i.e. amicable resolution, negotiation and mediation) to those where they do not (i.e. arbitration, litigation).[18] The focus of the contemporary conflict resolution movement has primarily been on developing and expanding the use of informal processes which leave decision-making authority with the disputants. This focus has been bolstered by a critique of formal processes where decision-making authority remains in a third party. The loss of decision-making authority results in a more intrusive 'foreign' element in the process, raises efficiency concerns and signals a shift away from a focus on rectifying (or avoiding further) damage to the long-term relationship between the disputants. Simply stated, autonomy is a positive criterion for measuring the value of a process.

Related to the autonomy criteria is the valuing of the flexibility which processes such as negotiation, mediation and arbitration facilitate, especially viewed in light of the formal requirements of litigation.[19] All of these processes are praised for allowing (to varying degrees) the disputants to dictate the tone, tenor and pace of the proceedings; to choose their degree of participation;

to engage in a multiplicity of modes of communication and dialogue; to seek out specialist advice, knowledge or expertise; and to accommodate cultural, racial and other differences that may impact on behaviours and choices. Flexibility is often seen as a benefit regardless of the school of thought one belongs to concerning the animating purposes of the contemporary conflict resolution movement. The 'better-quality' advocates highlight flexibility as providing more individualized and therefore satisfactory resolutions. The 'better-quantity' advocates see efficiency goals potentially advanced by flexible processes that may be quicker, less cumbersome and cheaper.[20]

While both the autonomy and flexibility values would provide for a relatively linear mapping of contemporary processes, the valuing of the public and private distinction manifests itself in a slightly more complex mapping. Litigation, of course, has an inevitable public dimension. It engages the parties within a public forum and through appeal to general instruments that are typically applicable to all. In some systems, the outcome of litigation has precedental repercussions, thus abstracting the specific resolution of the case into a general proposition with import for like cases. The rationale for this public nature of conflict resolution are multidimensional, ranging from the positioning of the courtroom as a forum for democracy to the affirmation and reinforcement that justice must be visible and to add ritualistic authority to ideals of fairness, equality and the rule of law.

Processes such as negotiation, mediation and arbitration often move conflict resolution from the public to the private sphere. This privatization of conflict resolution has been the object of critique. Feminist scholarship, for example, has expressed concern that both opportunities to affirm and strengthen rights and equality schemes, as well as the important process of public education concerning gender inequality which court decisions provide, are potentially undermined by privatization. As well, mediation has been critiqued as a vehicle for reproducing and perpetuating power imbalances and patterns of dominance.[21] Similarly, a number of scholars have contemplated what might have occurred if key civil rights disputes had been mediated.[22] Underlying these critiques one often finds theoretical commitment to the falsity of the public/private distinction. Even in the face of these critiques, however, the trend over the last decade has been to privatize dispute resolution in areas that we intuit as predominately private – most notably family disputes. Advocates of this trend often see privatization as a positive value, safeguarding the intimate nature of familial relationships and shielding individuals and relationships from exposure in the public forum.

These three values, utilized to articulate the essential elements of contemporary conflict resolution processes and their relationship to each other, are not easily applicable to consultation. The multiplicity of forms of consultation, noted earlier, denies the ascendancy of any of these values. For example, consultation can be practised with little disputant autonomy when an Assembly imposes a resolution or with great autonomy, such as when it is used by individuals to reach an amicable resolution. Similarly, it can occupy a range of positions on a flexibility spectrum. Autonomy, flexibility and valuing the public/private distinction all illustrate the predominance of particular values in conflict resolution discourse, values which, as noted earlier, do not map easily onto Bahá'í thought.

Take, for example, the issue of autonomy. Certainly individual empowerment and autonomy are relevant themes throughout the writings of Bahá'u'lláh and 'Abdu'l-Bahá. It must be remembered that the Bahá'í Faith was born into a Twelver Shí'í context where blind imitation *(taqlíd)* of the learned (*mujtahid*) was a central ethic of decision-making on the requirements of religious law. Frequently this practice of imitation is condemned in the Bahá'í writings and individuals are exhorted to embolden their autonomy.[23]

But this emphasis on autonomy does not appear to directly translate, as we have already seen, into a concern with architectures of intervention which give correspondingly more or less decision-making power to disputants as opposed to intervenors. Perhaps one reason for this is because of the centrality of unity in Bahá'í thought. Bahá'í ontology argues that the pattern underlying reality is one of unity in diversity – in which distinct entities are combined to form more complex entities. Unity is, as such, a propelling force of life and an aim and ambition of living organisms. This arguably suggests that in a process such as consultation – which aims to create unity – the value of autonomy is relative and contextually bound. In some circumstances, consultation and decision-making through a binding authority, with little disputant autonomy, is most appropriate. In other circumstances, more emphasis on disputant autonomy is beneficial. This determination will vary on the specific context and how the challenges to creating unity are present in that context.

Similar difficulties arise when trying to speak of consultation in relation to the other continua. Consultation is a nascent method of dialogue and decision-making within an infant religion. Like all religious systems in their early years, the public life of the community and the methods through which conflicts and disputes are settled is characterized by a high degree of informality, flexibility and diversity. This is a largely inevitable fallout of the social reality of religious systems, which often take centuries to develop relatively indigenous cultures and practices. Some might argue that the Bahá'í Faith, with its systematic pursuit of an administrative structure as well as its hyper-modern community-building through a succession of 'plans', is a unique historical case that has pursued a high degree of formality early in its evolution. Any claims to formality and inflexibility within the Bahá'í system, however, would appear to be ignorant of the actual reality of how the Bahá'í system currently functions as well as certain underlying precepts that inform it. Any keen observer will note extreme local differences in the use of consultation and the types of decisions made by both individuals and Assemblies. At the same time, it must be accepted that certain features that are associated with the informality and flexibility of outcomes using contemporary processes – such as not being bound by earlier decisions or the ability to pursue forms of remedies specifically suited to the needs of particular disputants – are prescribed features of any Bahá'í legal system that may emerge in the future.

What this illustrates is that consultation cannot be easily plotted on a spectrum of flexibility and formality. In some circumstances it will have many of the indicia of an informal process and in other contexts appear highly formal. Consultation is also a dynamic practice in this regard – the degree of formality that might emerge in certain contexts in the future is uncertain. It is, as such, not particularly helpful to think of consultation through the lens of flexibility.

The Nature of Conflict

A third method of illustrating the dissonance between the contemporary conflict resolution movement and Bahá'í consultation is to examine assumptions about the nature of conflict which inform each of them.

Conflict theory preaches the inevitability of inter-group competition. As Galtung and Jacobsen comment, 'Conflict, incompatible goals, are as human as life itself; the only conflict-free humans are dead humans' and 'war and violence are like slavery, colonialism, and patriarchy; however, they come and they go'.[24] This sentiment is typically accompanied by the view that conflict is desirable. 'Conflict is the spice that seasons our most intimate relationships' and 'it is woven into the fundamental fabric of nature'.[25] Conflict is seen as having numerous positive life-affirming effects – it can strengthen group identity, bring issues and problems to the surface and encourage positive action. These beliefs about conflict typically show fidelity to the idea that there are basic human needs that require satisfaction and attempts at needs satisfaction often give rise to conflict.[26] There is a symmetry between inner and outer conflict in this scheme. Internal dissonance is said to give rise to behaviours likely to result in social conflict. Alleviating social conflicts is thus also an attempt to reestablish inner peace and harmony.

Processes such as negotiation, mediation and arbitration typically incorporate these assumptions concerning the inevitable nature of conflict. This is seen in both conflict resolution literature as well as the training modalities used. It is also in the very language and structure of the process which reinforce assumptions concerning the naturalness and appropriateness of conflict.

Such assumptions appear antithetical to Bahá'í consultation. Within Bahá'í ontology is a commitment to the reality of unity underlying creation – implying that conflict may be understood as a result of disunity or absence of unity.[27] In consultation, unity exists both as a prerequisite to engaging in a process and as the desired outcome. As a prerequisite, unity refers, in essence, to a shared commitment or unity of purpose concerning engagement in a process and, within limits, the nature and character of that process. Achievement of a greater state of unity is the hoped for end result, even if the actual particulars of a dispute are not settled.[28] This primacy of unity also acts to deny commitment to the reality and inevitability of conflict. It is notable that terminology such as 'parties' and 'disputants' is not typically employed in consultation and those involved in the decision-making process are exhorted to focus on building unity as the proper form of response to conflict.

In other words, consultation appears to utilize a different mental map than contemporary conflict resolution processes. Approaching a situation of conflict through a process that preaches the inevitability of conflict potentially results in different behaviour than if we approach from an understanding of the possibility of unity.[29] How we understand the dimensions of time involved in the resolution of conflict, the ways in which we use space, the intended outcomes and the role an intervenor might play all radically change. A focus on unity similarly shifts an intervenor's focus towards understanding a conflict as an opportunity to create, or perhaps recreate, a strong and substantive condition of unity.

Developmentalism: A Framework for Analysis

The dissonance between Bahá'í consultation and some of the predominant trends in conflict resolution discourse suggests the need for alternative ways of talking if a critical analysis of the relationship between Bahá'í consultation and the contemporary conflict resolution movement is to take place. Indeed, there are some trends in current scholarship which are more helpful. The growing acceptance of a language of 'transformation', 'healing' and 'personal growth' illustrates a recognition of the individual and relational attitudinal and psychological dimensions of conflict and conflict resolution.[30] Similarly, the increasing focus on preventative and pro-active conflict resolution – or 'provention' as one scholar labels it[31] – indicates that historic unwillingness among some groups in the movement to devise models of conflict resolution that address underlying layers of a conflict is being replaced by the demand for more holistic and comprehensive models.

Such developments, simply because they entertain the more intimate dimensions of human life in crafting processes of resolution, are more attuned to consultation which places demands and expectations on the spiritual aspects of human beings. But it is a more subtle, and still as yet underdeveloped, aspect of these new voices that illustrates a shift to an alternative framework for thinking about conflict resolution which provides useful categories for analysing the relationship between consultation and contemporary processes. By saying that conflict resolution ought to be transformative for those involved in it or have a preventative effect by decreasing the intensity of a current conflict or decreasing future incidences of conflict, one is putting a new spin on the obvious maxim that not all conflict resolution processes are equal. It is clear that in a literature filled with slogans such as 'fit the forum to the fuss',[32] it is understood that the context and nature of a conflict dictates the appropriateness of particular modes of resolution. What is now being recognized is the need to factor in additional criteria to determine appropriate modes of resolution and the contexts in which they should be used. Among these are attitudinal and psychological criteria which are the foundations upon which transformation can occur, as well as social and cultural criteria which determine what will be preventative in a particular context.

One approach to understanding these current preoccupations is to view them as incorporating a concern with developmentalism into conflict resolution. Developmental psychology concerns itself with questions of the appropriate behaviours, skill-sets and emotional and intellectual make-up at various stages in human life, the relationship between those stages and movement between them. Developmentalism may be utilized to identify appropriate conflicting behaviours and conflict resolution modalities at various stages in human development and thus provide a basis for comparison which does not focus on the structural features of a process.

Utilizing a developmental model as the basis for analysing consultation in light of the contemporary conflict resolution movement is also logical because of the place of developmentalism within Bahá'í thought. Bahá'u'lláh and 'Abdu'l-Bahá employed developmental analogies frequently and in a number of contexts. The Bahá'í view of developmentalism is extensive and extends to all facets of life. Speaking of individual biology and psychology in developmental terms is not controversial or unique. Central to Bahá'u'lláh's social and political vision, however, is the idea of the collective maturation of humanity.[33] The idea of collective maturation in Bahá'í thought is unique in its linking of social development with spiritual evolution and the dynamics of divine revelation. Unlike many social theories that responded critically to the static nature of enlightenment thought by viewing society in dynamic and constructed terms, Bahá'u'lláh subjected revelation and religion to the same historical processes of change and construction. Revelation thus becomes a historical force and its modes of expression within society an object of history itself.

In the lives of individuals, the dynamism of divine will is parallelled in a process of individual spiritual development that occurs in response to the innate needs of the human soul for transcendence and universality.[34] The Bahá'í writings also appear to link individual spiritual growth with collective maturation.[35] Based on the Bahá'í writings one might argue that individual spiritual growth has important social dimensions, as it encourages individuals to relate with others and publicly and privately act in particular ways and in response to certain ethical precepts. In the Bahá'í writings, one term often used to describe many aspects of this ethical framework is 'service'.[36]

The comprehensive place of developmentalism within Bahá'í thought is, of course, a subject of study unto itself and few useful critical analyses have been written exploring its implications for social and political processes. The idea of collective maturation will, in particular, be a challenge to contemporary social thought.

While the Bahá'í use of developmentalism is far more comprehensive than would be generally accepted within political and social theory today, the above discussion suggests that Bahá'í thought would advocate developmental models of conflict resolution. Given the current trends in conflict resolution literature which illustrate a growing focus on the psychological dimensions of conflict and the place of conflict resolution in individual growth and change, a developmental framework appears to be well positioned to respond to the challenges of dissonance between consultation and contemporary processes identified earlier.

A Developmental Model of Conflict Resolution

The central unit of the developmental model of conflict resolution we propose in this paper is that of worldview. Developmental models often posit that individuals mature and act according to particular worldviews at various stages of development. A worldview refers to the predominant lens through which we construct, interpret and interact with all aspects of our reality. Worldviews are reflexive. They are shaped by our experience of reality and at the same time they reshape and act upon that reality. Worldviews are dynamic. They are typically the subjective comprehensions of exposure to a wide variety of external explanations and understandings of the world. These external arguments about the nature of the world come from myriad forces, including parents, culture and religion. Therefore, worldviews always have a distinct component – because they are shaped by our conceptions of our own experiences. However, they are also shared in a general sense, as the external forces are often overlapping and common in varying degrees.

General categories of shared worldviews can also be said to exist because human consciousness is the central factor that shapes both our worldview and the manner in which we engage and act as social beings. The human power of understanding – the main agent for the development of consciousness – involves cognitive, emotive and experiential forms of learning and is responsive to the forces of both nature and nurture. Development of consciousness and worldview is an evolving process with certain distinct stages that can be simplistically plotted as infancy, childhood, adolescence and maturity but could be made more complex through adaptation of Erikson's eight stages or the application of any other such scheme. Worldview thus helps us to focus on the social and interactive dimensions of human development. Development of consciousness as expressed through our worldviews alters not only ourselves but also the nature of all of our relationships. As our consciousness evolves and our worldviews develop, our social behaviours, including the conflicts we are involved in, our approaches to conflict resolution and the decision to be in conflict in the first place, will all be potentially altered.

The relevance of worldviews for conflict resolution is seen in their impact on individual and group decision-making. In any attempt at conflict resolution, individuals alone and with others make numerous decisions. Some of these are fundamental – Do I want to engage in this process? Do I agree with this proposed outcome? – while others are somewhat less significant. However, any process of conflict resolution can be thought of as a matrix of large and small decisions being made, sometimes by individuals involved and sometimes collectively by everyone involved together.

Three components of worldviews shape our decisions – perspective, principles and purpose. All human decisions are affected, framed and in some senses determined by these three aspects.

Perspective is the world-constructing dimension of worldview. It is innate for human beings to attempt to order their experiences and observations of the world around them. This ordering is done at both the individual and communal levels and typically manifests itself in a perception of how the world is organized (the descriptive perspective) and how it should be organized (the normative perspective). Perspectives affect decision-making because we use them to set expectations for outcomes and to predict the decisions or interests of others. Simple examples illustrate the role of perspective in decision-making. For example, decisions concerning our professional life will often be shaped by our constructed world. Is it a world of opportunity or deprivation? Is it a world of competition for scarce resources or of sharing and altruism? Or, more basically, is the world a friendly or hostile place?

Principles are the interactive component of worldview, the way in which the worldview is translated into concrete behaviours in life. In one sense, principles have historically been analysed through discussions of morality and ethics and refer to the values that guide our actions. Individuals often see within their actions a moral imperative – a sense of rightness and correctness. We choose to act in certain ways because we see those actions as reflecting our particular and partial notion of the truth. Principles are thus also sources of justification. They justify the particular decisions we make and the actions we undertake in the world – undergirding them with a degree of personal conviction.

Purpose is the interpretive component of worldview. Whereas our perspective is our understanding of how the world is ordered and our principles inform and shape our practices within that world, our purpose is what provides ultimate meaning to life and, as such, dictates the ends we seek. Purpose acts like a funnel for all our decisions and actions, guiding them towards particular outcomes. There exists both a microcosmic and macrocosmic dimension to purpose. The microcosmic dimension is seen in how purpose shapes the particular results we seek in day-to-day activities, conflicts and interactions. In the language of conflict resolution, it refers to both our positions and interests. The macrocosmic dimension lies in how purpose determines the plausible range of positions and interests we might contemplate pursuing in the first place. For example, consider a custody dispute between a divorcing couple. There are many potential outcomes that might be pursued. The contemplation of these outcomes is directed – interpreted – by the microcosmic dimension of purpose. The fact remains, however, that in any typical dispute certain rational outcomes are deemed wholly implausible or, more likely, never even contemplated. This narrowing of the range of possibilities is accomplished by the macrocosmic dimensions of purpose. Whenever we refer to purpose later in this paper, we are referring first and foremost to the broader, more general macrocosmic dimension and its funnelling effect on our decisions.

Utilizing this approach to the concept of worldview we have developed a nascent four-stage developmental model of conflict resolution.[37] The basic premises of the model are as follows:

1) The conflicting behaviours and modes of resolution people engage in will vary depending upon their worldview;

2) Certain worldviews are more prone to conflict, while others are more conducive to the creation of peace, harmony and unity; and

3) Particular structures, architectures of intervention and values correspond with particular worldviews.

Table 1 identifies four major stages in human development – infancy, childhood, adolescence and adulthood – and our arguments for their corresponding worldviews.

Decision Making	**Stage of Development**	**Perspective**	**Principles**	**Purpose**
Level 1	Infancy	World is . . . Me	Self-interest	Instinctual Self-Preservation
Level 2	Childhood	World is . . . Dangerous	Might is Right/Domination	Conscious Self-/Group Preservation
Level 3	Adolescence	World is . . . a Jungle	Survival of the Fittest/Competition	To 'Win'
Level 4	Adulthood	World is . . . One	Truth and Justice	Unity in Diversity

Table 1: The Developmental Stages of Decision-making

Within these levels one finds many common themes from the literature on human development. The worldview of infancy is distinguished from the later worldviews by the fact that the human being in infancy is unable to differentiate between the self and others, a trait that is generally accepted as typical of the human infant. Similarly, the plotting of a heightened tendency towards competition and conflict at the stage of adolescence reflects a typical description of that phase of human life. As well, the expansion of purpose to be all-encompassing reflects cognitive developments in our ways of understanding and relating to the world.

The basic directions in which perspective, principles and purpose develop are obvious. The development of perspective leads from an undifferentiated and self-consumed understanding of the world to an all-encompassing and inclusive one. This erosion of dichotomous perceptions fuels the potential to recognize the indivisibility of one's choices and actions from the surrounding world. Similarly, the development of principles is towards increasingly other-centred or altruistic behaviour (broken down into the ideas of truth and justice in Table 1) and a lessening of the tendency towards either authoritarianism (childhood) or competition (adolescence). Finally, the development of macrocosmic purpose is in the direction of expansion outwards from the self, to the point where unity itself becomes a desired outcome.

The initial relevance for conflict resolution is that whenever individuals sit down to resolve a conflict, they bring to the table a predominant worldview that will generally correspond to one of the four developmental levels. Just as people bring to the resolution table their positions and interests, they also bring with them the perspective, principles and purpose that are informing and shaping those positions and interests, as well as their behaviour. The developmental model thus provides a useful tool for analysing and responding to disputant behaviour. Anecdotes from a training and from an intervention help illustrate this.

After presenting the four worldviews, we often ask people about their own level of decision-making. Typically, the answers given are judgemental and self-delusional, such as the oft-repeated comment, 'I know a lot of people who operate at the childhood and adolescent levels but I'm glad to be at Level 4.' One interesting exchange occurred during a graduate seminar in conflict resolution.[38] After being presented with the four levels of decision-making, John, one of the group members, suggested the group operated according to Level 4 but that he had worked with many who were 'at Level 3'. At one point another class member, Jane, raised the issue of a particularly difficult set of political negotiations in which she had been involved outside of the class. John made the following comment in reply: 'I assume everyone involved in the discussions was operating in a pure Level 3 mode.'

Within this exchange we can observe the drawbacks and utility of a developmental model of conflict resolution. Developmental analogies are often accompanied by misplaced implications of 'better' or 'superior'. In reality, by referring to developmental stages, one should see connotations of cause and effect. Earlier stages cannot and should not be avoided or skipped. They are the building blocks of later ones and are fundamental for their attainment. However, it may be psychologically unhealthy to be in a particular stage of development for too long or at a particular period of life. It is not always appropriate to be primarily driven by the worldview of a child but that is not because of an innate problem with the worldview itself. Only in the context of time and space may worldviews be deemed appropriate or inappropriate, healthy or unhealthy. In their essence they are always needed and fundamental to human life and growth.

This danger aside, the anecdote reveals an important human impulse that lies at the root of all conflict resolution. Human beings want to be successful and be seen as successful; they want to do their best and be associated in other people's minds as the best. Humans innately strive to be better, to improve and to be affirmed in their improvement. John was both trying to associate himself with Level 4 and operating on the assumption that other individuals wanted to be at Level 4. Humans exposed to a developmental model, if it seems to resonate with their experience of being human, are driven to try to fulfil it. Our experience has been that the mere activity of trying to organize conflict resolution methods and processes developmentally for disputants has the effect of propelling them to try to utilize processes that are more likely to result in peaceful, long-standing resolution – whether it is mediation over the courts, the courts over violence or an attempt to create unity as opposed to just reaching an amicable outcome.

The second anecdote is the unfortunately familiar situation of an intervention between a divorcing couple in order to achieve a financial settlement. Throughout the attempted intervention Frank, the husband, exhibited the following behaviours: initially refused to take part; later agreed to take part but tried to set conditions and terms on his participation; tried to commandeer the process from the outset by demanding to make the first opening statement; either failed to listen when others were speaking or attempted to interrupt and challenge noisily; and tried to belittle the mediator on a number of occasions. Based on the developmental model, Frank was exhibiting behaviours typical of a predominantly childhood worldview. His tendency towards control and authoritarianism resonated with the insecurities and fear typical of that stage of development. The tools a mediator typically has at his or her disposal to deal with this situation – caucusing, time-outs, more evaluative tools – while often helpful, nonetheless avoid addressing the real motivations that are prompting Frank's behaviour and making the process difficult. If a resolution is reached under such conditions, there are nagging dilemmas that remain – have we just reinforced Frank's aggressive authoritarian tendencies? Were the outcomes skewed to meet the demands of Frank's behaviour? Won't Frank, given his worldview, be engaged in new, and perhaps related, conflicts that require intervention very soon? By contrast, the developmental model potentially offers a whole other set of techniques and approaches to this situation. At the very least a structured scheme to diagnose Frank's behaviour is provided. This model opens the door to techniques including worldview education and challenging participants to engage in Level 4 conflict resolution that can be used in a way that may be pro-active and lead to long-term resolutions and results.

However, our argument goes even further. Step two in the developmental model of conflict resolution involves recognizing that someone with a particular worldview will correspondingly tend to try to resolve conflict in a particular way (the nature of conflict resolution) employing a particular modality (the mode of conflict resolution). Moreover, it is even possible to speculate how particular contemporary processes might reflect a particular level as opposed to others. The nature of conflict resolution is that it can be survival based, force based, power based or unity based.

We have labelled the modes of conflict resolution as the Self-Centred Mode (S-Mode), the Authoritarian Mode (A-Mode), the Power Struggle Mode (P-Mode) and the Consultative Mode (C-Mode). Table 2 summarizes the nature and modes of conflict resolution.

Decision-Making	Stage of Development	Nature of Conflict Resolution	Mode of Conflict Resolution
Level 1	Infancy	Survival Based	Self-Centred (S-Mode)
Level 2	Childhood	Force Based	Authoritarian (A-Mode)
Level 3	Adolescence	Power Based	Power Struggle (P-Mode)
Level 4	Adulthood	Unity Based	Consultative[39] (C-Mode)

Table 2: The Developmental Modes of Conflict Resolution

When an individual or group attempts to resolve a conflict in the S-Mode, their sole objective is to fulfil self-centred needs apart from any awareness or concern for the needs, interests and issues that the other parties to the conflict face. These self-centred needs have their roots in the extreme vulnerability and dependency of those involved. The S-Mode is not just that a person or a group is 'looking out for their own interests' or 'taking care of number one first' but that they are actually oblivious to the harmful effects on other people of their pursuit of self-interest. Usually, we do not find many examples of pure S-Mode behaviour. Self-interest is also present in the A-Mode and P-Mode but individuals functioning in those two modes are more conscious of its presence. The A-Mode of conflict resolution is associated most intimately with physical and psychological forces as tools for resolving conflicts. Underlying the worldview of childhood is a profound sense of insecurity and by consequence A-Mode conflict resolution often has the disjointed appearance of mediating between moments of force and moments of strained calm.

The moments of calm, just like the moments of force, serve to reinforce the power position of the authority figure by alleviating his or her insecurity.

The association of the A-Mode with force, which often translates into violence, arguably means there are significant remnants of the A-Mode in contemporary peaceful processes. For example, one central critique of adversarial adjudicative processes that contributed to the rise in popularity of mediation was that mediation allowed for a shift in decision-making authority away from legal actors to the disputants themselves. The movement away from imposed resolutions to chosen ones perhaps represents a struggle with the A-Mode and force-based conflict resolution within an otherwise nonviolent process.

The P-Mode corresponds to the adolescent worldview that is characterized by an internal struggle of identity formation and an external competition for autonomy and independence. Such a worldview invites competition and a power struggle with those around them but rarely descends into physical confrontation. Conflict resolution processes that stress winning and positioning seem to fit comfortably with this worldview, as would many aspects of traditional adversarial legal cultures. At the National Conference on Peacemaking and Conflict Resolution held in Phoenix, Arizona, in 1999, we presented the developmental model of conflict resolution to a group of experienced mediators and negotiators. With almost no dissent they agreed on two things. First, and unsurprisingly, they unanimously agreed that when they are engaged in mediation and negotiation, the majority of the parties – whether there are lawyers present or not – behave in the P-Mode. Those who did not behave in the P-Mode were often described as being in the A-Mode. Second, and very surprising, is that they all agreed that mediation and negotiation were both processes that are designed in accordance with a P-Mode mentality. Without exception, mediation and negotiation were termed adolescent processes of conflict resolution. When we challenged them on this classification, they stated that while there are elements within certain forms of negotiation and mediation that perhaps transcend the adolescent mindset (transformative mediation was often mentioned), the processes themselves are adolescent. Many issues were mentioned as evidence for this opinion.

Mediation's focus on party autonomy and mediator neutrality – while important improvements over some of the authoritarian tendency of adjudication – nonetheless embodies ideals of open competition and the importance of winning. Also, many expressed dissatisfaction with mediation's inability to be structured in a manner that is other than the divisive party/party mentality that suffuses almost all conflict resolution processes. This issue speaks to a general concern over whether we have to view conflict resolution in an 'us versus them' and 'either-or' mentality. In other words, when there is a conflict, inevitably it is required that we analyse the conflict as a point of contention between competing parties with different interests who need to resolve the specific issue before them. Even further, popular rhetoric such as 'win/win' outcomes were interpreted by the group of conflict resolution practitioners as embodying the adolescent attitude that the purpose of conflict resolution is to fulfil one's desired end(s) as fully as possible, ideally with the least amount of difficulty or resistance.

The C-Mode of conflict resolution is typified by a movement towards a mature worldview in which unity is recognized as fundamental to individual and collective existence. The goal and purpose of conflict resolution, in this mode, is to achieve a higher degree of unity between individuals, in recognition of the fact that individuals' lives and the conflicts which one faces in life are embedded within larger social patterns and relationships and are indivisible from other contexts and events. As well, concomitant with the mature stage of individual human development, C-Mode processes operate on the assumption that the surface elements of conflict often mask more significant and underlying causes. C-Mode processes aim to encourage a deepened consciousness of these underlying causes and encourage reflection within the process about how this consciousness should impact on conflicting behaviour. In more mundane ways, the distinction between P-Mode and C-Mode processes may be exemplified by a shift in ways of speaking. A C-Mode worldview renders obsolete a language of 'parties', 'disputants' and 'intervention' and encourages language that reinforces harmony and unity while denying the dichotomous perceptions of early stages of development. At the same time, the C-Mode encourages a general fidelity to the creation of higher states of unity.

Bahá'í Consultation and the Developmental Model

The four-stage developmental model of conflict resolution provides an alternative axis for analysing and evaluating conflict resolution processes. It is particularly helpful for studying the relationship between consultation and contemporary conflict resolution processes as it has commonalities with both Bahá'í thought as well as emerging trends within conflict resolution scholarship.

Plotting Bahá'í consultation on the four-stage developmental model illustrates that consultation aspires to embody certain elements of the C-Mode worldview. We have already noted the importance of unity within Bahá'í thought and the comprehensive view of development and maturation in the Bahá'í Faith. To this can be added the willingness of the Bahá'í writings to employ discourses of truth, justice and unity when discussing social ordering and conflict resolution.

The C-Mode characteristics of Bahá'í consultation may be seen more specifically through analysis of the prototypical use of consultation – by a Bahá'í Assembly engaged in a decision-making situation. As described in the Bahá'í writings and generally practised, consultation involves steps of self-preparation, group preparation, open discourse aimed at truth-seeking, decision-making and action. The two preparation stages, which typically involve prayer and meditation, are aimed at reminding participants of the worldview in which they should engage in the upcoming consultation and the framework of unity which they have with the other participants in the process. Consider, for example, one of the prayers typically read at the beginning of Bahá'í Assembly meetings:

> O God, my God! We are servants of Thine that have turned with devotion to Thy Holy Face, that have detached ourselves from all

> besides Thee in this glorious Day. We have gathered in this Spiritual Assembly, united in our views and thoughts, with our purposes harmonized to exalt Thy Word amidst mankind. O Lord, our God! Make us the signs of Thy Divine Guidance, the Standards of Thine exalted Faith amongst men, servants to Thy mighty Covenant, O Thou our Lord Most High, manifestations of Thy Divine Unity in Thine Abhá Kingdom, and resplendent stars shining upon all regions. Lord! Aid us to become seas surging with the billows of Thy wondrous Grace, streams flowing from Thine all-glorious Heights, goodly fruits upon the Tree of Thy heavenly Cause, trees waving through the breezes of Thy Bounty in Thy celestial Vineyard. O God! Make our souls dependent upon the Verses of Thy Divine Unity, our hearts cheered with the outpourings of Thy Grace, that we may unite even as the waves of one sea and become merged together as the rays of Thine effulgent Light; that our thoughts, our views, our feelings may become as one reality, manifesting the spirit of union throughout the world. Thou art the Gracious, the Bountiful, the Bestower, the Almighty, the Merciful, the Compassionate.[40]

In the context of the discussion so far this prayer can be seen to be giving the participants a common point of unity (in this case worship of the divine) which acts as the starting point for building unity through the decision-making process to come. This point of unity is present within the process as a baseline to which participants can turn to refocus the process if needed. This prayer also appears to orient participants to a transcendent object and outcome, a higher level of unity – which is immaterial and intangible – and apart from the particulars of any issue or conflict which they face. This prayer also aims at consciousness-raising – driving those involved to a higher degree of self-awareness concerning the nature of human beings and the place of love, transcendence and unity in human life.

There are also limits on compromise-seeking in consultation which are an aspect of the C-Mode. Compromise, which is ingrained in the give and take cultures of negotiation and mediation, is sometimes in tension with a truth-seeking process. The oft-cited requirement for individuals to be 'detached' from their ideas within the consultation process is intended to facilitate a distinction between truth-seeking and compromise. The 'detachment' requirement facilitates individuals' ideas and stories to be maintained in a comprehensive and whole manner within the process, to see how they fit and interact with the ideas and stories of others. It is from the totality of this information that the process of decision and resolution then commences, in a manner where individuals are encouraged to recognize the impact and importance of other ideas and stories and how they contribute to a more comprehensive understanding of the situation at hand. This is at odds with some compromise-based modalities, in which individuals' stories and ideas are slowly carved until a mutually beneficial story is agreed upon. This quest for the mutually beneficial story is at odds with the quest for the resolution that is based on the most factually complete understanding of the events, a full account of the issues involved and a well-rounded consideration of the individual and collective dimensions of various outcomes.

A full analysis of consultation as a C-Mode process also requires a distinction between participants and process. While consultation was designed as an expression of an ontology that stresses the centrality of unity in human reality, the degree of structural flexibility which it affords indicates that it is a process which can be easily co-opted and transformed by the worldviews of the participants who are engaged in it. In other words, while the process of consultation as designed reflects in substantial ways the C-Mode worldview, in practice it often appears as an A-Mode or P-Mode process. Thus in certain contexts and incidences consultation is in important ways inseparable from other contemporary processes. However, it also contains the structural potential to facilitate a conflict resolution practice that could transcend some of the limitations of current processes. It is in this distinction between participants and process that the gap between 'consultation talk' and 'consultation practice' could be the subject of further critical analysis. Consultation is spoken of in the ambitious rhetoric of the C-Mode but typically practised using modalities, methods and understandings of the A-Mode and P-Mode. Thus the practice of consultation often appears disjointed from our expectations and discourse and as such is a potential source of tension, disillusionment and alienation.

This has important implications for how Bahá'ís think and speak about consultation. The discourse of consultation within the popular religion, focusing on the process and the individual skills and meta-skills of those who participate within it, fails to draw any coherent distinction between consultation and other processes. Conceived in worldview terms, however, consultation can be coherently compared with other processes, and critiques of current consultation practices can be articulated along the axis of worldview. Further, while these arguments are not fully developed in this paper, claims of distinctiveness are given strong support through a worldview analysis.

It is important to note that the claim being made is not that Bahá'í consultation is the only C-Mode process. Indeed, it is implicit within the developmental model that a range of processes and modalities exist at any given stage. In our discussions of these concepts with scholars, practitioners and students of conflict resolution strong arguments have been made that other current modalities and processes – including transformative mediation – are animated by many aspects of the C-Mode worldview. Further, the developmental model suggests that in addition to being described as worldview, if process language must be employed in reference to consultation it should be of a plurality of techniques, stages and skills which take a variety of forms. The unifying element of these plural forms is the worldview dimension which informs how a process might be structured in a particular context as well as the framework within which participants are intended to operate.

Conclusion

Bahá'ís have been encouraged to make a contribution to the conflict resolution movement. In order to fulfil this mandate Bahá'ís must identify and articulate developments within current conflict resolution scholarship and practice which provide coherent frameworks for comparison and analysis of consultation and other processes. The first attempts to do this have been important starting points but more work is needed. Further, it appears that the popular Bahá'í religion, Bahá'í institutions and Bahá'í scholars need to problematize their assumptions about the nature of consultation, to move beyond the conventional ways of talking and thinking about consultation. The focus on worldview and developmentalism is one possible framework that may contribute to this discussion but there are others – including insights from communication theory, political thought, psychology and law. It is hoped that a rejuvenated discourse over the nature of Bahá'í consultation will explore these and other approaches and help account for the claims concerning consultation found in the Bahá'í writings.

Bibliography

'Abdu'l-Bahá. *The Secret of Divine Civilization.* Wilmette, IL: Bahá'í Publishing Trust, 1990.

— *Tablets of Abdul-Baha Abbas.* Chicago: Bahá'í Publishing Society, vol. 1, 1909.

Bahá'í International Community. *Bahá'u'lláh.* London: Bahá'í Publishing Trust, 1991.

Bahá'í Prayers: A Selection of Prayers revealed by Bahá'u'lláh, the Báb and 'Abdu'l-Bahá. Wilmette, IL: Bahá'í Publishing Trust, 2002.

Bahá'í World 1993–94, The. Haifa: Bahá'í World Centre, 1994.

Bahá'u'lláh. *The Kitáb-i-Aqdas.* Haifa: Bahá'í World Centre, 1992.

Baruch Bush, Robert A. and Joseph P. Folger. *The Promise of Mediation: Responding to Conflict Through Empowerment and Recognition.* The Jossey-Bass Conflict Resolution Series, Consulting ed. Jeffrey Z. Rubin. San Francisco: Jossey-Bass, 1994.

Bryan, Penelope E. 'Killing Us Softly: Divorce Mediation and the Politics of Power'. *Buffalo Law Review*, vol. 40, 1992.

Burton, John. *Conflict: Resolution and Provention.* The Conflict Series. New York: St Martin's Press, 1990.

Compilation of Compilations, The. Prepared by the Universal House of Justice 1963–1990. 2 vols. [Sydney]: Bahá'í Publications Australia, 1991.

Currie, Chris M. 'Opinion Wanted: A Theoretical Construct for Mediation Practice'. *Dispute Resolution Journal*, August 1998, pp. 70–5.

Danesh, H.B. *The Psychology of Spirituality*. Ontario: Nine Pines Publishing, 1994.

— *Unity: Creative Foundation of Peace.* Ottawa and Toronto: Bahá'í Studies Publications and Fitzhenry & Whiteside, 1986.

Danesh, Hossain B. and Roshan Danesh. 'A Consultative Conflict-Resolution Model: Beyond Alternative Dispute Resolution'. *International Journal of Peace Studies*, vol. 7, no. 2, Autumn/Winter 2003, pp. 17–33.

—'Has Conflict Resolution Grown Up?: Toward a New Model of Decision Making and Conflict Resolution'. *International Journal of Peace Studies*, vol. 7, no. 1, Spring/Summer 2002, pp. 59–76.

Danesh, Roshan. 'Religious Renewal and Public Order: Law, Politics, and Religion in the Bahá'í Faith'. Unpublished thesis, Harvard Law School, 2003.

Einstein, Albert and Sigmund Freud. *Why War?* Redding: CAT Publishing, 1991.

Galtung, Johan, and Carl G. Jacobsen. *Searching for Peace: The Road to TRANSCEND*. London: Pluto Press, 2000.

Gonzales, Steven. 'The Conflict Resolution Movement'. *Journal of Bahá'í Studies*, vol. 9, no. 2, 1999, pp. 1–46.

Hatcher, William S. 'The Kitáb-i-Aqdas: The Causality Principle in the World of Being', in *The Bahá'í World 1993–94*. Haifa: Bahá'í World Centre, 1994.

Menkel-Meadow, Carrie. 'Ethics in Alternative Dispute Resolution: New Issues, No Answers from the Adversary Conception of Lawyer's Responsibilities'. *South Texas Law Review*, May 1997, pp. 407–54. [Symposium: The Lawyer's Duties and Responsibilities in Dispute Resolution]

— 'The Trouble with the Adversary System in a Postmodern, Multicultural World'. *William and Mary Law Review*, October 1996, pp. 5–44. [Symposium: W.M. Keck Foundation Forum on the Teaching of Legal Ethics]

— 'When Dispute Resolution Begets Disputes of its Own: Conflicts Among Dispute Professionals'. *UCLA Law Review*, August 1997, pp. 1871–1933. [Symposium on Alternative Dispute Resolution]

Moore, Christopher W. *The Mediation Process: Practical Strategies for Resolving Conflict.* San Francisco: Jossey-Bass, 2nd edn. 1996.

Muldoon, Brian. *The Heart of Conflict.* New York: Perigee, 1996.

Sander, Frank E. A. and Stephen B. Goldberg. 'Fitting the Forum to the Fuss: A User-Friendly Guide to Selecting an ADR Procedure'. *Negotiation Journal*, vol. 10, 1994.

Shoghi Effendi. *Guidance for Today and Tomorrow.* London: Bahá'í Publishing Trust, 1953.

The Universal House of Justice. *Messages from the Universal House of Justice 1963-1986: The Third Epoch of the Formative Age.* Wilmette, IL: Bahá'í Publishing Trust, 1996.

Notes

1. Certain portions of this paper, in particular the section entitled 'A Developmental Model of Conflict Resolution', appeared previously with minor differences as a part of the article 'Has Conflict Resolution Grown Up?: Towards a Developmental Model of Conflict Resolution and Decision Making' published in *International Journal of Peace Studies*, vol. 7, no. 1, Spring/Summer 2002, pp. 59–76. Reprinted with permission.
2. The authors thank Kimberly Syphrett for her research assistance and Christine Zerbinis for her editorial comments.
3. 'Consultation bestoweth greater awareness and transmuteth conjecture into certitude. It is a shining light which, in a dark world, leadeth the way and guideth. For everything there is and will continue to be a station of perfection and maturity. The maturity of the gift of understanding is made manifest through consultation.' (Bahá'u'lláh, in *Compilation*, vol. 1, no. 168, p. 93)
4. 'Say: no man can attain his true station except through his justice. No power can exist except through unity. No welfare and no well-being can be attained except through consultation.' (Bahá'u'lláh, in ibid. no. 167, p. 93)
5. 'Man must consult on all matters, whether major or minor, so that he may become cognizant of what is good. Consultation giveth him insight into things and enableth him to delve into questions which are unknown. The light of truth shineth from the faces of those who engage in consultation. Such

consultation causeth the living waters to flow in the meadows of man's reality, the rays of ancient glory to shine upon him, and the tree of his being to be adorned with wondrous fruit. The members who are consulting, however, should behave in the utmost love, harmony and sincerity towards each other. The principle of consultation is one of the most fundamental elements of the divine edifice. Even in their ordinary affairs the individual members of society should consult.' ('Abdu'l-Bahá, in ibid. no. 180, p. 97)

6. Consultation is a formal part of Bahá'í community decision-making meetings called 'nineteen day feasts'. Feasts are composed of three parts: spiritual, administrative and social. The central component of the administrative part is intended to be a forum for consultation among members of the community.
7. There has been little published scholarly discussion of this gap. However, it is a topic of discussion among Bahá'ís. Discussions range in content from cynical reflections on the utility of consultation as practised to substantive debates exploring difficulties with the current Bahá'í practice of consultation and its limitations.
8. These anecdotes are firsthand observations of the authors. The authors have heard countless similar observations.
9. 'Abdu'l-Bahá writes, 'The prime requisites for them that take counsel together are purity of motive, radiance of spirit, detachment from all else save God, attraction to His Divine Fragrances, humility and lowliness amongst His loved ones, patience and long-suffering in difficulties and servitude to His exalted Threshold. Should they be graciously aided to acquire these attributes, victory from the unseen Kingdom of Bahá shall be vouchsafed to them.' ('Abdu'l-Bahá, in *Compilation*, vol. 1, no. 175, p. 95)
10. Currie, 'Opinion Wanted', *Dispute Resolution Journal*, pp. 70–5; Menkel-Meadow, 'Ethics in Alternative Dispute Resolution', *South Texas Law Review*, pp. 407–54. [Symposium: The Lawyer's Duties and Responsibilities in Dispute Resolution]; Menkel-Meadow, 'When Dispute Resolution Begets Disputes of its Own', *UCLA Law Review*, pp. 1871–933. [Symposium on Alternative Dispute Resolution]
11. A good example of this is the National Conference on Peacemaking and Conflict Resolution (NCPCR) held every two years in the United States. At these conferences, one often

finds sessions conducted by Bahá'ís on Bahá'í consultation, faith-based facilitation and issues related to unity-building.

12. Gonzales, 'The Conflict Resolution Movement', in *Journal of Bahá'í Studies*, vol. 9, no. 2, p. 23.
13. ibid.
14. For example, the Universal House Justice wrote the following comment in a letter to Landegg Academy: 'The Universal House of Justice . . . [expresses] its pleasure in learning of the forthcoming launching of your new Master's Degree programme. Such an initiative holds the promise of contributing significantly to the Bahá'í community's efforts to promote an ever deeper understanding of the complementarity and inseparability of the spiritual and material dimensions of reality. The House of Justice is encouraged, too, by the programme's intention of focusing on [the] study [of] moral development and conflict resolution, which must rank high on humanity's agenda in the decades immediately ahead.' (Letter written on behalf of the Universal House of Justice to Landegg Academy, 5 September 1997)
15. The Bahá'í Faith is administered through elected bodies currently known as Assemblies. These bodies are elected annually, are made up of nine individuals and exist at the local (municipal), regional and national levels. The international elected Assembly is called the Universal House of Justice. The Universal House of Justice has nine members and is elected every five years.
16. For example, the 1955–6 Annual Report of the National Spiritual Assembly of the Bahá'ís of the United States comments that '[t]he local Assembly, as the Guardian has stated, can act as a board of arbitration if the couple disagrees about the terms and conditions of divorce, and when it so acts the couple are to abide by its decision'.
17. For more discussion of Bahá'í political thought see Danesh, *Religious Renewal and Public Order*, unpublished thesis, 2003.
18. Moore, *Mediation Process.*
19. See also Baruch Bush, 'What Do We Need a Mediator For?', *Ohio Journal of Dispute Resolution*, pp. 1–36; Menkel-Meadow, 'The Trouble with the Adversary System in a Postmodern, Multicultural World', *William and Mary Law Review*, pp. 5–44. [Symposium: W.M. Keck Foundation Forum on the Teaching of Legal Ethics]

20. For a discussion of the 'quantitative' and 'qualitative' streams of the conflict resolution movement see Menkel-Meadow, 'When Dispute Resolution Begets Disputes of its Own', *UCLA Law Review*, no. 1871, August 1997, p. 44.
21. For an example of feminist critique of mediation see Bryan, 'Killing Us Softly', *Buffalo Law Review*, vol. 40, p. 441.
22. For an example, in their summary of the 'Oppression Story' of the conflict resolution movement, Baruch Bush and Folger write: 'The overall effect of the movement has been to neutralize social justice gains achieved by the civil rights, women's and consumer's movements, among others, and to help reestablish the privileged position of the stronger classes and perpetuate their oppression of the weaker.' (Baruch Bush and Folger, *Promise of Mediation*, p. 23)
23. For example, 'Abdu'l-Bahá writes: 'O People of Persia! Open your eyes! Pay heed! Release yourselves from this blind following of the bigots, this senseless imitation which is the principal reason why men fall away into paths of ignorance and degradation. See the true state of things. Rise up; seize hold of such means as will bring you life and happiness and greatness and glory among all the nations of the world.' ('Abdu'l-Bahá, *Secret of Divine Civilization*, p. 104)
24. Galtung and Jacobsen, *Searching for Peace*, p. vii.
25. Muldoon, *Heart of Conflict*, p. 9.
26. The work of Abraham H. Maslow is a good example. Also, Freud's assertions that the only hope for a reduction of war is in the displacement of instinctual aims and impulses. (Einstein and Freud, *Why War?*)
27. William S. Hatcher, echoing 'Abdu'l-Bahá's descriptions of the nature of reality, writes that 'the Bahá'í writings affirm that reality is an integrated whole but that this wholeness is a unity in diversity, not a uniformity'. (Hatcher, 'The Kitáb-i-Aqdas: The Causality Principle in the World of Being', in *Bahá'í World* 1993–94, p. 190.) For further discussion of the relationship between unity and conflict see Danesh and Danesh, 'Has Conflict Resolution Grown Up? Towards a Developmental Model of Conflict Resolution and Decision Making'. For a discussion of the concept of unity in the Bahá'í Faith and its relationship to peace see Danesh, *Unity: Creative Foundation of Peace*.
28. For example, in Bahá'í consultation it is emphasized that it is

better for an Assembly to reach a flawed decision but be united in the outcome than to reach a better decision but be disunited.

29. The Universal House of Justice emphasizes the importance of using unity as the frame of reference for approaching social situations: 'When Bahá'u'lláh proclaimed His Message to the world in the nineteenth century He made it abundantly clear that the first step essential for the peace and progress of mankind was its unification. As He says, "The well-being of mankind, its peace and security are unattainable unless and until its unity is firmly established." To this day, however, you will find most people take the opposite point of view: they look upon unity as an ultimate almost unattainable goal and concentrate first on remedying all the other ills of mankind. If they did but know it, these other ills are but various symptoms and side effects of the basic disease – disunity.' (From a letter of the Universal House of Justice to an individual, 8 December 1967, in The Universal House of Justice, *Messages from the Universal House of Justice 1963 to 1986*, para. 55.3, p. 125)
30. For example, see Baruch Bush and Folger, *Promise of Mediation*.
31. Burton, *Conflict: Resolution and Provention*.
32. Sander and Goldberg, *Fitting the Forum to the Fuss*.
33. A good summary of this idea is the following statement from the Bahá'í International Community: 'One of the most suggestive analogies to be found in the writings not only of Bahá'u'lláh, but of the Báb before Him, is the comparison between the evolution of the human race and the life of the individual human being. Humanity has moved through stages in its collective development which are reminiscent of the periods of infancy, childhood, and adolescence in the maturation of its individual members. We are now experiencing the beginnings of our collective maturity, endowed with new capacities and opportunities of which we as yet have only the dimmest awareness.

    'Against this background, it is not difficult to understand the primacy given in Bahá'u'lláh's teachings to the principle of unity.' (Bahá'í International Community, *Bahá'u'lláh*, p. 30)
34. 'Abdu'l-Bahá summarizes the life transformation that occurs as one spiritually matures in the following terms: 'Know thou, verily, man before reaching (spiritual) maturity passes his days and only apprehends trivial things which are clear on account of their exoteric indications, but when he attains full

development, then he grasps the reality of things and their esoteric facts. Every day after maturity is equivalent to one year before it, on account of man's perception, understanding, apprehension and discoveries.' ('Abdu'l-Bahá, *Tablets of Abdul-Baha*, vol. 1, p. 166)

35. This linking of individual spiritual growth and collective change and maturation is a theme echoed in various ways in the Bahá'í writings. For example, Bahá'u'lláh often asserts hegemony over the 'hearts of men', which alludes, amongst other things, to His intention to lead people closer to God. Yet, Bahá'u'lláh makes it clear that social ordering and the pattern of collective life are not distinct from the processes of spiritual growth and change. For example, after making the assertion that He does not 'wish to lay hands on your kingdoms' (Bahá'u'lláh, *Kitáb-i-Aqdas*, para. 83), Bahá'u'lláh appears to assert that the world of kings – the world of order, society and politics – must also respond and submit to the processes of change and development: 'How great the blessedness that awaiteth the king who will arise to aid My Cause in My kingdom, who will detach himself from all else but Me! Such a king is numbered with the companions of the Crimson Ark – the Ark which God hath prepared for the people of Bahá. All must glorify his name, must reverence his station, and aid him to unlock the cities with the keys of My Name, the omnipotent Protector of all that inhabit the visible and invisible kingdoms. Such a king is the very eye of mankind, the luminous ornament on the brow of creation, the fountainhead of blessings unto the whole world.' (ibid. para. 84)

36. This idea is captured in Shoghi Effendi's introduction to the Bahá'í Faith in which he succinctly states that the Bahá'í Faith 'exalts any work performed in the spirit of service to the level of worship'. (Shoghi Effendi, *Guidance for Today and Tomorrow*, p. 4)

37. This developmental model of conflict resolution forms the basis of an innovative new process of conflict resolution called Conflict-free Conflict Resolution (CFCR). Implications of this model have been more fully discussed in Danesh and Danesh, 'Has Conflict Resolution Grown Up?', *International Journal of Peace Studies*, vol. 7, no. 1, Spring/Summer 2002, pp. 59–76; Danesh and Danesh, 'A Consultative Conflict-Resolution Model', *International Journal of Peace Studies*, vol. 7, no. 2, Autumn/Winter 2002, pp. 17–33.

38. The recounted events occurred in the graduate seminar 'Conflict-Free Conflict Resolution' taught by the authors at Landegg International University in June 2000. The names of the participants have been changed, as is the case throughout this article.
39. The term 'consultative' in this chart does not refer to Bahá'í consultation specifically. It is being employed as a general descriptive term.
40. 'Abdu'l-Bahá, in *Bahá'í Prayers*, pp. 300–1.

3

Contemporary Governance and Conflict Resolution: A Bahá'í Reading

Graham Hassall

It is an age of universal reformation. Laws and statutes of civil and federal governments are in process of change and transformation. Sciences and arts are being moulded anew. Thoughts are metamorphosed. The foundations of human society are changing and strengthening.[1]

A new world order is emerging in the wake of the post-Cold War realities. As America awaits the fifth 'big change', reinterpretation of the 'cultural pantheon of several distinct realities' assumes special meaning for global well-being, for peaceful coexistence and global prosperity. The triumphal globalist notion of 'the end of history' is repudiated by the appalling contradictions of the Cold Victory. The search for a 'prophetic paradigm' – beyond nationalistic idolatry, utopian hubris, and liberal democratic complacency – continues for the sake of peace, justice, freedom, love, and the prosperity of all humankind.[2]

'Religion as Critique'

Religion has traditionally played a role in overcoming conflict.[3] Prophetic law has, additionally, served as an undeniable basis, a statement of the social *grundnorm* (now referred to as 'natural law') on which contemporary legal codes have been based. The 'revealed laws' are supplemented by laws established through human reason and by reference to tradition. As the purpose of law is promotion of the well-being of the masses rather than 'chains that bind them', ancient codes of law, whether written or customary, require reform if they prove detrimental to the welfare and interests of peoples in a period of rapid social evolution.

In this article I explore the conflict-resolving capacities of contemporary political processes in the context of Bahá'í writings on governance and conflict. The article adopts a 'religion as critique' approach to the practices of modernity and identifies a number of challenges of contemporary government that must sooner or later be addressed in the inevitable move to more effective governmental norms and processes.[4] To state my thesis in brief, the Bahá'í writings provide the foundations for a 'critique of modernity' at the same time that they suggest possible paths to the future. A major criticism of modernist government is its inability to solve conflicts. In fact, current structures of government contribute in many circumstances to the production of conflict rather than its resolution. These conflict-laden structures are accompanied by conflict-enhancing attitudes which tolerate high levels of conflict owing to a belief that such conflict is inevitable.

Religious critique of modernity takes many forms, from discourse to political action, to violent confrontation.[5] Obviously, this essay advocates the pursuit of change through dialogue and discourse. Less obvious may be its normative approach, as opposed to idealistic: it proposes pursuit of change in desired directions through both intellectual and social engagement and not through intellectual idealization alone.

Governance in the Bahá'í Writings

The term 'governance' refers to the structures that are established by societies for the purpose of regulating their affairs and promoting their welfare. The history of the diverse peoples of the world is in one sense a vast pool of experience with different systems of governance, each having its strengths and weaknesses and each contributing something to the practice of governance in our day. From remnants of splendid empires the nations of the first, second and third worlds have emerged, each commending the victories of their own style. From despotisms to authoritarian democracies to anarchical, stateless societies; from laissez-faire capitalism to communalism and communism; from narrow nationalisms and ethno-nationalisms to socialist and liberal internationalisms – world history records many and diverse experiments in social and political organization.[6]

The Bahá'í writings, no less than earlier prophetic religions, concern themselves with governance. In numerous of His Tablets, Bahá'u'lláh refers to the 'lamentably defective' condition of the contemporary order.[7] But this critique differs from other critiques of modernity, particularly the post-modern, which 'void' meaning through deconstruction of contemporary paradigms of power without suggesting alternatives.[8] Rather, it points to limitations in modern ideologies, structures of government and systems of values while acknowledging signs of positive social and political change.

The need for reform was a constant refrain in the discourse of 'Abdu'l-Bahá.[9] Public talks in North America highlighted the 'call to freedom' that challenged the 'dogma, creeds and hereditary beliefs' which could not withstand 'the analysis of reason in this century'.[10] His essay addressed to the Hague Conference for A Durable Peace questioned the adequacy of the nation state as a basis for peace.[11] His treatise *The Secret of Divine Civilization* and Shoghi Effendi's letters *The World Order of Bahá'u'lláh* expand on Bahá'u'lláh's general themes. Shoghi Effendi explained that the 'animating purpose' of Bahá'u'lláh's teachings is to broaden the basis of society's foundations and to 'remould its institutions in a manner consonant with the needs of an ever-changing world'.[12]

The Bahá'í model of governance presents itself, He suggests, as a 'pattern' of 'divine civilization'[13] that challenges many institutions of contemporary society and rejects conflict built into such current processes and structures as the adversarial structure of civil government, the advocacy principle informing most of civil law, the struggle between classes and other social groups and the competitive spirit in much of modern life.

The 'alternative' model of governance offered in the Bahá'í writings seeks to transform current practices rather than replace them. According to the 'organic' theory of social evolution, such interventions, combined with the current systems' inherent instabilities, will assist in realizing fundamental change, which will include changes in values as well as in structures and procedures, to an extent that systems theorists call a 'paradigm shift'.

As long ago as the 1930s Shoghi Effendi commented on the detrimental effect of narrowly defined national policies on global order. His letters *The Promised Day is Come* and *The World Order of Bahá'u'lláh* contrast the destructive forms of nationalism that emerged in the 19th and 20th centuries with a positive form of nationalism that must characterize future states. Shoghi Effendi traced 'intolerant and militant nationalism' to Hegelian philosophy which deifies the state.[14] 'Abdu'l-Bahá's view was that if the predominant conception of patriotism remains 'limited within a certain circle, it will be the primary cause of the world's destruction'.[15] Following World War One national leaders who feared that allegiance to any form of internationalism would 'sap the loyalty' required for the continued existence of the nation states, opposed such developments as the Geneva Protocol, the idea of a United States of Europe, and an Economic Union of Europe. We now observe, of course, that each of these institutions has come to pass. Economically, 'narrow' and 'brutal nationalism', which had been reinforced by the post-war theory of self-determination, had resulted in 'high and prohibitive tariffs' which in turn inhibited the 'healthy flow of international trade' and finance.[16] In short, was Shoghi Effendi's conclusion as early as the 1930s, national leaders had failed to adapt national processes which were 'suited to the ancient days of self-contained nations' to present-day needs.[17]

Shoghi Effendi also associated the rise of nationalism with the demise of religious belief, noting that in some instances nationalist movements had included a 'conscious, avowed, organized attack' on Christianity;[18] had been associated with a 'systematized work of defamation against all forms of ecclesiastical influence', and had 'contributed to the de-Christianization of the masses'; and 'a notable decline in the authority, the prestige and power of the Church'.[19] The resulting secularization of society in modernism has been described as a 'disenchantment' of public life, a reduction of meaning to social good which leads to cynicism, to despair and to hypocritical uses of power by elites who deny the existence of any duties higher than their own selves and their constituencies. Even the rights of coming generations are sacrificed to the interests of those currently in power. Public office is no longer held 'in trust', on behalf of those who came before and those of future generations. Conflicts between competing social, political and economic interests are considered unavoidable and for the most part unresolvable (hence, to be 'managed', rather than 'resolved'). In this modernist view, conflict between states is as inevitable as conflict within states. In the international arena there is also the expectation that conflict can be managed in accordance with the interests of each sovereign state. Where interests coincide, states may agree to multilateral or bilateral treaty arrangements but in cases of conflict most states reserve the right, ultimately, to defend their interests militarily.

Shoghi Effendi has explained that the Bahá'í model cannot be associated with any single known model of governance but 'embodies, reconciles and assimilates within its framework'[20] the best features of each classical model while remaining free of their defects. It is unlike any form of government, whether democracy, autocracy, dictatorship, monarchy or republic; and as such cannot be wholly likened to such historic religious legal systems as the Hebrew Commonwealth or the governmental orders developed in the Christian and Islamic civilizations. It is, in other words, a unique Administrative Order, both in theory and in practice, and in both secular and religious traditions.[21] Bahá'u'lláh commended the 'republican form' of government but preferred that the role of monarchy be retained[22] and praised the British system for being 'adorned with the light of both kingship and of the consultation of the people'.[23]

In recent years the Universal House of Justice and its agencies have elaborated on such subjects as the future of the United Nations Organization[24] and the challenges of social development. *The Prosperity of Humankind* suggests that reassessment of structures and processes of government will include redefinition of the terms 'power' and 'authority'; formulation of laws that are 'universal in both character and authority';[25] reformulation of consultative practices and of concepts of justice; a conscious effort to ensure that 'technological breakthroughs' and 'limited resources' are not reserved for 'privileged minorities';[26] and the continued development of laws protecting human rights and the whole range of civil, political, social and economic rights.[27] Among specific observations of current practice, it criticizes the lack of citizen involvement in local-level decision-making.[28]

Modernity and the Exhaustion of Possibilities

Giddens describes modernity as the 'institutions and modes of behaviour established first of all in post-feudal Europe but which in the twentieth century increasingly have become world-historical in their impact'.[29] Modernity, in other words, is a term used to describe the industrial, capitalist societies of the 20th century and the social relations experienced within them, principally based on the nation state but also on 'dis-embedded social relations' that have evolved from the individualization and eventually the alienation of individual existence.[30]

Nationalism continues to frame most thinking about the quest for order in modernity and modernists continue to regard the social and political technologies of liberal democracy and international relations as being adequate for managing conflict. With the decline of the communist system, some have proclaimed the 'end of history' and the victory of liberal democracy. But this supposes an 'exhaustion of possibilities' that attempts closure of debate on political innovation. The idea that 'there are no more solutions left' to combat the world's problems is simply a prejudice.[31]

Although nationalism has provided the key ideological motif in the modern period, it has not been without significant limitations. Communism, similarly, has proved an ideological programme unable to deliver genuine social, political and economic advance. The cause of fascism flowered for a time in mid-century but proved so extreme as to bring opposition to itself from all directions. Towards the end of the 20th century ethnonationalisms emerged as key ideological forces. The structures of governance that have been built on these predominant ideologies of modernism have reached the limits of their effectiveness and are in disarray. Philosophically the confidence of the 'moderns' has been replaced by the scepticism of the post-moderns and even where revolutionaries have replaced their former hegemonic overlords the challenges of governance remain.

If liberal democracy perfects the science of governance, how do we account for the vast gap in social indicators between humanity's present condition and the ability of governments to meet its needs? The few apparently successful liberal democracies must be seen against a far more encompassing background. Mohan summarizes the present impasse in this way:

> Capitalism and communism represent two diametrically opposed schools of thought. The strength and weakness of the two systems stem from the inherent nature of materialism. Communism has failed, and socialism is fighting for its survival in the material culture that is apparently pervasive and successful. Capitalism's claim that it has been ultimately victorious over the ruins of the Marxist ideologies is both unscientific and pretentious . . . In a way, the post-material consciousness is, rather, a rediscovery of lost values: basic empowerment (democratization), fundamental authenticity (good faith), primitive innocence (freedom from oppression), and primordial justice (ethics of action and values). These four elements will serve as the tenets of social praxis and help define the paradigm of a rational and humane society that is both responsible and compassionate.[32]

Progress under Conditions of Modernity

The modern period has undoubtedly made considerable progress in its approaches to government. The ideal of democracy has been extended and strengthened,[33] adherence to the ideas of the rule of law and of constitutionalism has spread and the concept of justice as the basis of governmental authority has matured. Elected representatives make law and change law, courts resolve disputes and bureaucratic agencies aim to deliver government programmes throughout the state. Although most decision-making occurs at the national level, decision-making and problem-solving at the global level is becoming more comprehensive, as indicated in the rapid maturation of international law.

The expression of competing voices within parliaments concerning matters of government invented by liberal democracy is an advance over the lack of such representation under feudalism and the absolute monarchies. The provision of courts of law from local to national levels, with yet other courts in which to appeal decisions of lower courts, is similarly an advance over earlier judicial bodies that were poorly equipped to assess evidence and to dispense justice. So, too, the elaboration of modern bureaucracies to administer every aspect of government policy provides a level of public support unmatched at any time in history.

Similar advances can be reported for most parts of the globe. Societies that were traditionally stratified, based on class, caste, even slavery, are undergoing modification. There has been propagation, too, of the institutions and values of democracy and of such qualities of civil societies as expansion of print and electronic media and the emergence of significant numbers of private citizens actively involved in public life. This social change has been aided by the spread of technology and communications including satellites, and most recently, the Internet.[34]

The Limits to Modernity

The adequacy of this modernist framework is being challenged in several ways. The traditional notion that the nation is the supreme political unit, possessing such sovereign rights as the right to wage war, to control the flow of goods and people across its borders, and to legislate and carry out domestic law, is inconsistent with the growing practice of international commerce and trade. Nationally organized forms of government and state are increasingly impotent in the face of global problems that include environmental deterioration, population explosion, the depletion of resources of energy, the outbreak of war and the conclusion of peace, the establishment of security, and of economic and social justice.[35] The right to wage war is incompatible with the expanding regime of humanitarian law and human rights protection.[36] It is also too costly and the impact of modern weaponry too devastating to achieve any political objectives. Descent into military conflict only indicates an inability to adopt effective conflict resolution techniques.

Additional tasks that remain include improving electoral processes to ensure that public affairs are handled by leaders with the requisite qualities;[37] improving the performance of the various constitutional organs, such as the parliaments, courts and executive branches of government;[38] and strengthening other mechanisms of accountability.[39] Yet another task requires redistribution of constitutional powers, some to a global state, others to local authorities. Most importantly, constitutional changes must be accompanied by a transformation in the values of leaders and peoples alike. Without a consciousness of the 'wholeness of humankind' and a desire for unity, other essential reforms in leadership selection, global constitutionalism and citizen participation will be insufficient and national, ideological and partisan interests will continue to control state power.[40] The suffering and underdevelopment of the majority of the world's people will continue, as will disparities between rich and poor. The fact that the current models of government are failing to meet human needs indicates that additional models will be established through necessity.[41] The task is to choose between alternative possible futures.

Four Challenges of Contemporary Governance

Taken as a whole, the critiques mentioned above highlight the fact that modern governments, whether liberal democratic or socialist, face four major challenges: establishing and maintaining legitimacy, promoting democracy, solving disputes effectively and ensuring social and economic development. These challenges incorporate the values of unity, democracy, justice and prosperity. Governments that do not respond effectively to these challenges risk serious internal conflicts and social instability.

Legitimacy

Legitimacy refers to the acceptance of the foundational principles of a state and to the constitution of a state. A people that sees its state and government as having legitimacy has a sense of constitutional unity. Without this sense of unity, a state is in danger of serious conflict and even collapse. A government can establish this sense of legitimacy over time by meeting the needs of the people and by building a sense of purpose and unity amongst them. The ability to build legitimacy depends partly on the quality of dialogue between the people and the state. The legitimacy of a state provides the foundation for the operation of democracy.[42]

Many states emerged from the break-up of colonial empires, from colonial intrusion or from inadequate peace treaties at the conclusion of unjustified wars. The 'nation' was the form adopted for anti-colonial struggle and perhaps a majority of the nations are identical with the boundaries of colonial states established by the European powers. The legacies of these origins include continuing uncertainty and dispute as to the relationship between ethnicity and statehood and hence uncertainty as to the status of minorities and 'first peoples'. Given that the boundaries of many contemporary states were determined arbitrarily, the lack of an authority to adequately settle boundary disputes is a serious hindrance to peace between states.[43]

Anderson's observation that nations are no more than 'imagined communities'[44] that require considerable social and political engineering to propagate echoes 'Abdu'l-Bahá's much earlier observation of nations and peoples as 'limited unities' that were 'imaginary and without real foundation'.[45] The artificial and arbitrary nature of national boundaries, coupled with insufficient mechanisms for handling boundary disputes, has been one of the major sources of international conflict in the past two centuries.[46]

The historical moments in which a great many nations were formed – through treaties or declarations of independence, left 'the people' out of negotiations concerning their own destiny and launched their nations in undemocratic circumstances which have not necessarily been remedied. Most current conflicts related to claims of ethno-nationalism, or separatism, have as their root cause a legitimacy deficit.[47]

The legitimacy of many contemporary states may currently be under challenge for one of several other reasons: in many places they are not meeting the basic human needs of their peoples. Ironically, while states are spending large proportions of their income on defence, they are failing to provide security. The 'global order' lacks legitimacy through lack of participation by citizens in decisions taken by nation states in the international arena.

Democracy

In a broad sense democracy refers to the election of leaders by the people. People who elect their own leaders are said to be 'free', although this 'freedom' refers to their agreement to act as they wish within the bounds of the rights and responsibilities that are determined by the society's legal system and public culture. The idea of democracy is not to achieve 'total freedom' – for such a thing is impossible – but to provide a social and political society in which individuals are able to pursue goals of their own choosing, to fully develop their personalities, abilities and talents, and to contribute the fruits of their efforts back to their society. Democracy offers both legitimacy and accountability, since the people have control over their leaders and over the laws that bind them. Where these conditions are met, a government acquires authority, and possessing authority, becomes effective in governing with a sense of justice.[48]

Democracy is a core Bahá'í value. But in the Bahá'í conception it does not refer merely to 'freedom of speech' or to the articulation of individual human rights. It refers rather to a culture in which the individual feels free to set forth views in an atmosphere of tolerance; in which the people's elected representatives see themselves as trustees of the public will; in which the people have respect for the decisions of the duly elected authorities; in which the values of diversity, reciprocity and mutuality are appreciated. Democracy therefore refers to a culture rather than to rules.

'Consultation' exemplifies a practice of governance that is given considerable attention in the Bahá'í writings. Open consultation is acknowledged as an essential component of a united society. Through it, each can know the thoughts of others. Any interference with the expression of thoughts leads to distortion of messages, to misunderstandings and ultimately to disunity.[49]

The Bahá'í approach to consultation recognizes the power of discourse to influence to either positive or negative effect. Bahá'u'lláh counsels on the proper use of language. The consultative principle, already found in most systems of government, is applauded as a 'lamp of guidance which leadeth the way'.[50] A principle with which it must be associated – albeit an association as yet unappreciated by theories of bureaucratic effectiveness – is that of compassion. The presence of these two capacities allows governments to 'fully acquaint themselves with the conditions of those they govern'.[51]

Bahá'u'lláh encourages free association between peoples,[52] since familiarity between people leads to 'concord', which is 'conducive to the maintenance of order'.[53] But this policy requires 'tolerance and righteousness'.[54] Bahá'u'lláh refers at length to the promotion of 'fellowship, kindliness and unity'[55] and continually warns of the need to 'flee' from 'anything whatsoever from which the odour of mischief can be detected'.[56] An additional aspect of the principle of tolerance concerns treatment of minorities, who live in all societies. The Bahá'í writings reject insistence on uniformity and encourage appreciation of diversity.[57]

Current principles of democratic government contain some, but not all, elements of the Bahá'í model. At a fundamental level, for instance, the Bahá'í approach retains the principle of elected leadership while abandoning current notions of electoral 'campaigning' and upholds the necessity for contestation of important issues while denying the necessity for institutionalized opposition. 'In every country where any of this people reside,' is Bahá'u'lláh's injunction, 'they must behave towards the government of that country with loyalty, honesty and truthfulness.'[58]

Electoral Design

Ironically, the 'representative democracy' practised in many states contains a number of elements that hinder rather than stimulate democratic activity. The nomination of a limited number of candidates, for instance, limits the choices placed before the elector and favours the interests of dominant personalities.[59] Furthermore, it hinders the 'spirit of initiative' in society and discourages inclinations toward individual responsibility.[60] Party systems also intervene between the individual voter and public offices in determining policy options and in controlling legislatures through, for example, controlling the voting preferences of party members.

In majoritarian systems the ability to restrict the number of candidates is related to the need for the winner to obtain at least 50 per cent of the vote. Rather than being free to vote from the eligible population at large, the voter must select one of the nominated candidates, whose approval generally rests with a political party. The operation of majoritarian systems, in the name of democracy, creates permanent minorities whose interests can never gain the support of such a majority and whose interests are never therefore fully considered by the elected representatives.[61]

Campaigns associated with political elections generate considerable conflict and violence. The process whereby candidates seek support from the electorate by publicizing their policy platforms in order to win voter approval has become increasingly distorted and subject to abuse. Problems include 'negative' campaigns (to turn an electorate against one's opponents), the making of promises in order to procure votes without the intention of keeping them and outright electoral corruption. Parties also now rely on sophisticated polling to identify electoral sentiments so that candidates can address them in order to win votes. Increasingly, parties are seeking out 'high profile' candidates from the entertainment and sports industries to attract public attention.

The extreme cost of obtaining a preeminent position, given that competing parties are seeking a similar goal, has dramatically increased the cost of political participation and party financing has become a major ethical issue. Without extensive funding, the political project becomes impossible but obtaining the required level of funding on a regular basis is a major task and has frequently led to the use of illegal strategies.

In sum, with the elaboration of electoral campaigns leaders are increasingly self-referring. In other words, candidates propose themselves and seek to minimize the worth of their rivals. Much selection has occurred prior to the ballot. Party campaigns are increasingly based on sophisticated market research. The lack of integrity in contemporary electoral systems has reduced the calibre of candidates willing to participate. Party systems are divisive at fundamental levels.[62] This can be verified empirically, with elections throughout the world increasingly being marred by 'electoral violence' between supporters of rival parties and candidates. For all these reasons democracy has become associated with partisanship, with cynicism, apathy and corruption. It has to be raised above these results of the 'political theatre' produced by nominations, candidature, electioneering and solicitation.

Moral courage has always been a virtue of the leadership. With growth in social complexity and the size of moral dilemmas, the capacity to lead with moral clarity is all the more desirable. 'Abdu'l-Bahá extolled the incorruptible leader schooled in both religious and worldly knowledge[63] and expanded on the qualities of the 'spiritually learned'[64] in his early work *The Secret of Divine Civilization*.

New communicative capacities are emerging to fill the need for 'active citizenry' formally provided by the processes of nominations and campaigns. The absence of electoral campaigning in the Bahá'í process eliminates problems of determining influences on candidates through donations to campaign funds, for none exist. Also, the problem of monitoring election expenses does not exist. Voters are to take part in elections 'consciously and diligently' and not be aloof or assume an indifferent or independent attitude.[65]

The institutions of representative democracy purport to represent 'the people'. Increasingly, however, 'the people' are voicing their own opinions and stand in less need of representation. New technologies of communication are allowing 'we the people' to mobilize and to articulate their views. This has led to an increase in the range of views being broadcast and a decrease in the representative power of the elected representatives. The task now is to be able to hear this increased range of voices and to do so in a manner that still allows decisions to be made in a timely manner. The rapid rise of the NGO movement also suggests that citizens desire to air their views other than through their elected representatives.

Many important issues are no longer decided by national parliaments and citizens are voicing their concerns directly to governments other than their own. They have become, in other words, active in a supranational civil society. The notion of 'the people' of a nation being in some way a united collective was thus shattered in the last century by the emergence of extra voices, such as stateless peoples deprived of recognition by international law. The inability of the nation-state system to recognize these peoples was a source of aggravation throughout the 20th century.

Parliamentary Design

The separation of members of the legislature into 'the government' and 'the opposition' is another problematic feature of the Westminster tradition. Whereas the intention of the division was to ensure that parliament, as the legislature, held the executive accountable for its actions while at the same time providing an alternative group of representatives to develop and demonstrate their capacity to become an 'alternative government', the logic of the system has taken its toll on theory. 'Abdu'l-Bahá stated what everyone knows:

> Parliamentary procedure should have for its object the attainment of the light of truth upon questions presented and not furnish a battleground for opposition and self-opinion. Antagonism and contradiction are unfortunate and always destructive to truth.[66]

However, Westminster-derived parliaments are regarded as arenas of political point-scoring rather than deliberation and rarely provide an opportunity for all members to consult 'fully and frankly' on issues of public concern. The 'Westminster divide' also inhibits the utilization of all human resources in parliament by assigning a substantial minority to 'opposition' status.

The division of powers that features in most modern constitutions, while based on the meritorious search for a check on absolute power, also promotes conflicts within the constitutional offices, such as between a head of executive and head of judiciary. While such conflicts are often held to indicate that the 'separation of powers' is being tested and strengthened, it can also mean that the interests of the masses are being neglected while members of the elect and elite who are in public office idly dispute the allocation of powers, functions and privileges.

The 'separation of powers' doctrine also introduces problems into the possible emergence of global thinking about governance. In the western tradition, the separation of powers as achieved over time in England, France and the United States served the purpose of limiting the potential of any one branch of government from exercising total power. It was a 'check on governmental authority'. The constitutional doctrine of limiting state authority has come to occupy a position of dogma. In the spread of constitutional ideas around the world it is now being applied with less success in cultures unfamiliar with the idea of the separability of authority. But whereas this institutionalization established a certain degree of order in political life, it is not a universally valid construct and has led to levels of conflict that threaten the very fabric of states and societies. The method of debate in most contemporary parliaments does not constitute consultation in pursuit of answers to complex problems but political discourse having other objectives, particularly survival and conquest within the system.

Parliamentary design and the behaviour of political parties are linked. Law is associated with power and state law is viewed as a medium for marshalling the resources of the state to conduct competition with all other states. Political power has come to be shaped as a 'prize' which, when won by the leading party, can be exercised in that party's interests. A 'conservative party', for instance, may win power and act on policies that favour the privileged, while elsewhere a 'labour party' in government privileges the rights of workers. Power is viewed as an opportunity to force change in the direction of their desires.[67] A very different view of law sees it as a medium for setting standards.[68]

Political parties emerged from the desire of interest groups to act with a united voice in public life and in parliament. But parties have come to dominate legislatures in ways that were unimaginable a century ago. With the decline of democratic consultation in parliaments, parliamentarians quickly became dissatisfied with mere representation in parliament and sought control of the executive. By the late 20th century the rationale of the 'party machine' had become little more than a way to capture a majority in the legislature. The artificiality of two-party systems is evident in the decline of the effectiveness of two-party systems within democratic political systems. The rise of third and fourth parties has been accommodated through changes to proportional representation systems, which continue to place the interests of parties above those of citizens. Party coherence invariably depends on specific ideological and public policy programmes, whereas the complexity of public life is rendering ideologies inadequate. No party is able to generate policies that cater to the needs of all members of society and the futility of attempting to do so *in advance* of the party's participation in the legislature points to a further failing of the present system: a pattern of parliamentary debate – and political discourse in general – which ignores all the principles of consultation and privileges coercive and aggressive styles of debate intended to drown dissenting voices rather than to entertain them.

Justice

In communities of disenchantment, legality need not be coupled with justice. To create just laws a system of governance must find some way of identifying and co-opting just leaders. Just laws can only derive from close understanding of the conditions of society. In some political systems the elected leaders are known for their familiarity with their 'electorates'. In others, however, their notoriety stems from the fact of their ignorance of the circumstances of those whom they purport to represent.

The purpose of law is to ensure the well-being of all. Laws protect the rights and interests of individuals and of the community as a whole by outlining systems of obligations and duties and providing sanctions when the laws are transgressed.[69] Laws also provide for the transfer of wealth within a society, through systems of taxation and other levies, for the purpose of redistribution of wealth among those who are more and less needy in society. When laws provide certainty and are based on principles of fairness, they can contribute to a sense of well-being and harmony in society. A justice system based on an adversarial mode of decision-making is less a quest for truth or justice than a quest for victory in the eyes of the law.

The promotion of human rights requires a fundamental redefinition of human relationships and movement in this direction has barely begun. Elements in the redefinition include consultation (requiring standards far beyond current practices of negotiation and compromise, and the 'culture of protest' that one associates with debate, propaganda, the adversarial method and paradigms of partisanship); far greater access to knowledge and to the opportunity to apply it to the shaping of human affairs.

The reformulation of consultative practices includes recognition of the interrelationship between justice, consultation and the attainment of social and economic development. Justice is best achieved when those in power are motivated by concern for their own spiritual progress.[70] Bahá'u'lláh exhorts governments to hold in highest regard the principles of reward and punishment, these being the 'two pillars' which 'traineth the world'.[71] When this principle is recognized, public offices are best filled according to 'desert and merit'.[72] He stressed the need for structures of government led by the learned and the wise, yet responsive to the will of the masses.

Prosperity

A final challenge of contemporary governance is the generation of social and economic prosperity. This challenge requires more than 'economic development', more than industrialization and increased consumption and more than the spread of material benefits. It refers to the attainment of the well-being of the people, through their acquisition of material development in accordance with their own plans, activities and priorities. It refers, that is, to the development of the peoples' personalities in accordance with their own volition and choice. In the Bahá'í perspective, justice on a world scale is not possible given the existing nation-state system that has no intention of remedying the disparities between the nations and makes no effective inroads, furthermore, into disparities that exist within them.

Modernity in Transition: Why Change is Inevitable

Transition towards more global and more conflict-resolving governance has commenced and further change is inevitable. Whether focused on reforms to electoral systems, parliaments, courts or the use of executive power, such change is invariably motivated by the need to minimize conflict and enhance legitimacy and effectiveness. There is also urgent need for reform of governance at the global level. Traditional constitutional law has been critical law because it has been limited in scope to government structure and has not opened itself to consideration of international law and diplomacy. If constitutional law is to concern itself with human dignity and with freedom and welfare, it must now address global issues. Humanity faces the collective task of navigating its way into the future through a fundamental review of its existing frameworks of organization and action. The quest for global security is not a utopian one. The fact that global peace has been threatened since the advent of the nuclear age demonstrates that the need for security on a global level is real. The Commission on Global Governance has issued a call for a concept of global security broader than one focusing on military issues alone.[73] This may signal a move towards the notion of collective global security advocated in the Bahá'í writings.[74]

Reduction in conflict is linked to the creation of effective measures for confidence-building at global level but this in turn is linked to the complexities of entrenched interests. Late 20th century economies became trapped in a weapons culture, in which defence industries account for significant proportions of national economies. Whereas violent political instruments of warfare must be abolished through international and national law, there is also need to review the application of science and technology to ensure that rapidly expanding scientific capacity is used for the public good and not for evil purposes related to warfare and destruction. Nation states have a role but their scale, function, will and capabilities are not equal to the challenges of globalism. Some form of global federation is required, with power distributed between and among levels of states.[75]

There is growing recognition of the complexity of human affairs, in which opposing agents of chaos and order, of growth and decay, generate 'open' historical moments in which the destinies of whole peoples and nations are determined. There is, also, growing recognition of the 'relationality' that exists between all peoples and between peoples and the ecosystem as a whole. This is sometimes described as a 'unity in diversity' in which each individual has a legitimate place in the functioning of the whole. Reciprocal relations between 'the people' and 'the state' are often formulated and expressed in terms of rights and responsibilities. Consciousness of the oneness of humanity, if taught to the next generation, could protect it from ethnic and religious conflict and encourage processes of collaboration and conciliation. It could generate a desire to base decisions on just principles and lead to the development of laws that are 'universal in both character and authority'. Certainly, it would foster a more even spread of access to knowledge of science and technology.

So-called commitment to both 'democracy' and 'economic development' presents a paradox: if so much power is now in the hands of 'the people', why is it that they have not been able to change their material conditions? Partly, this shows flaws in the 'roles' played by the 'protagonists'. Governments have viewed the masses as recipients of aid and of development programmes; future models of democracy will transfer powers of decision-making to the grass roots. How is 'people power' effective? Through unity, cooperation and reciprocity. These processes are activated through consultation, dialogue and acknowledgement of the legitimacy of each other's aspirations. The inability of nation states to grant citizens democracy at the international level has contributed to the emergence of civil society at both national and international levels consisting of non-governmental activities and coverage of public interest issues by a now world-encircling media.

Governance and Conflict Resolution: Keys to Participation

Bahá'í scriptures anticipate 'far-reaching changes in the governance of human affairs and in the institutions created to carry it out'.[76] The systems of government elaborated during the modern period have laid the crude foundations for such changes but have exhausted the possibilities for progress within modernity's paradigm. Working beyond that paradigm the outlines of an emerging practice of governance are appearing. They embrace a greater consideration of the aspirations and ideas of individuals while also recognizing group rights, foster consultation at all levels of decision-making, add responsibilities to the rights enjoyed by both the individual and the state, add mediation to the traditional forms of dispute resolution, transcend national boundaries to consider the impact of decisions on citizens and states beyond one's own and accept accountability as a practice that benefits the public interest.

Bahá'í perspectives on conflict resolution have at least three points of departure. In the first, the individual believer, seeking to align her behaviour with the fundamental tenets of her faith, inevitably incorporates conflict resolving practices as aspects of her interpersonal demeanor, whether consciously or otherwise, and regardless of what labels she gives these attitudes and skills.

At community level, Bahá'ís similarly adopt conflict resolving processes as they strive to conduct their affairs in conformity with the rules imposed on them by the Bahá'í writings and in conformity with the customs surrounding the treatment of conflicts that are emerging through the praxis of Bahá'í institutions. Finally, Bahá'ís engage with the problem of conflict in the world at large, both as an intellectual problem requiring analysis and as a spiritual condition requiring regeneration through participation. At three distinct levels, therefore, Bahá'ís share an interest in questions of conflict and conflict resolution. This does not mean, on the other hand, that each and every Bahá'í individual or community possesses competence in problem-solving. On the contrary, it is the need to gain such competence that fuels closer consideration of this subject.

Bibliography

'Abdu'l-Bahá. *Foundations of World Unity*. Wilmette, IL: Bahá'í Publishing Trust, 1945.

— *Paris Talks*. London: Bahá'í Publishing Trust, 1967.

— *The Promulgation of Universal Peace*. Wilmette, IL: Bahá'í Publishing Trust, 1982.

— *The Secret of Divine Civilization*. Wilmette, IL: Bahá'í Publishing Trust, 1990.

— *Selections from the Writings of 'Abdu'l-Bahá*. Haifa: Bahá'í World Centre, 1978.

'Abdu'l-Bahá in London. London: Bahá'í Publishing Trust, 1987.

Alston, P. (ed.). *Human Rights Law*. Aldershot: Dartmouth, 1996.

Anderson, B. *Imagined Communities: Reflections on the Origin and Spread of Nationalism*. London: Verso, 1983.

Arjomand, Said Amir (ed.). *The Political Dimensions of Religion*. New York: State University of New York Press, 1993.

Bahá'í International Community. *The Prosperity of Humankind*: A statement prepared by the Bahá'í International Community Office of Public Information, Haifa, first distributed at the United Nations World Summit on Social Development,

Copenhagen, Denmark, 3 March 1995; http://www.bic-un.bahai.org/95-0303.htm and *The Prosperity of Humankind*. London: Bahá'í Publishing Trust, 1995.

— *Turning Point for All Nations: A Statement of the Bahá'í International Community on the Occasion of the 50th Anniversary of the United Nations*. New York: Bahá'í International Community United Nations Office, 1995.

Bahá'u'lláh. *Tablets of Bahá'u'lláh*. Wilmette, IL: Bahá'í Publishing Trust, 1988.

Commission on Global Governance. *Our Global Neighbourhood*. New York: Oxford University Press, 1995.

Giddens, Anthony. *Modernity and Self-Identity: Self and Society in the Late Modern Age*. Stanford: Stanford University Press, 1991.

Habermas, J. *Between Facts and Norms: Contributions to a Discourse Theory of Law and Democracy*. Cambridge: Polity Press, 1996.

Harris, P. and B. Reilly. *Democracy and Deep-Rooted Conflict: Options for Negotiators*. Stockholm: International Institute for Democracy and Electoral Assistance, 1998.

Held, D. *Prospects for Democracy: North, South, East, West*. Cambridge: Polity Press, 1993.

Imai, Ryukichi. 'Global Governance: Some Reflections'. Institute for International Policy Studies (Tokyo), Policy Paper 191E, December 1997.

Inter-Parliamentary Union. *Democracy: Its Principles and Achievement*. Geneva: Inter-Parliamentary Union, 1998.

Jessop, B. 'Putting States in Their Place: State Systems and State Theory', in *New Developments in Political Science: An International Review of Achievements and Prospects*. Cheltenham: Edward Elgar, 1990.

Johnston, D. and Cynthia Sampson (eds.). *Religion, The Missing Dimension of Statecraft*. Oxford: Oxford University Press, 1994.

Lights of Guidance: A Bahá'í Reference File. Compiled by Helen Hornby. New Delhi: Bahá'í Publishing Trust, 5th edn. 1997.

Lijphart, A. *Electoral Systems and Party Systems 1945–1990: A Study of Twenty-seven Democracies*. Oxford: Oxford University Press, 1994.

Mohan, Brij. *Global Development: Post-Material Values and Social Praxis*. Westport, CT: Praeger, 1992.

Prescott, J. R. V., H. J. Collier and D. F. Prescott. *Frontiers of Asia and*

Southeast Asia. Carlton: Melbourne University Press, 1977.

Richardson, J. M. and Jianxin Wang. 'Peace Accords: Seeking Conflict Resolution in Deeply Divided Societies', in K.M. de Silva and S. W. R. de A. Samarasinghe (eds.), *Peace Accords and Ethnic Conflict*. London: Pinter Publishers, 1993.

Rosenfeld, M. *Constitutionalism, Identity, Difference, and Legitimacy: Theoretical Perspectives*. Durham: Duke University Press, 1994.

Sciulli, David. *A Theory of Societal Constitutionalism: Foundations of a Non-Marxist Critical Theory*. Cambridge: Cambridge University Press, 1992.

Shoghi Effendi. *Bahá'í Administration*. Wilmette, IL: Bahá'í Publishing Trust, 1968.

— *The Light of Divine Guidance: Messages from the Guardian of the Bahá'í Faith to the Bahá'ís of Germany and Austria*. 2 vols. Hofheim-Langenhain: Bahá'í-Verlag, 1982.

— *The Promised Day is Come*. Wilmette, IL: Bahá'í Publishing Trust, rev. edn. 1980.

— *The World Order of Bahá'u'lláh*. Wilmette, IL: Bahá'í Publishing Trust, 1991.

Smooha, S. and Theodor Hanf. 'The Diverse Modes of Conflict Regulation in Deeply Divided Societies', in A. D. Smith, *Ethnicity and Nationalism*. Leiden: E. J. Brill, 1992.

Star of the West. rpt. Oxford: George Ronald, 1984.

Websites:

http://www.eur.nl/frg/iacl/index.htm

http://www.idea.int

http://www.ipu.org

http://www.transparency.de

http://www.un.org

Notes

1. 'Abdu'l-Bahá , *Promulgation*, p. 144.
2. Mohan, *Global Development*, p. xvi.
3. 'It is evident that the fundamentals of religion are intended to

unify and bind together; their purpose is universal, everlasting peace. Prior to the time of Jesus Christ the World of God had unified opposite types and conflicting elements of human society; and since His appearance the divine Teachers of the primal principles of the law of God have all intended this universal outcome.' ('Abdu'l-Bahá, *Promulgation*, p. 97)

4. See also Johnston and Sampson, *Religion, The Missing Dimension of Statecraft.*
5. See Arjomand, *Political Dimensions of Religion.*
6. Toynbee's *A Study of History* can be read as a study of governance east and west. The political philosophies of Locke, Hobbes, Adam Smith, Burke and Rousseau can be seen as the foundations of governance by the modern (western) states. The writings of Marx can be viewed similarly, as the beginning of a critique of governance in the contemporary era.
7. Bahá'u'lláh, *Tablets*, p. 171.
8. My view is that post-modernists, far from merely 'celebrating difference' and exploring the transgression of the social codes of modernism, promote a philosophy of despair by espousing the impossibility of establishing meaning in the life-world.
9. 'Ethical precedents and principles cannot be applied to the needs of the modern world. Thoughts and theories of past ages are fruitless now. Thrones and governments are crumbling and falling. All conditions and requisites of the past unfitted and inadequate for the present time, are undergoing radical reform.' ('Abdu'l-Bahá, *Foundations of World Unity*, p. 18)
10. 'Will the despotism of former governments answer the call for freedom which has risen from the heart of humanity in this cycle of illumination? It is evident that no vital results are now forthcoming from the customs, institutions and standpoints of the past. In view of this, shall blind imitations of ancestral forms and theological interpretations continue to guide and control the religious life and spiritual development of humanity today? Shall man, gifted with the power of reason, unthinkingly follow and adhere to dogma, creeds and hereditary beliefs which will not bear the analysis of reason in this century of effulgent reality? ('Abdu'l-Bahá, *Promulgation*, pp. 140–1)
11. 'Every one can live in any spot on the terrestrial globe. Therefore all the world is man's birthplace. These boundaries and outlets have been devised by man. In the creation, such

boundaries and outlets were not assigned . . . No wise and just person will acknowledge these imaginary distinctions. Every limited area which we call our native country we regard as our motherland, whereas the terrestrial globe is the motherland of all, and not any restricted area.' ('Abdu'l-Bahá, *Selections*, p. 300)

12. Shoghi Effendi, *World Order,* p. 41. The passage commences: 'Far from aiming at the subversion of the existing foundations of society . . .' – a reminder, if one were needed, that the Bahá'í programme is transformative more than revolutionary and certainly not seditious.
13. ibid. p. 152.
14. ibid. p. 182.
15. 'Abdu'l-Bahá, *Selections*, p. 300.
16. Shoghi Effendi, *World Order*, p. 35.
17. ibid. p. 36.
18. ibid. p. 182.
19. ibid. Shoghi Effendi refers to the 'forces of a blatant nationalism and racialism' which have 'usurped the rights and prerogatives of God Himself' (Shoghi Effendi, *Promised Day is Come*, p. 16); elsewhere nationalism is described as 'excessive', 'blind', 'intolerant' and 'militant' (ibid. p. 104); as one of the three 'false gods' (together with racialism and communism) (ibid. p. 113); and as 'intolerant and militant'. (Shoghi Effendi, *World Order*, p. 182)
20. Shoghi Effendi, *World Order*, p. 154.
21. To equate the Bahá'í model with any current or historical model would be, in the estimation of Shoghi Effendi, not merely 'misleading' but misplaced, given the model's 'divinely-conceived', as opposed to humanly, constructed origins: 'Such an attempt would in itself betray a lack of complete appreciation of the excellence of the handiwork of its great Author . . . The hereditary authority which the Guardian is called upon to exercise, the vital and essential functions which the Universal House of Justice discharges, the specific provisions requiring its democratic election by the representatives of the faithful – these combine to demonstrate the truth that this divinely revealed Order, which can never be identified with any of the standard types of government referred to by Aristotle in his works, embodies and blends with the spiritual verities on which it is based the beneficent

elements which are to be found in each one of them.' (Shoghi Effendi, *World Order*, pp. 152–4)

22. Bahá'u'lláh, *Tablets*, p. 28.
23. Bahá'u'lláh, *Tablets*, p. 93.
24. Bahá'í International Community, *Turning Point for all Nations.*
25. Bahá'í International Community, *Prosperity of Humankind*, p. 8.
26. ibid. p. 10.
27. ibid. pp. 9–13.
28. 'Future generations . . . will find almost incomprehensible the circumstance that, in an age paying tribute to an egalitarian philosophy and related democratic principles, development planning should view the masses of humanity as essentially recipients of benefits from aid and training. Despite acknowledgment of participation as a principle, the scope of the decision making left to most of the world's population is at best secondary, limited to a range of choices formulated by agencies inaccessible to them and determined by goals that are often irreconcilable with their perceptions of reality.' (ibid. p. 4)
29. Giddens, *Modernity and Self-Identity*, pp. 14–15.
30. Giddens further explains: 'In respect of both social and natural scientific knowledge, the reflexivity of modernity turns out to confound the expectations of Enlightenment thought – although it is the very product of that thought. The original progenitors of modern science and philosophy believed themselves to be preparing the way for securely founded knowledge of the social and natural worlds; the claims of reason were due to overcome the dogmas of tradition, offering a sense of certitude in place of the arbitrary character of habit and custom. But the reflexivity of modernity actually undermines the certainty of knowledge, even in the core domains of natural science. Science depends not on the inductive accumulation of proofs, but on the methodological principle of doubt. No matter how cherished, and apparently well established, a given scientific tenet might be, it is open to revision – or might have to be discarded altogether – in the light of new ideas or findings. The integral relation between modernity and radical doubt is an issue which, when exposed to view, is not only disturbing to philosophers but is existentially troubling for ordinary individuals.' (ibid. p. 21)
31. Sciulli, *Theory of Societal Constitutionalism*, p. 2.
32. Mohan, *Global Development*, p. xvi.

33. 'Consider what a vast difference exists between modern democracy and the old forms of despotism. Under an autocratic government the opinions of men are not free, and development is stifled, whereas in democracy, because thought and speech are not restricted, the greatest progress is witnessed.' ('Abdu'l-Bahá, *Promulgation*, p. 197)
34. Access by the individual to the activities and findings of the United Nations symbolizes the 'new' communications and information era. Website <http://www.un.org>
35. This is the basis on which some Japanese analysts are now advocating the need for global governance. See, for instance, Ryukichi Imai, 'Global Governance: Some Reflections', Institute for International Policy Studies (Tokyo), Policy Paper 191E, December 1997.
36. See Alston, *Human Rights Law.*
37. Such goals are at the heart of such agencies as the Inter-Parliamentary Union (website <http://www.ipu.org>) and the International Institute for Democracy and Electoral Assistance (website <http://www.idea.int>).
38. This is being undertaken by a large number of agencies, both governmental and non-governmental. One global association interested in advancing constitutional design and process is the International Association of Constitutional Law. Website <http://www.eur.nl/frg/iacl/index.htm>
39. One agency focused on strengthening accountability is Transparency International. Website <http://www.transparency.de>
40. In modernist societies, 'unity' is upheld through such external symbols as slogans, flags and doctrines of uniformity and conformity.
41. See Jessop, 'Putting States in Their Place: State Systems and State Theory', in *New Developments in Political Science: An International Review of Achievements and Prospects*, pp. 43–60.
42. See Rosenfeld, *Constitutionalism, Identity, Difference, and Legitimacy*.
43. 'Abdu'l-Bahá envisaged the formation of an 'impartial, international Commission' to formalize state boundaries: '. . . every country must be properly delimited, its exact frontiers marked, its national integrity secured, its permanent independence protected, and its vital interests honoured by the family of nations . . . In this manner all causes of friction and differences will be removed. And in case there should arise

some disputes between them, they could arbitrate before the Parliament of Man, the representatives of which should be chosen from among the wisest and most judicious men of all the nations of the world.' ('Abdu'l-Bahá, in *Star of the West*, vol. 5, no. 8, p. 117)

44. See Anderson, *Imagined Communities.*
45. 'Abdu'l-Bahá, *Foundations of World Unity*, p. 66.
46. See Prescott, *Frontiers of Asia and Southeast Asia.*
47. See: Smooha and Hanf, 'The Diverse Modes of Conflict Regulation in Deeply Divided Societies', in Smith, *Ethnicity and Nationalism*; Richardson and Wang, 'Peace Accords: Seeking Conflict Resolution in Deeply Divided Societies', in Samarasinghe, *Peace Accords and Ethnic Conflict*; and Harris and Reilly, *Democracy and Deep-Rooted Conflict.*
48. See Inter-Parliamentary Union, *Democracy: Its Principles and Achievement.*
49. The implications of this insight are explored in depth in Habermas's 'theory of communicative action'; see Jurgen Habermas, *Between Facts and Norms* and other literature about 'deliberative democracy'; see Held, *Prospects for Democracy.*
50. Bahá'u'lláh, *Tablets*, p. 168.
51. ibid. p. 127.
52. ibid. p. 36.
53. ibid.
54. ibid.
55. ibid. p. 90.
56. ibid. p. 94.
57. Utilization of this principle has resulted in a resurgence of Native American culture in the Bahá'í communities of North, Central and South America: e.g., Marian Steffes Council, Continental Indigenous Council series covering the Bahá'ís of Alaska, Canada and the United States.
58. Bahá'u'lláh, *Tablets*, pp. 22–3.
59. See a letter written on behalf of Shoghi Effendi to an individual, 4 February 1935, in *Lights of Guidance*, p. 9, no. 31.
60. 'To be able to make a wise choice at the election time, it is necessary for him to be in close and continued contact with all of his fellow-believers, to keep in touch with all local activities, be they teaching, administrative or otherwise, and to fully and whole-heartedly participate in the affairs of the local as well as national committees and assemblies in his country. It is only in

this way that a believer can develop a true social consciousness, and acquire a true sense of responsibility in matters affecting the interests of the Cause. Bahá'í community life thus makes it a duty for every loyal and faithful believer to become an intelligent, well-informed and responsible elector, and also gives him the opportunity of raising himself to such a station. And since the practice of nomination hinders the development of such qualities in the believer, and in addition leads to corruption and partisanship, it has to be entirely discarded in all Baha'i elections.' (From a letter written on behalf of Shoghi Effendi to an individual, 4 February 1935, in *Lights of Guidance*, p. 10, no. 34)

61. See Lijphart, *Electoral Systems and Party Systems 1945–1990*.
62. 'Party systems are based on national interests, and the involvement of Bahá'ís in political programmes in one country, however meritorious, may place them in opposition to political programmes being advocated by Bahá'í members of parties in other countries.' (From a letter written on behalf of Shoghi Effendi, 24 June 1947) 'We Bahá'ís are *one* the world-over, we are seeking to build up a New World Order, Divine in origin. How can we do this if every Bahá'í is a member of a different political party – some of them diametrically opposed to each other? Where is our unity then? We would be divided because of politics, against ourselves, and this is the opposite of our purpose.' (From a letter written on behalf of Shoghi Effendi to a National Spiritual Assembly, 24 June 1947, in *Light of Divine Guidance*, vol. 1, p. 123)
63. 'While the setting up of parliaments, the organizing of assemblies of consultation, constitutes the very foundation and bedrock of government, there are several essential requirements which these institutions must fulfil. First, the elected members must be righteous, God-fearing, high-minded, incorruptible. Second, they must be fully cognizant, in every particular, of the laws of God, informed as to the highest principles of law, versed in the rules which govern the management of internal affairs and the conduct of foreign relations, skilled in the useful arts of civilization, and content with their lawful emoluments.' ('Abdu'l-Bahá, *Secret of Divine Civilization*, p. 17)
64. 'Abdu'l-Bahá, *Secret of Divine Civilization*, p. 33.
65. Shoghi Effendi, *Bahá'í Administration*, p. 39.

66. 'Abdu'l-Bahá, *Promulgation*, p. 72.
67. And yet, which leader has achieved his ends through coercive use of public authority? The leaders of capitalist economies are no more able to bend their economies in desired directions than were their socialist and communist rivals. Such coercive applications of power achieved a certain degree of economic growth and progress but even this is fading, as currently in Russia and increasingly in the 'Asian Tigers' – Japan, Malaysia, South Korea.
68. 'It is impossible for a country to live properly without laws. To solve this problem rigorous laws must be made, so that all the governments of the world will be the protectors thereof.

    'In the Bolshevistic principles equality is effected through force. The masses who are opposed to the people of rank and to the wealthy class desire to partake of their advantages.' ('Abdu'l-Bahá, *Foundations of World Unity*, p. 44)
69. 'Abdu'l-Bahá said: '. . . Equality and Brotherhood must be established among all members of mankind. This is according to Justice. The general rights of mankind must be guarded and preserved. All men must be treated equally. This is inherent in the very nature of humanity.' (*'Abdu'l-Bahá in London*, p. 29)
70. 'If administrators of the law would take into consideration the spiritual consequences of their decisions, and follow the guidance of religion, "They would be Divine agents in the world of action, the representatives of God for those who are on earth, and they would defend, for the love of God, the interests of His servants as they would defend their own". If a governor realizes his responsibility, and fears to defy the Divine Law, his judgements will be just. Above all, if he believes that the consequences of his actions will follow him beyond his earthly life, and that "as he sows so must he reap", such a man will surely avoid injustice and tyranny.' ('Abdu'l-Bahá, *Paris Talks*, pp. 157–8)
71. Bahá'u'lláh, *Tablets*, pp. 128–9.
72. Bahá'u'lláh, *Tablets*, p. 127.
73. 'The primary goals of global security policy should be to prevent conflict and war and to maintain the integrity of the planet's life-support systems by eliminating the economic, social, environmental, political, and military conditions that generate threats to the security of people and the planet, and by anticipating and managing crises before they escalate into

armed conflicts.' (Commission on Global Governance, *Our Global Neighbourhood*, pp. 84–5)

74. 'They must make the Cause of Peace the object of general consultation, and seek by every means in their power to establish a Union of the nations of the world. They must conclude a binding treaty and establish a covenant, the provisions of which shall be sound, inviolable and definite. They must proclaim it to all the world and obtain for it the sanction of all the human race. This supreme and noble undertaking – the real source of the peace and well-being of all the world – should be regarded as sacred by all that dwell on earth. All the forces of humanity must be mobilized to ensure the stability and permanence of this Most Great Covenant. In this all-embracing Pact the limits and frontiers of each and every nation should be clearly fixed, the principles underlying the relations of governments towards one another definitely laid down, and all international agreements and obligations ascertained. In like manner, the size of the armaments of every government should be strictly limited, for if the preparations for war and the military forces of any nation should be allowed to increase, they will arouse the suspicion of others. The fundamental principle underlying this solemn Pact should be so fixed that if any government later violate any one of its provisions, all the governments on earth should arise to reduce it to utter submission, nay the human race as a whole should resolve, with every power at its disposal, to destroy that government. Should this greatest of all remedies be applied to the sick body of the world, it will assuredly recover from its ills and will remain eternally safe and secure.' ('Abdu'l-Bahá, *Secret of Divine Civilization*, pp. 64–5)

75. When asked whether universal peace required 'political democracy in all the countries of the world' 'Abdu'l-Bahá replied: 'It is very evident that in the future there shall be no centralization in the countries of the world, be they constitutional in government, republican or democratic in form. The United States may be held up as the example of future government – that is to say, each province will be independent in itself, but there will be federal union protecting the interests of the various independent states. It may not be a republican or a democratic form. To cast aside centralization which promotes despotism is the exigency of the time. This

will be productive of international peace.' ('Abdu'l-Bahá, *Promulgation*, p. 167) 'With it, too, rests the decision whether a certain point at issue is strictly local in its nature, and should be reserved for the consideration and decision of the local Assembly, or whether it should fall under its own province and be regarded as a matter which ought to receive its special attention. The National Spiritual Assembly will also decide upon such matters which in its opinion should be referred to the Holy Land for consultation and decision.' (Shoghi Effendi, *Bahá'í Administration*, pp. 40–1)

76. Bahá'í International Community, *Prosperity of Humankind*. p. 14.

4

Beyond Linguistic Conflict: Spiritual Foundations of a Universal Auxiliary Language[1]

Jeffrey S. Gruber

In this paper we consider spiritual principles and teachings expounded in the writings of the Bahá'í Faith that lie at the heart of the selection, adoption and development of a universal auxiliary language. These principles are essential for resolution of the linguistic conflicts that have naturally arisen at the worldwide interface of language contact today. The significance of the adoption of a universal language relates to the attribute of justice, which is the essence of the Bahá'í Revelation, and to the advent of mankind's maturity, which characterizes the present age. Spiritual principles underlying its purpose include the objectives of world peace and unity as well as the worldly pragmatic. The provision of a new milieu, collective consultation and a motivation for justice and unity comprise the means for its achievement. Its fairest fruits are reflections of the principles of the progressive unfoldment of civilization and the inherent divinity of natural processes.

Significances

Justice: The Essence of the Laws of the Age

Writing in the latter half of the 19th century, Bahá'u'lláh, Prophet-Founder of the Bahá'í Faith, enjoined and foretold the imminent adoption of a universal auxiliary language. This He did in several places of His writings, notably the Kitáb-i-Aqdas, or Most Holy Book, the repository of His laws and ordinances, in the Tablet of Bis͟hárát, or Glad-Tidings, and in His later summary book *Epistle to the Son of the Wolf*. In these passages He exhorts the leaders of men to come together in agreement to select and adopt a language to be spoken, in addition to their mother tongues, by all the peoples of the world. These are His words in the Glad-Tidings:

> It behoveth the sovereigns of the world – may God assist them – or the ministers of the earth to take counsel together and to adopt one of the existing languages or a new one to be taught to children in schools throughout the world, and likewise one script. Thus the whole earth will come to be regarded as one country. Well is it with him who hearkeneth unto His Call and observeth that whereunto he is bidden by God, the Lord of the Mighty Throne.[2]

Bahá'u'lláh taught that the present age constitutes a new stage in the social and spiritual evolution of the planet, the stage of world civilization and unity. Since His time on earth, that vision of a global community has been gradually unfolding. Intrinsic to it, the new stage, Bahá'u'lláh proclaimed, had of necessity to be a new social order of justice. 'Bestir yourselves,' He said ' . . . in anticipation of the days of Divine justice.'[3] Indeed, justice pervades all of Bahá'u'lláh's revelation and teachings for this day and is associated with a maturity of vision detached from past prejudices and limitations:

> The essence of all that We have revealed for thee is Justice, is for man to free himself from idle fancy and imitation, discern with the eye of oneness His glorious handiwork, and look into all things with a searching eye.[4]

It stands as the essence of His laws and teachings, whose aim is the establishment of oneness and unity on earth:

> The purpose of justice is the appearance of unity among men . . . Verily I say, whatever is sent down from the heaven of the Will of God is the means for the establishment of order in the world and the instrument for promoting unity and fellowship among its peoples.[5]

'Abdu'l-Bahá, eldest son of Bahá'u'lláh and Centre of His Covenant, further affirms:

> . . . the human world will adapt itself to a new social form, the justice of God will become manifest throughout human affairs, and human equality will be universally established.[6]

The teaching that humanity must today adopt a universal auxiliary language, as one of the signal features of Bahá'u'lláh's Faith, is fundamentally, then, an outpouring of divine justice. In contrast, linguistic diversity has been characteristic of human society for millennia past. Thus we may surmise that a universal language is possible in the present era precisely because universal justice can now be made manifest. In this connection, consider the biblical account of the origin of linguistic diversity, the story of the Tower of Babel:

> And the whole earth was of one language, and of one speech . . .
>
> And they said, Go to, let us build us a city and a tower, whose top may reach unto heaven; and let us make us a name, lest we be scattered abroad upon the face of the whole earth.
>
> And the Lord came down to see the city and the tower, which the children of men builded.
>
> And the Lord said, Behold, the people is one, and they have all one language; and this they begin to do: and now nothing will be restrained from them, which they have imagined to do.
>
> Go to, let us go down, and there confound their language, that they may not understand one another's speech.
>
> So the Lord scattered them abroad from thence upon the face

> of all the earth: and they left off to build the city.
>
> Therefore is the name of it called Babel; because the Lord did there confound the language of all the earth: and from thence did the Lord scatter them abroad upon the face of all the earth.[7]

In some sense Bahá'u'lláh confirms this biblical account:

> The divers and widely-known languages now spoken by the peoples of the earth were originally unknown, as were the varied rules and customs now prevailing amongst them. The people of those times spoke a language different from those now known. Diversities of language arose in a later age, in a land known as Babel. It was given the name Babel, because the term signifieth 'the place where the confusion of tongues arose'.[8]

The biblical account suggests that the purpose of this diversity has been to protect humanity during the early stages of its civilized development – its childhood – by limiting human collective power and preventing the widespread tyranny it could have then implied. It was, for those times, a limited resolution of the conflict between the need for peace and unity and a justice that could not yet be fully realized. One research linguist at least (Mark Baker[9]) has proposed an interpretation of the Bible's account along these lines and its explanatory value for language diversity.

Today, however, according to the Revelation of Bahá'u'lláh, the condition of linguistic diversity is to change. If, through His Revelation, humankind reaches the stage in which universal justice is possible, then the conflict can, and must, be fully resolved: unity becomes a reflection of justice, without tyranny, and a universal language becomes thereby not only permissible but necessary. We may say that the legacy of Babel is in this day abrogated by a mandate for divine justice.

A Sign of Maturity

Bahá'u'lláh identifies both justice and the adoption of a universal auxiliary language with mankind's attainment of maturity. The stage which humanity is now entering is described as that of its collective maturity. In 'Abdu'l-Bahá's words:

> The world of humanity has, heretofore, been in the stage of infancy; now it is approaching maturity. Just as the individual human organism, having attained the period of maturity, reaches its fullest degree of physical strength and ripened intellectual faculties . . . likewise the world of humanity in this cycle of its completeness and consummation will realize an immeasurable upward progress . . .[10]

Similarly, the appearance of justice, which characterizes this new age, is likened to the weaning of a child from its mother's milk:

> Know verily that the essence of justice and the source thereof are both embodied in the ordinances prescribed by Him Who is the Manifestation of the Self of God amongst men, if ye be of them that recognize this truth . . . Were His law to be such as to strike terror into the hearts of all that are in heaven and on earth, that law is naught but manifest justice. The fears and agitation which the revelation of this law provokes in men's hearts should indeed be likened to the cries of the suckling babe weaned from his mother's milk, if ye be of them that perceive.[11]

So too, the adoption of a universal language will be a cardinal sign that humanity's maturity has been reached. As Shoghi Effendi, the Guardian and head of the Bahá'í Faith from 1921 to 1957, explains:

> [Bahá'u'lláh] in His Most Holy Book, has enjoined the selection of a single language . . . an injunction which, when carried out, would, as He Himself affirms in that Book, be one of the signs of the 'coming of age of the human race'.[12]

The passage referred to is the following:

> We have appointed two signs for the coming of age of the human race: the first, which is the most firm foundation, We have set

> down in other of Our Tablets, while the second hath been revealed in this wondrous Book.[13]

The second of these signs, that of a universal auxiliary language, is referred to by Bahá'u'lláh in His book in these words:

> O members of parliaments throughout the world! Select ye a single language for the use of all on earth, and adopt ye likewise a common script . . . This will be the cause of unity, could ye but comprehend it, and the greatest instrument for promoting harmony and civilization, would that ye might understand![14]

The Universal House of Justice explains that the first sign is 'the emergence of a science which is described as that "divine philosophy" which will include the discovery of a radical approach to the transmutation of elements'.[15]

What language is chosen to be the universal auxiliary language is less important than that some language is chosen. Nevertheless a choice must eventually be made. The question of which language, or the nature of the language, thus becomes almost immediately an unavoidable issue and conflicting positions inevitably arise. In fact, although all might agree that the adoption of a universal language is beneficial, or even essential, the main problem for humanity in its implementation could well be agreement on a particular language. The issue impedes steps towards the decision to adopt some language. On the one hand, natural languages may come with unwanted ethnic or national associations and traditions that would favour a particular group. This has been an argument for choosing an ethnically neutral artificial or planned language (e.g. Esperanto).[16] Such an artificially constructed language has the advantage of being purposely free of cultural and linguistic traditions. On the other hand, the lack of such traditions, including literature, in an artificial language may be seen as a disadvantage and imply a disregard and loss of ethnic literatures. Its adoption may also seem to some unnatural, evoking fears of undesirable communicative and cognitive effects.[17]

It is essential, then, to overcome the prejudices and fears that block steps towards committing to a universal auxiliary language.

This requires justice and maturity. Perhaps for this reason the adoption of a universal auxiliary language, whenever it occurs, is to be a sign of the collective coming of age of humanity.

Purpose

Peace and Unity

The primary spiritual purpose of a universal auxiliary language, like justice, is world unity. Referring to the adoption of a universal language in *Epistle to the Son of the Wolf*, Bahá'u'lláh stated: 'Were men to take fast hold on that which hath been mentioned, the whole earth would come to be regarded as one country . . .'[18] Again, elsewhere, He said: 'When this [a universal language] is achieved, to whatsoever city a man may journey, it shall be as if he were entering his own home.'[19]

The emergent global community offers the prospect of world peace and unity but it is hindered by the lack of direct communication between the world's peoples. Beyond filling this need, the adoption of a universal auxiliary language will dynamically encourage the development of feelings of trans-national identification, unity and brotherhood. As Bahá'u'lláh further said: '. . . the greatest means for the promotion of that unity is for the peoples of the world to understand one another's writing and speech.'[20]

It is well known that a common script alone has a unifying effect, even when the spoken forms of the languages differ and are not mutually intelligible. For example, Chinese is not a single language in the sense of mutual intelligibility but distinct 'dialects' share a writing system and so are socially regarded and psychologically felt as part of one language. In contrast, to have different scripts serves to differentiate peoples and cultures, even when the languages are virtually the same. For example, religious communities speaking the same language distinguish themselves by adopting (and adapting) the writing system, together with loan vocabulary, from the language(s) of their parent religious community and scriptures. Hindi and Urdu are fundamentally the same language but are distinguished not only by their religious ties but commonly by script and Sanskrit or Persian loan words, including Arabic and Turkish loans by way of the Persian. Similarly, Serbo-Croatian is a single language with Cyrillic writing for the Serbian Eastern Orthodox community and Roman writing for the Croat Roman Catholic community.

Thus people identify themselves with a community that is viewed as linguistically homogeneous. On a planetary scale, a universal auxiliary language is thus able to sustain world peace through open communication within the global community. It has the power to engender a spirit of oneness by a popular transcendence to trans-national identity.

Ease and Practicality

Pragmatic purposes of social benefit and service also reflect spiritual principle. This is also an aim of Bahá'u'lláh in promulgating a universal auxiliary language. By adopting it, He wrote in *Epistle to the Son of the Wolf*, people would need to acquire 'only two languages, one their own native tongue, the other the language in which all the peoples of the world would converse'. He continued:

> Were men to take fast hold on that which hath been mentioned . . . the people would be relieved and freed from the necessity of acquiring and teaching different languages . . . Our purpose is that all men may cleave unto that which will reduce unnecessary labour and exertion, so that their days may be befittingly spent and ended.[21]

There are indeed immense practical and material benefits in the adoption of a single international language. These include huge savings of administrative costs, time and effort spent in translation in the areas of business, governance, education and other enterprises going beyond linguistic, ethnic and national boundaries. Andrew Large, in his book treating the movement towards an international language,[22] notes that nearly 50 per cent of administrative costs incurred by the European Community are related to language. For instance, for a visit of the European

Parliament to Columbia in 1980, a staff of 90 consisting of 47 interpreters, 12 translating staff and four translation equipment technicians supported a 49-member delegation. Moreover, devising fully satisfactory translation-interpretation systems for the six official languages in the United Nations clearly poses problems that would be obviated by the adoption of a single language for all its internal operations.[23] Areas of concern that are becoming increasingly cooperative and global today, such as efforts against crime, drugs, violence and poverty and for protection of the environment, also require a universal auxiliary language.[24]

Reaping the benefits inherent in the emergent global community itself make the adoption of a universal auxiliary language essential. For example, there is the promise of technological transfer among members of the global community. A universal auxiliary language is needed to provide the medium for this. Moreover, the promise of the global community is for a grander mutual enrichment between all peoples, not only for transfer from the so-called technologically developed to the technologically developing. Facile and immediate interchange of ideas at all levels is needed. Such a pervasive positive shift in the state of world communication can only come about through the adoption of a universal auxiliary language. As 'Abdu'l-Bahá said early in the last century:

> . . . the very foremost service to the world of man is to establish an auxiliary international language. It will become the cause of the tranquillity of the commonwealth of man. It will become the cause of the spread of sciences and arts amongst the nations of the world. It will be the cause of the progress and development of all the races.[25]

Means

New Wine, New Bottles

The Voice of God, proceeding through Bahá'u'lláh, proclaimed the advent of the new age in these words:

> The Divine Springtime is come, O Most Exalted Pen, for the Festival of the All-Merciful is fast approaching. Bestir thyself, and magnify, before the entire creation, the name of God, and celebrate His praise, in such wise that all created things may be regenerated and made new.[26]

'Abdu'l-Bahá also declared:

> Now the new age is here and creation is reborn. Humanity hath taken on new life. The autumn hath gone by, and the reviving spring is here. All things are now made new. Arts and industries have been reborn, there are new discoveries in science, and there are new inventions; even the details of human affairs, such as dress and personal effects – even weapons – all these have likewise been renewed. The laws and procedures of every government have been revised. Renewal is the order of the day.[27]

The following well-known verse from the Bible is related thematically and is pertinent to the matter of how a universal auxiliary language will come to be adopted.

> Neither do men put new wine into old bottles: else the bottles break, and the wine runneth out, and the bottles perish: but they put new wine into new bottles, and both are preserved.[28]

Auxiliary languages have arisen in response to national and international linguistic needs many times in the past, as well as in recent times, but on less than global scale. On the one hand there has been the historic natural emergence of languages serving as lingua francas, for example Hindustani, Swahili, forms of Latin and Arabic, and pidgins and creoles[29] arising in situations of language contact, such as trade or empire.[30] On the other hand, there has been the widespread adoption by national governments of international languages as official languages, usually amongst numerous ethnic languages.

By 'international language' we refer to a language used for international communication, and as a major language, such as for government or education, in a number of distinct nations, while not necessarily being universal. Because of such languages, we have preferred to refer to the language to be adopted worldwide by the term 'universal auxiliary language' rather than 'international auxiliary language'. The latter are today primarily the European languages English, French, Spanish, Portuguese, German and Russian, whose influence originally spread largely through colonialization. In West Africa every country has adopted some international language as its official language.[31]

A principal facilitator in the spread of an auxiliary language, like that of lingua francas in the past, is the inception of a new, broader social milieu. At various times and places, often at historic turning points, there emerges a new social entity or milieu that crosses existing linguistic boundaries, creating communicative conflicts, as well as new opportunities, at the interfaces of language contact. The situation requires and encourages the adoption of an auxiliary language to resolve the conflicts and permit partaking of the benefits. Today, as in the past, a similar response is necessitated: an auxiliary language must be adopted for the new milieu which, in this case, is the entire global community. We may say that the new wine of world civilization needs the new bottle of a universal auxiliary language to contain and convey it.

In a sense the new milieu aids in the resolution of the very conflicts that its emergence has engendered. A lingua franca or auxiliary language is not adopted so much by coercion or force as by the attraction the new social entity presents. The process can occur without a sense of loss, since the adopted language is seen as specifically for the new milieu, while the old contexts remain. The new language does not initially 'replace' the old languages in the contexts in which they have been used. Thus there may be no felt threat to the existing languages in their own contexts. It is simply the desire to attain the benefits of the new milieu that leads to the willing adoption of the new language.

The new social entity today, the emergent global community, carries with it the material and spiritual benefits of the spread of technology and the arts and the prospect of world peace. Its elements are typified by such institutions as the United Nations, particularly its internal operations. Besides the substantial benefits that would follow from the adoption of a single official auxiliary language to be used in all its fora, it provides a new context for the adoption of such a language transcending ethnic and national ones, not implying any loss to the latter.

No less an example is the international community of the Bahá'í Faith. Ian Semple, a member of the Universal House of Justice, discussed in an interview in *English Today*[32] the use of English as an administrative language at the Bahá'í World Centre in Haifa, Israel. This has been necessitated for practical reasons, English and Persian being the official languages at the Centre. However, the Bahá'í Faith itself states no preference for which language should be chosen as a universal auxiliary language. Although the Universal House of Justice may in the future determine an auxiliary language to be used by the Bahá'í world community as a whole, this is not now possible, as it would place an unfair burden on those who, in many parts of the world, already have to learn a regional lingua franca or national language in addition to their mother tongues. For the present, the needs of regional milieux take precedence over the universal one.

Consider also the Internet, another striking constituent of the emergent global community. To participate in it and for it to function efficiently, the use of a single language is essential. This language is willingly adopted in the context of the Internet. Internet guru John Quarterman[33] has discussed in an essay the emergence of communities and a new society through the Internet characterized by its transcendence of traditional barriers – spatial, temporal, political, as well as linguistic. Even for an unfamiliar language, for example, time can be taken to read and compose messages. He noted the predominance of English on the Internet and speculated on its further spread, the increased use of national languages and the possible evolution of a new creole English as a lingua franca there. The essay stimulated a discussion on a forum of the Internet itself.[34]

An observer, also writing in *English Today*, stated:

> [The] trend is for most national networks to present at least part of their connection to the Internet in some form of English . . .

> Messages on the Usenet newsgroups are overwhelmingly written in English, and the bulk of the moderated mailing lists . . . are conducted in English . . . [But] growing numbers of users with no English language skills are joining the net and the dominance of English in message forums, mail lists, and remote access user interfaces . . . can be expected to diminish . . . Perhaps the clearest expression of concerns about the intrusion of the English language . . . can be found on the French Gopher server . . . The French Minister of Culture has posted a series of documents there . . . asserting the need to preserve and maintain the French language on the net.[35]

The observer concluded that the stage in humanity's communicative evolution signalled by the advent of computer networking is comparable to those reached by the successive advents of speech, writing and print.

Consultation and Collective Action

Although, as in the past, a natural process is now inevitably leading to the adoption of a universal auxiliary language, nevertheless the principle of conscious consultative decision and collective action is required as a part of the process today.

The adoption of a universal auxiliary language through consultation and collective action is explicitly called for by Bahá'u'lláh, in passages such as those quoted above and the following:

> It is incumbent upon all nations to appoint some men of understanding and erudition to convene a gathering and through joint consultation choose one language from among the varied existing languages, or create a new one, to be taught to the children in all the schools of the world.[36]

'Abdu'l-Bahá similarly referred to 'agreement' in the adoption of a universal auxiliary language: 'A language shall be agreed upon by which unity will be established in the world.'[37]

It is clear from a social and spiritual perspective that the eventual adoption of a universal auxiliary language should flow from the forces of justice and not, as has more often been the case in the past and currently, be driven by an impulse toward 'linguistic imperialism'. This is the tendency for disproportionate power and resources to accrue to speakers of some favoured language, thereby asserting and maintaining its social dominance. The international use of English has been described as exhibiting linguistic imperialism.[38] Indeed, one of the driving forces of the recent spread of international languages has been the desire to attain to the benefits of dominance, which the spread then reinforces. The spread of an international language in this way produces and sustains political and social inequalities, oppressing peoples with dominated languages and cultures. The development of the potential of these languages is thereby also prevented, compromising their 'language rights' to use and maintain their mother tongues, while love-hate attitudes are generated towards the international language. These factors have been given as reasons for favouring a constructed universal language, such as Esperanto, over natural international ones, such as English.[39]

The situation is different for a lingua franca with neutral socio-economic connotations, as, for example, present-day Swahili, which is preferred in common usages to the official international language, often English, for this reason.[40] Also, where the international language is regarded as 'adopted', rather than as culturally 'other', the sense of linguistic imperialism dissipates. Additionally, there are reciprocal egalitarian effects concomitant with the spread of a dominant international language, such as English.[41] Although spread by linguistic imper-ialism, the use of English has had the positive effects of any international language, such as empowering its users in the assertion of their cultural rights, in turn affecting and enlightening its initial promoters. A universal auxiliary language collectively adopted in a spirit of justice will have the support of all peoples, while empowering all to contribute to the forging of world culture. A recent statement by the Bahá'í International Community, the consultative Bahá'í office at the United Nations, reflects the character and needs of the current process:

> . . . endowed with the wealth of all the genetic and cultural diversity that has evolved through past ages, the earth's inhabitants are now challenged to draw on their collective inheritance to take up, consciously and systematically, the responsibility for the design of their future.[42]

> Justice is the one power that can translate the dawning consciousness of humanity's oneness into a collective will through which the necessary structures of global community life can be confidently erected.[43]

Unity and Justice as Motives

Along with the need for consultative decision and action, the motivation to adopt and promulgate a universal auxiliary language must be a spirit of unity and justice. The result otherwise, as in the case of linguistic imperialism, is oppression.

An aspect of linguistic justice is the concept of the right to communicate[44] – a universal human right to two-way communication in the society in which one lives. In the international context, a universal auxiliary language must be adopted with a view to provide the means for all human beings to exercise their right to communicate in the world community. All the peoples of the world have the right to partake of and contribute to the emerging world society and its affairs. Implicit in this is the necessity for interchange at grass roots level. There are perhaps 5000 languages and major dialects in the world.[45] All but a handful are spoken by less than two per cent of the world's population, a great many being the languages of minorities. In 1997 only 12 languages had more than 116 million speakers (native, or first-language, plus non-native) out of a world population of 5.8 billion: Mandarin, English, Hindi, Spanish, Russian, Arabic, Bengali, Portuguese, Malay-Indonesian, French, Japanese and German.[46] International languages function for communication, cultural exchange and integration in national and regional contexts.[47] In the same way, a universal auxiliary language is essential in the empowerment of linguistic minorities to contribute to and participate in world society.

An indication of the growing consciousness of the need to adopt a universal auxiliary language is the phenomenon of constructed interlanguage movements. Some beginning in the 19th century, that of Volapük, meaning 'world speech', in 1880, and Esperanto, which means 'one who hopes', in 1887, were instilled with an aspiration for unity and justice.[48] Intellectual stirrings of this awakening actually appeared earlier, in the 17th century, which witnessed a florescence of artificial 'philosophical' language schemes. These included projects by Descartes and Leibniz. One of the most concretely developed, based on thesaurus-like principles, was that of John Wilkins, a British clergyman and popular scientist.

It was not until the 19th century, however, with the introduction of Volapük by the German parish priest Martin Schleyer, that the concept of a universal language demonstrated an ability to attract masses of people. The period also marked a shift in emphasis from proposals of a priori language type to those of a posteriori type. The latter, more pragmatically concerned with ease of learning and use, based vocabulary and grammatical structure on natural languages. Volapük, with an English-based vocabulary but employing a copious system of affixes, grew meteorically in one decade (283 societies throughout the world in 1889) and then sharply declined. Esperanto, with its mere '16 rules' and more recognizable vocabulary, replaced it as a movement. Its author, Ludwig Zamenhof, a Polish physician of Jewish descent, sought world brotherhood and the reconciliation of religions and saw language differences as a major cause of injustice. Numbers reached a peak before World War One (1800 societies in 1914). Today the Universal Esperanto Association has members in over a hundred countries with more than 1250 clubs and societies and an estimated two million speakers worldwide.[49]

Among more recent proposals, Interlingua, introduced in 1951, emphasized immediate ease of use in international settings. Other relatively prominent planned interlanguages during the period include Ido, Latino sine Flexione, Occidental, Novial, Basic English and Glosa. Most of the proposals following Esperanto aimed at creating what was thought to be a more natural interlanguage. A posteriori constructed languages of the 'schematic' or 'autonomistic' type, such as Esperanto, stress regularity of word formation from roots within the language itself, sometimes resulting in seeming unnaturalness (e.g. patr-in-o 'mother'). Those of the 'naturalistic' type have familiarity of word forms a priority, sometimes at the expense of regularity. Controversy over this issue brought about an initial schism, with the presentation of Ido as a revision to Esperanto put forth by the 'Delegation for the adoption of an International Language' meeting in Paris in 1907. Later, Latino sine Flexione was developed by the mathematician Giuseppe Peano and by 1915, renamed Interlingua, came to feature a vocabulary of word roots common to Latin and European languages. Occidental, invented by Edgar von Wahl, appeared in 1922 with the focus of ease of use by the western world. The renowned linguist Otto Jespersen, himself wrestling with the problem of naturalness, created Novial, presented in 1928.[50] In 1924 the International Auxiliary Language Association formed in New York with the objective of combining previous interlanguages and investigating experimentally to decide between schematic and naturalistic solutions. Their product, in 1951, promoted especially by linguist Alexander Gode, was again called Interlingua.

Another tack, to create simplicity by radically constraining the basic vocabulary of the language, resulted in Basic English, produced by British educator C. K. Ogden in 1930. A modified natural language like Latino sine Flexione, it limited vocabulary to 850 English words with fixed meanings essential for expression. Glosa, introduced in 1981, a modification of Lancelot Hogben's Interglosa of 1943 by Wendy Ashby, features a core of 1000 Romance and Greek roots recognizable from scientific vocabulary.[51] Also worthy of note is Loglan, a modern a priori constructed language with a grammar based on *ad hoc* logical principles and a vocabulary systematically resolved from roots of the world's languages: its purpose is avowedly for 'research' rather than international communication.[52]

All together as many as 900 artificial or planned languages have been proposed, most quite ephemeral.[53] The specific number depends on how much of a particularized grammar, vocabulary or speakership a project must have in order to be considered a distinct language. Nevertheless, throughout all this, Esperanto seems to have stood unique in the strength of its 'inner idea' to promote a sense of oneness and world community, bearing a message of peace and justice for all humankind. Its spirit as a movement in this respect, together with its demonstrated viability in a living speech community, has been said to account for its special success.[54] Zamenhof explicitly preferred unity over linguistic perfection. Pursuing the latter at the expense of unity has indeed led to the multiplication of interlanguage projects, schisms and dissolution. Zamenhof stated in the introduction to his *Fundamento de Esperanto*, 1905, that modification of Esperanto's core grammar was absolutely forbidden. He allowed, however, that when the language would be firmly agreed upon by the major world governments, it could then adopt universal modifications without fear of schism.[55]

Here the spiritual principle of the preservation of unity in collective decision-making even if wrong is clear; for this ensures peaceful and just relationships that quickly resolve conflicts and lead to truth, while disunity retards and obscures it. 'Abdu'l-Bahá said:

> [If parties] agree upon a subject, even though it be wrong, it is better than to disagree and be in the right, for this difference will produce the demolition of the divine foundation. Though one of the parties may be in the right and they disagree that will be the cause of a thousand wrongs, but if they agree and both parties are in the wrong, as it is in unity the truth will be revealed and the wrong made right.[56]

Fruits and Development

Progressive Unfoldment

> Know of a certainty that in every Dispensation the light of Divine Revelation hath been vouchsafed unto men in direct proportion to their spiritual capacity. Consider the sun. How feeble its rays the moment it appeareth above the horizon. How gradually its warmth and potency increase as it approacheth its

> zenith, enabling meanwhile all created things to adapt themselves to the growing intensity of its light. How steadily it declineth until it reacheth its setting point. Were it, all of a sudden, to manifest the energies latent within it, it would, no doubt, cause injury to all created things . . . In like manner, if the Sun of Truth were suddenly to reveal, at the earliest stages of its manifestation, the full measure of the potencies which the providence of the Almighty hath bestowed upon it, the earth of human understanding would waste away and be consumed; for men's hearts would neither sustain the intensity of its revelation, nor be able to mirror forth the radiance of its light. Dismayed and overpowered, they would cease to exist.[57]

Bahá'u'lláh foresees a two-stage process in the adoption of a universal language. In the initial stage, which is now imminent, some one language will be universally accepted as an auxiliary to all mother tongues. Not until the final stage, in the far future, will there be one single language for all mankind. The Universal House of Justice stated:

> Bahá'u'lláh enjoins the adoption of a universal language and script. His Writings envisage two stages in this process. The first stage is to consist of the selection of an existing language or an invented one which would then be taught in all the schools of the world as an auxiliary to the mother tongues . . . The second stage, in the distant future, would be the eventual adoption of one single language and common script for all on earth.[58]

The two-stage process in the adoption of a universal language reflects the principle of the progressive and gradual unfoldment of civilization. Since the concept of a universal auxiliary language and script is for a language supplementary to existing ethnic and national languages and scripts, for the imminent, initial stage, a single language, replacing existing languages worldwide, is not advocated or foreseen. All people will need to learn a single auxiliary language, while at the same time they will be empowered to preserve their ethnic languages or mother tongues. Circumventing forces of linguistic imperialism, collective action will determine what language is to be learned by all, while all other local, national or regional languages will be on an equal footing. Thus, in the first stage, local, ethnic and minority languages will be encouraged to flourish alongside national and international ones. Paradoxically, the adoption of a universal language will, at least initially, stimulate the development of local languages.

Indeed, in relation to social conditions, the contemporaneous use of ethnic languages with a universal language is, in the present period, important and to be promoted. The situation is similar to the use of native or ethnic languages alongside international languages or lingua francas today. In such circumstances, the ethnic language has value as a medium of education, especially elementary education, even to the extent of fostering competence, at a later stage, in the lingua franca itself. The use and maintenance of the mother tongue, viewed as a basic human right, also has an elevating social and economic effect, contributing to positive feelings of self-identity as well as towards integration into the multilingual society as a whole.[59]

Moreover, from the perspective of world civilization, the diverse languages of the world should not now simply cease to exist. Each language is the result of thousands of years of linguistic and cultural development. Linguistic conservation is at the present time of inestimable value for its potential to enrich humanity's cultural and linguistic inheritance. By the adoption of a universal auxiliary language to be taught alongside all mother tongues in the first stage, the fruition of human capacity represented by the languages of the world will not be annulled but rather will be allowed to contribute to this heritage.

These considerations can to a certain extent be compared with concerns for the conservation of biodiversity. But biological species tend to differentiate from each other when in contact, seeking to fill distinct ecological niches. In contrast, languages in contact exhibit convergence and tend to assimilate each other in various ways, drawing from and enriching each other.[60] A well-known example is the vocabulary enrichment of English by Old French following the Norman conquest. The term 'linguistic area' is commonly used to refer to such a group of contiguous (but genetically relatively unrelated) languages that have come to resemble each other by the 'diffusion' of various linguistic features, usually as a result of a long period of bilingual contact. Another case is South Asia, where 'centuries of language contact have resulted mainly in enriching and expanding the verbal repertoire of the Indian speech community . . . Two [examples] are "Urdu", a result of the interface of KhaRiiBolii with Persian, and "Indian English", a result of contact between English and the Indian languages.'[61] Another recent example is the convergence of syntactic structures in the 'Englishization' of Korean.

We may muse that the ultimate linguistic importance of diverse languages today lies not so much in their strict preservation as in their potential for finally enriching, through contact, humanity's linguistic heritage in a developing universal language.

Nature: An Expression of the Divine Will

> Say: Nature in its essence is the embodiment of My Name, the Maker, the Creator. Its manifestations are diversified by varying causes, and in this diversity there are signs for men of discernment. Nature is God's Will and is its expression in and through the contingent world. It is a dispensation of Providence ordained by the Ordainer, the All-Wise.[62]

Bahá'u'lláh's utterance – 'The day is approaching when all the peoples of the world will have adopted one universal language and one common script'[63] – not only proclaims the unfoldment of part of God's plan for humanity but also testifies to a natural sociolinguistic process occurring on a worldwide scale. The movement towards the adoption of a universal auxiliary language today is a natural response to the exigencies of global contact among the peoples and languages of the world.

The nature of language is also by no means static. Languages continually change and evolve. Just as the many languages of the world have developed within different cultures in past ages, we must expect evolution of whatever universal auxiliary language is adopted to take place in the arena of world civilization in the future. In particular, during the first stage, the centuries of contact of the universal auxiliary language with the diverse languages of the world will lead to their mutual enrichment. The universal auxiliary language would, interacting in a situation of contact with these diverse languages, inevitably become imbued with their influences, reflecting the varied linguistic developments of all of humanity.

Such a process is a common occurrence on a limited scale in pidginization and creolization. In pidginization, a dominant international language, in contact with a local one, typically provides much of the vocabulary base, while sentence patterns often carry over from the local 'substrate' language or arise from innate strategies. This results in a linguistic system of usually reduced structure with local influences and variation. Subsequent creolization involves expansion and convergence of forms,[64] plausibly following universal patterns,[65] producing a consistently defined and fully elaborated new language.

Thus the universal auxiliary language, whatever its origin or initial nature, could, through the convergent effects of contact, come to reflect the diverse linguistic developments of the world. Even an artificially constructed language would be subject when actually in use to influences from the natural languages with which it is in contact and in conformity with the human faculty of language. In the fullness of time, this evolution could lead to the second stage, in which one single language, embodying the linguistic heritage of humankind, will be adopted by the world.

That each separate language is a manifestation of the same innate and universal human cognitive capacity is a premise of modern linguistic science.[66] To disclose the nature of this capacity is its ultimate goal. Different languages that seem very unlike each other have merely developed different aspects of the same linguistic faculty as tools of linguistic expression. Languages cluster around types,[67] being more or less pure as to type or showing mixed characteristics, as they tend to do through contact. In this respect language distinctions are rather like the distinctions of biological race rather than species. Just as racial types involve a concentration of certain genetic characteristics, language types may represent a compression of linguistic parameters, resulting from historic isolation and adaptation but susceptible to convergence and integration through contact.

There are two matters at issue for scientific investigation here: one a part of sociolinguistics, the other of universal linguistic structure. The latter asks how and to what extent divergent structures can be combined in a single language. The question relates to the validity of 'implicational' universals of language, i.e. characteristics of languages whose occurrences depend on the occurrences of others.[68] However, to some researchers it has seemed that 'as far as the strictly linguistic possibilities go, any linguistic feature can be transferred from any language to any other language; and implicational universals that depend solely on linguistic properties are . . . invalid'.[69] In the same way, the clustering of properties together that characterize types seem often to be violated, so that there is a continuum of language patterns exhibiting various degrees of inclusion of the correlated properties.

The sociolinguistic question is to what extent conditions in the unified humanity of the future will be conducive to the diffusion of linguistic features through a universal auxiliary language. Borrowing occurs in contact situations of bilingualism in languages spoken by bilinguals, with the more prestigious, populous or functionally necessary language more likely to maintain its identity and tending to lend more of its features to the other. These are most readily items of vocabulary. When the languages are equal in social respects, so that there is stable and mutual bilingualism, the languages maintain their identity by distinct vocabulary but become similar in syntactic pattern. Borrowings in either language often seem to occur so as to increase its own expressiveness.[70]

Subsequent diffusion of linguistic features beyond the bilingual area of the feature's source and throughout a linguistic community is effected by the movements and contacts of population segments. It has been proposed that such diffusion is more rapid where the linguistic community exhibits a widespread but less dense communicative network, where communicative ties are largely single-purpose. In contrast, in dense networks of isolated communities where the communicative ties are multi-purpose, language change is conservative.[71] As an example, Icelandic exhibits close strong ties and has changed little from its early Germanic origins, while English communities exhibit open weak ties and English has changed rapidly and considerably. If this proposition is correct, we may surmise that, in the case of the universal auxiliary language developing in the global village of the future, the widespread open nature of communicative contacts will be conducive to the rapid spread of linguistic features and consequent language evolution.

Evolutionary Planning

Bahá'í sources suggest that the universal auxiliary language, whether natural or artificially constructed, should be planned in some way:

> It must be made by a Council representing all countries, and must contain words from different languages. It will be governed by the simplest rules, and there will be no exceptions; neither will there be gender, nor extra and silent letters. Everything indicated will have but one name. In Arabic there are hundreds of names for the camel![72]

> Thou hast written regarding the language of Esperanto. This language will be spread and universalized to a certain degree, but later on a language more complete than this, or the same language will undergo some changes and alterations and will be adopted and become universal.[73]

> Perhaps the main consideration in future will be the specific qualities of a [universal] language as being exact, rich and easy to learn for both East and West.[74]

An initially constructed or planned universal language could attempt at the outset to incorporate within it the potentialities of the human language faculty and an inheritance from the languages of the world.[75] But planning need not, and should not, be an initial operation only. Moreover, planning is not necessarily in conflict with evolution and need not oppose natural language change. Rather language planning can complement the natural evolution of the universal auxiliary language, aiming at making it more learnable, expressive and reflective of the world's linguistic inheritance.

Suppose the natural process of evolution stimulated by contact with the diverse languages of the world is supported and guided globally by conscious decision and continued planning. Constructed language movements, such as that of Esperanto and Interlingua, have done this in some degree by progressively determining vocabulary without imposing many rules of syntax. In that case, usage is to some extent free to follow the patterns of mother tongues. This has also been advocated in some quarters in the use of natural international languages.[76]

Research is, of course, also required to determine standards (such as communicability) in the international use of the universal language, without the imposition of any one national standard. English is felt by some to be already truly internationalized, no longer belonging to any particular country, and comprising 'nativized' varieties, including recognized national standard varieties whose institutionalized teaching may be fully justified. The process of convergence, such as the 'nativization' of English, has in fact been described as eliminating language conflict and establishing a new identity. Half jokingly, it has been said that the worldwide academic and scientific use of 'bad English' could lead to a new standard which would 'serve the purposes of its community of speakers better than any existing standard of English would, since it would be far less culture-bound and ethnocentric than all the other Englishes we can choose today'.[77]

The institution of a universal auxiliary language, however, will be deliberately taught and utilized in a single world-encompassing linguistic community, with no parts isolated from others.[78] While variations of use and (perhaps rapid) change would occur, fragmentation into mutually unintelligible dialects or daughter languages will not. Moreover, varieties of use of the universal language would converge globally, both through its natural tendency to do so and the process of institutionalized planning and instruction. The latter would involve codification and incorporation of significant grammatical usages into the educational textbooks of the universal language as they occur, such as is now done for vocabulary in the lexicographic development of dictionaries. The process will enrich the universal auxiliary language in expressive power and as a manifestation of the human linguistic potential.

A language manifesting such a development of the human language faculty will be incomparably 'rich' in expressive power. It will have the capacity for both 'exact' and more fluid modes of expression. Initial learning of the universal auxiliary language will also be relatively 'easy' for all speakers, as optional use of what is innately possible will allow speakers to use basic patterns familiar to their mother tongues. Such a language will have the 'simplest' set of rules, which, as in some constructed interlanguages, means the absence of stated rules.

Bahá'u'lláh in *Epistle to the Son of the Wolf* alludes to a new language devised and offered as a universal auxiliary language:

> At present, a new language and a new script have been devised. If thou desirest, We will communicate them to thee.[79]

No one asked and so we do not know the language to which Bahá'u'lláh was referring. However, if devised by God's Manifestation, that language is an expression of the divine Will, hence a 'natural' language and one which, we might conjecture, embodies the full expressive potential of the linguistic faculty. Perhaps the ultimate form of the auxiliary language, responding to innate and universal influences, may evolve, in the second stage, into the single language of all humanity and regain a semblance of that perfect language proffered by the Manifestation of God of this age.

Bibliography

'Abdu'l-Bahá. *The Promulgation of Universal Peace.* Wilmette, IL: Bahá'í Publishing Trust, 1982.

— *Tablets of Abdul-Baha Abbas*. Chicago: Bahá'í Publishing Society; vol. 1, 1909; vol. 2, 1915; vol. 3, 1916.

'Abdu'l-Bahá in London. London: Bahá'í Publishing Trust, 1987.

Bahá'í International Community. *The Prosperity of Humankind*. London: Bahá'í Publishing Trust, 1995.

Bahá'í World Faith. Wilmette, IL: Bahá'í Publishing Trust, 2nd edn. 1976.

Bahá'u'lláh. *Epistle to the Son of the Wolf*. Wilmette, IL: Bahá'í Publishing Trust, 1988.

— *Gleanings from the Writings of Bahá'u'lláh*. Wilmette, IL: Bahá'í Publishing Trust, 1983.

— *The Kitáb-i-Aqdas*. Haifa: Bahá'í World Centre, 1992.

— *Tablets of Bahá'u'lláh*. Wilmette, IL: Bahá'í Publishing Trust, 1988.

Baik, M. J. 'Syntactic Features of Englishization in Korean'. *World Englishes*, vol. 12, no. 2, July 1994, pp. 155–66.

Baker, M., *The Polysynthesis Parameter*. New York: Oxford University Press, 1995.

Bhatt, Rakesh Mohan. 'Language Identity, Conflict, and Convergence in South Asia'. *Studies in the Linguistic Sciences*, vol. 22, no. 1, Spring 1992, pp. 17–37.

Bickerton, D. *Roots of Language*. Ann Arbor, MI: Karoma Publishers, 1981.

Braga, Giorgio. 'International Languages: Concept and Problems'. *International Journal of the Sociology of Language*, vol. 22, 1979, pp. 27–49.

Brann, C. M. B. 'Functions of World Languages in West Africa'. *West African Journal of Modern Languages*, vol. 3, June 1978, pp. 6–28.

Brown, James Cooke. *Loglan 1: A Logical Language*. Gainesville, FL: Loglan Institute, 1989.

Buono, John W. 'Why a World Language?' *Eco-logos*, vol. 18, no. 65, 1972, pp. 1–3.

Chomsky, Noam. *Knowledge of Language: Its Nature, Origins and Use*. New York: Praeger, 1986.

Cumming, John D. 'The Internet and the English Language'. *English Today*, vol. 11, no. 1, January 1995, p. 4.

Dulicenko, Aleksandr D. 'Ethnic Language and Planned Language: On the Particulars of the Structural, Genetic and the Functional Aspect', in Klaus Schubert (ed.). *Interlinguistics: Aspects of the Science of Planned Languages*. Berlin: Mouton de Gruyter, 1989, pp. 47–61.

Esperanto League for North America: <www.esperanto-usa.org>

Fettes, Mark. 'Europe's Babylon: Towards a Single European Language?' Esperanto Documents, no. 41A, 1991, pp. 1–16.

Foliaki, Lopeti. 'The Search for Unity: A Proposal of Instituting a Universal Language to Help Unravel World Problems'. *TESL Reporter*, vol. 7, no. 4, 1974 , pp. 12–18.

Forster, Peter G. *The Esperanto Movement.* The Hague: Mouton, 1982.

Golden, Bernard. 'The Social Factor in the International Language Movement'. *Eco-logos*, 23, 83.1, 1977, pp. 12–16.

Greenberg, Joseph. *Universals of Human Language.* Stanford, CA: Stanford University Press, 1987.

Gruber, Jeffrey S. 'On the Selection of an International Auxiliary Language'. *World Order*, vol. 1, no. 3, 1967, pp. 19–25.

Haberland, Hartmut. 'Whose English, Nobody's Business'. *Journal of Pragmatics*, vol. 13, 1989, pp. 927–38.

Harrison, Richard K. 'A Bibliography of Planned Languages (excluding Esperanto)'. <www.geocities.com/Athens/5383/bibliog.html>, 1997.

The Holy Bible, King James Version.

'An International Auxiliary Language'. *English Today*, vol. 9, January 1987, pp. 18–19.

Kachru, Braj B. 'Englishization and Contact Linguistics'. *World Englishes*, vol. 12, no. 2, July 1994, pp. 135–54.

— et al. 'Symposium on Linguistic Imperialism'. *World Englishes*, vol. 12, no. 3, 1993, pp. 335–73.

Large, Andrew. *The Artificial Language Movement.* Oxford: Blackwell, 1985.

Larsen, Fritz. 'Jespersen's New International Language', in Arne Juul (ed.). *Otto Jespersen: Facets of His Life and Work.* Amsterdam: John Benjamins Publishing Company, 1989, pp. 101–22.

Lieberman, E. James. 'Esperanto and Trans-National Identity: The Case of Dr Zamenhof'. *International Journal of the Sociology of Language*, vol. 20, 1979, pp. 89–107.

Linguist List: 'Lingua Franca on the Internet'. <http://www.linguistlist.org/>, December 1993–January 1994. 5.8.1–5.147.2.

McMahon, April S. *Understanding Language Change*. Cambridge: Cambridge University Press, 1994.

Milroy, James. *Linguistic Variation and Change: On the Historical Sociolinguistics of English*. Oxford: Blackwell, 1992.

— and L. Milroy. 'Linguistic Change, Social Network, and Speaker Innovation'. *Journal of Linguistics*, vol. 21, 1985, pp. 339–84.

Mohanty, Ajit K. 'Psychological Consequences of Mother-Tongue Maintenance and the Language of Literacy for Linguistic Minorities in India'. *Psychology and Developing Societies*, vol. 2, no. 1, 1990, pp. 31–51.

Ornstein, Jacob. 'Reflections of a Linguist on the Unending Quest for a World Language: Negatives, Positives and Prospects'. *ITL, Review of Applied Linguistics*, no. 38, 1977, pp. 3–30.

Panharipande, Rajeshwari. 'Counteracting Forces in Language Change: Convergence vs. Maintenance'. *Studies in the Linguistic Sciences*, vol. 12, no. 2, Fall 1982, pp. 97–116.

Pennycook, Alastair. *The Cultural Politics of English as an International Language*. London: Longman, 1994.

Phillipson, Robert. *Linguistic Imperialism*. Oxford: Oxford University Press, 1992.

Quarterman, John S. 'The Global Matrix of Minds', in Linda S. Harasim, (ed.). *Global Networks: Computers and International Communication*. Cambridge, MA: MIT Press, 1993.

Romaine, Suzanne. *Pidgin and Creole Languages*. London: Longman, 1988.

Scotton, Carol M. M. 'Towards a sociolinguistic theory of choosing a lingua franca'. *Studies in African Linguistics*. Suppl. 2, 1971, pp. 109–29.

Shoghi Effendi. *God Passes By*. Wilmette, IL: Bahá'í Publishing Trust, rev. edn. 1974.

Smith, Larry E. 'English as an International Auxiliary Language'. *RELC Journal*, vol. 7, no. 2, December 1976, pp. 38–42.

Star of the West. rpt. Oxford: George Ronald, 1984.

Thomason, Sarah Grey and Terrance Kaufman. *Language Contact, Creolization and Genetic Linguistics*. Berkeley: University of California Press, 1988.

Todd, Loreto. *Pidgins and Creoles*. London: Routledge and Kegan Paul, 1974.

Tonkin, Humphrey. 'The Future of Modern Languages in English-speaking Countries'. Esperanto Documents no. 18, 1979, pp. 3–14.

— 'Language and International Communication: The Right to Communicate'. Lecture presented at the United Nations, 4 April 1978. Esperanto Documents no. 15A, 1979, pp. 1–12.

The Universal House of Justice. Research Department. Memorandum, 7 July 1994.

World Almanac and Book of Facts. Mahwah, NJ: World Almanac Books, 1998.

Notes

1. This paper, less some revisions, was first presented as a class of the Wilmette Institute, Wilmette, Illinois, under its programme 'Spiritual Foundations for a Global Civilization', on 28 July 1999 and entitled 'Spiritual Foundations of Universal Auxiliary Language'. A related paper, with a somewhat different focus, 'Language as Justice in the New World Order', appeared in *World Order*, Spring 1999. Much of the substance of this work was initially presented under the title 'A Universal Auxiliary Language: Humanity's Inheritance' at the International Seminar on United Nations Restructuring: Turning Point for All Nations, held on 18 October 1995, by the Bahá'í International Community, United Nations Plaza, New York. A later version, 'Language in the New World Order' was presented at the New World Order in Bahá'í Perspective Conference, 26–8 January 1996, Bahá'í National Center, Evanston, Illinois. I wish to express thanks to Dr C. O. Lerche for suggestions on the earlier versions and to *World Order* reviewers for constructive criticisms incorporated in this and other versions, especially to Dr Betty J. Fisher, Associate and Managing Editor, for her professional editorial expertise, and to Dr Howard B. Garey, Professor Emeritus of French and Romance philology, Yale University, for substantive contributions. All shortcomings remain my own.
2. Bahá'u'lláh, *Tablets*, p. 22.
3. Bahá'u'lláh, *Gleanings*, p. 17.
4. Bahá'u'lláh, *Tablets*, p. 157.

5. ibid. pp. 66–7.
6. 'Abdu'l-Bahá, *Promulgation*, p. 132.
7. Genesis 11:1, 4–9
8. Bahá'u'lláh, *Gleanings*, p. 173.
9. Baker, *Polysynthesis Parameter*, pp. 512–15.
10. 'Abdu'l-Bahá, *Promulgation*, pp. 37–8.
11. Bahá'u'lláh, *Gleanings*, p. 175.
12. Shoghi Effendi, *God Passes By*, p. 211.
13. Bahá'u'lláh, *Kitáb-i-Aqdas*, para. 189.
14. ibid.
15. Universal House of Justice, in ibid. 'Notes', p. 250, note 194.
16. For example, Tonkin, *Future of Modern Languages in English-speaking Countries.*
17. Ornstein, 'Reflections of a Linguist on the Unending Quest for a World Language: Negatives, Positives and Prospects'.
18. Bahá'u'lláh, *Epistle to the Son of the Wolf*, p. 138.
19. Bahá'u'lláh, *Gleanings*, p. 250.
20. Bahá'u'lláh, *Tablets*, p. 128.
21. Bahá'u'lláh, *Epistle to the Son of the Wolf*, pp. 138–9.
22. Large, *Artificial Language Movement*, p. 199.
23. Foliaki, 'The Search for Unity: A Proposal of Instituting a Universal Language to Help Unravel World Problems'.
24. Buono, 'Why a World Language?'
25. 'Abdu'l-Bahá, in *Star of the West*, vol. 2, no. 18, p. 304.
26. Bahá'u'lláh, *Gleanings*, p. 27.
27. 'Abdu'l-Bahá, *Selections*, pp. 252–3.
28. Matthew 9:17
29. See Todd, *Pidgins and Creoles.*
30. Typically, in a pidgin, vocabulary is chosen from a culturally dominant language while much of the syntax derives from a native substrate language. A creole is commonly distinguished from a pidgin in having become the sole language of a community.
31. Brann, 'Functions of World Languages in West Africa'.
32. 'An International Auxiliary Language', *English Today* 9 [January 1987], pp. 18–19.
33. Quarterman, 'The Global Matrix of Minds', pp. 52–3.
34. Linguist List: 'Lingua Franca on the Internet' <http://www.linguistlist.org/>, December 1993–January 1994, 5.8.1–5.147.2.
35. Cumming, 'The Internet and the English Language', p. 4.

36. Bahá'u'lláh, *Tablets*, pp. 165–6.
37. 'Abdu'l-Bahá, *Promulgation*, p. 300.
38. Phillipson, *Linguistic Imperialism.*
39. Fettes, 'Europe's Babylon: Towards a Single European Language?'
40. Scotton, 'Towards a Sociolinguistic Theory of Choosing a Lingua Franca'.
41. See Kachru et al. 'Symposium on Linguistic Imperialism'; Kachru, 'Englishization and Contact Linguistics'; and Pennycook, *Cultural Politics of English as an International Language.*
42. Bahá'í International Community, *Prosperity of Humankind*, p. 2.
43. ibid. p. 9.
44. Tonkin, 'Language and International Communication: The Right to Communicate'.
45. Collier's Encyclopedia (1988 edition) estimates that there are anywhere from 2500 to 5000 languages in the world, depending on how language and dialect are distinguished.
46. *World Almanac and Book of Facts.*
47. Braga, 'International Languages: Concept and Problems'.
48. See, for example, Large, *Artificial Language Movement.*
49. Esperanto League for North America: <http://www.esperanto-usa.org>
50. Larsen, 'Jespersen's New International Language'.
51. Harrison, 'A Bibliography of Planned Languages (excluding Esperanto)', <www.geocities.com/Athens/5383/bibliog.html>, 1997.
52. Brown, *Loglan 1.*
53. Dulicenko, 'Ethnic Language and Planned Language: On the Particulars of the Structural, Genetic and the Functional Aspect'.
54. Lieberman, 'Esperanto and Trans-National Identity: The Case of Dr. Zamenhof' and Golden, 'The Social Factor in the International Language Movement'.
55. Forster, *Esperanto Movement*, p. 111.
56. 'Abdu'l-Bahá, *Bahá'í World Faith*, p. 411.
57. Bahá'u'lláh, *Gleanings*, pp. 87–8.
58. The Universal House of Justice, in Bahá'u'lláh, *Kitáb-i-Aqdas*, 'Notes', p. 250, note 193.
59. Mohanty, 'Psychological Consequences of Mother-Tongue Maintenance and the Language of Literacy for Linguistic Minorities in India'.

60. Baik, 'Syntactic Features of Englishization in Korean'.
61. Bhatt, 'Language Identity, Conflict, and Convergence in South Asia'.
62. Bahá'u'lláh, *Tablets*, p. 142.
63. Bahá'u'lláh, *Gleanings*, pp. 249–50.
64. See, for example, Romaine, *Pidgin and Creole Languages*.
65. Bickerton, *Roots of Language*.
66. Chomsky, *Knowledge of Language: Its Nature, Origins and Use*.
67. Baker, *The Polysynthesis Parameter*.
68. Greenberg, *Universals of Human Language*.
69. Thomason and Kaufman, *Language Contact, Creolization and Genetic Linguistics*.
70. Panharipande, 'Counteracting Forces in Language Change: Convergence vs. Maintenance'.
71. Milroy, *Linguistic Variation and Change*; Milroy and Milroy, 'Linguistic Change, Social Network, and Speaker Innovation'. See McMahon, *Understanding Language Change*.
72. Attributed to 'Abdu'l-Bahá, in *'Abdu'l-Bahá in London*, p. 94.
73. 'Abdu'l-Bahá, *Tablets*, vol. 3, p. 692.
74. From a letter written by Shoghi Effendi to an individual, 18 May 1928, in a memorandum by the Research Department of the Universal House of Justice, 7 July 1994.
75. Gruber, 'On the Selection of an International Auxiliary Language'.
76. Smith, 'English as an International Auxiliary Language'.
77. Haberland, 'Whose English, Nobody's Business'.
78. Smith, 'Spread of English and Issues of Intelligibility'.
79. Bahá'u'lláh, *Epistle to the Son of the Wolf*, p. 138.

5

International Human Rights: A Common Code in Resolving Intra-state and Inter-state Conflicts?

Nazila Ghanea

This essay examines the question of minorities, human rights and conflict resolution. It explains the linkage between these apparently disparate issues and provides a Bahá'í reading of the challenges they give rise to. In covering these issues, the essay is divided into three sections. The first is a historical background, contrasting the protection of minorities under the League of Nations and the United Nations. It also looks at how the advent of the end of the cold war catapulted the issue to the top of the international agenda once again. The second section examines the connection between conflict resolution and human rights and how this may respond to the question of minorities. The third and final section outlines some Bahá'í responses to these themes.[1]

Conflict and Minorities

An obvious dimension in which the pertinence of human rights to peace has been indisputably demonstrated in recent times is that of the issue of minorities. This link between the minority issue as a threat to peace had explicitly been recognized as far back as 1919 when President Wilson stated, 'Nothing, I venture to say, is more likely to disturb the peace of the world than the treatment which might, in certain circumstances, be meted out to minorities.'[2]

Minorities Under the League of Nations

In the immediate aftermath of the first world war, numerous politicians spoke in the tone of minority rights. It was in this spirit that Woodrow Wilson proclaimed his 'Fourteen Points', which led to the European Minority Treaties and the Mandate principle of the League of Nations. The main reason for international interest in the situation of minorities was a pragmatic one: the strong belief that 'minority–majority relations could destabilize not only countries where these minorities lived but they could drag into conflicts other states as well'.[3] Indeed, it was widely believed at the time that 'unhappy minorities in central Europe had contributed to the war's outbreak in 1914'.[4] The attempt was therefore made to provide channels for the protection of Central and Eastern European minorities through a complex network of insertions in treaties of peace, specific bilateral and multilateral treaties dealing with particular minorities and national declarations. Many of the various peace treaties concluded after the first world war contained minority protection clauses. As the establishment of the new state boundaries clearly divided certain peoples, forcing them to exist as ethnic, linguistic or religious minorities in new states, treaties were concluded between the Allied Powers and concerned states in order to secure the protection of the civil and political rights of their minorities. Such treaties included those with Poland, Czechoslovakia, Romania and Greece and provisions in peace treaties with Austria,[5] Hungary, Bulgaria and Turkey. League of Nations membership also demanded states such as Finland, Albania, Latvia and Lithuania,[6] Estonia and Iraq to make declarations on the protection of minorities. The League of Nations assumed responsibility for this international concern for minority rights with complaint procedures and a guarantee system for the rights of petition by individuals and groups. This, in certain cases, included autonomy rights such as those extended to the Aaland islanders.[7] 'Receivable' cases could be referred from the League Secretariat to the Council of the League. After the adoption of a resolution by the Council it would be sent to the *ad hoc* Minorities Committee. Between 1920 and 1929, 345 petitions had been referred to the League, 143 of which were deemed 'receivable' and 18 of which were finally forwarded to the Council for consideration.[8]

Under the League of Nations, the question of minorities was registered as a matter of international concern for the first time and given its organizational guarantee. The aim was twofold. In the words of the Permanent Court of International Justice in 1935, it was for states to

> ensure that nationals belonging to . . . minorities shall be placed in every respect on a footing of perfect equality with the other nationals of the State. The second is to ensure for the minority elements suitable means for the preservation of their racial peculiarities, their traditions and their national characteristics.[9]

However, this League experience with minorities was seriously tainted by the Nazi use of German minorities to destabilize the Versailles settlement and rise to power. This led to the collapse of the minorities system within just two decades of its establishment, 'under the pressure of persistent local animosities, not to mention Nazi expansionism and absorption of German peoples into the Third Reich'.[10] Another factor was the inconsistency and lack of 'consistent overall purpose'[11] under which the system had operated. The political survival of the importance of the rights of minorities was therefore severely disgraced for decades to come.

Minorities Under the United Nations System: Various Phases and Perspectives

After this debacle and yet another world war, the United Nations sidelined minorities and shifted its attention to universal human rights. The political climate of the times, and the immediate precedence of Hitler's abuse of minority rights, had led to this new United Nations emphasis. Minority provisions had been exploited by Hitler for continuous challenges to state boundaries, hence the whole scheme was now discredited as being inherently destabilizing.

It is therefore not surprising to note that there is no reference to minorities in the Charter of the United Nations or the Universal Declaration of Human Rights; though the Charter does prohibit distinctions on the grounds of race, language or religion. This more individualistic but universal regime was to provide a better basis of full equality for both minorities and majorities. No additional body of laws and rights relating specifically to minorities was seen to be necessary or politically viable. This was a deliberate omission, as a conscious attempt by the United Nations to recognize and promote individual human rights on a non-discriminatory basis. Other factors that encouraged a general promotion of universal human rights, rather than minority rights, was the fact of minority rule in South Africa and serious fears about similar circumstances arising in other colonized states.

Despite the United Nations's initial reticence regarding minority rights, over time a body of references to minority rights did gradually build up. Traces of references to minority rights appeared in the Convention on the Prevention and Punishment of the Crime of Genocide of 1948 Article 2, which referred to the right to existence and prohibition of 'acts committed with intent to destroy, in whole or in part, a national, ethnic, racial or religious group as such'. The UNESCO Convention against Discrimination in Education of 1960, the UN Declaration on the Elimination of All Forms of Intolerance and of Discrimination Based on Religion or Belief of 1981, the Convention on the Rights of the Child of 1989, various International Labour Organization conventions and the Covenant of Civil and Political Rights of 1967 also referred to more collective readings of human rights. For example, Article 27 of the International Covenant on Civil and Political Rights stated: 'In those States in which ethnic, religious or linguistic minorities exist, persons belonging to such minorities shall not be denied the right, in community with the other members of their group, to enjoy their own culture . . .' The Sub-Commission also recognized the need of minorities for protection, above and beyond the provision of non-discrimination reflected in individual human rights.

It gradually came to be realized that treating minorities purely on an equal basis with majorities still amounts to discrimination against minorities. In the same way that positive discrimination is sometimes deemed necessary in national legislation, recognition grew of the fact that non-discrimination, when imposed on the starting point of cultural, linguistic, educational and economic disadvantage for minorities, can still lead to the weakening, or even extinction, of minority groups. The United Nations Sub-Commission on Prevention of Discrimination and Protection of Minorities has explained it in this way:

> Protection of minorities is the protection of non-dominant groups which, while wishing in general for equality of treatment with the majority, wish for a measure of differential treatment in order to preserve basic characteristics which they possess and which distinguish them from the majority of the population . . . It follows that differential treatment of such groups, *or individuals* belonging to such groups, is justified when it is exercised in the interest of their contentment and the welfare of the community as a whole.[12]

Minority Rights as Human Rights: The Post Cold War Dilemma

With the thawing of the bipolar conflict in which the world had been gripped for nearly five decades began a violent reassertion of minorities on the international scene. These did not only stem from Soviet republics but from communities as diverse as those in the heart of Europe, Asia and Africa. The complexity of these assertions evaded prevalent approaches to conflict, how to contain it and attempts to resolve it. This was no longer a response to familiar cold war challenges such as nuclear build-up, military arms races and the disturbance of the balance of power. Even the term 'violent nationalism' failed to do credit to the new scenario, bringing previous diplomatic procedures and the

United Nations machinery to its knees. As the Bahá'í International Community observed, 'No sooner had improved relations between the superpowers removed the ideological motivation for such conflicts, than long-smoldering ethnic and sectarian passions surfaced as a new source of conflagration.'[13] They also spoke of 'underlying passions' that could lead to 'planet-wide destruction' and the continuing gravity of problems such as 'militant racialism' and 'religious fanaticism'.[14] With the end to the 'discipline'[15] imposed by the cold war on the international system and the emergence of a much 'looser'[16] international system, 'factors [such as extreme nationalism and religious extremism], which have mainly domestic roots, have a tendency to spill over and affect the stability of international relations'.[17] This scenario made the linkage between conflict, minorities and human rights painfully evident.

> Recent developments in the former Yugoslavia, Rwanda and Liberia . . . earlier crises in Cambodia . . . and in Uganda . . . as well as many other events which have had a disruptive effect on international relations, have all had human rights violations as a factor which contributed to the emergence of threats to international stability. Neglect of interests or violation of the rights of ethnic minorities in Eastern and Central Europe as well as in some former Soviet republics have contributed either to breaches of peace . . . or to strained relations between neighbouring countries.[18]

One writer summed up the contradictions of the early nineties in this way:

> The postmodern 'deconstructed' era . . . is characterized by apparently contradictory trends. On the one hand, there is a movement towards the internationalization or globalization of environmental, resource, humanitarian and rights issues which transcends Cold War inhibitions. On the other hand, we are witness to the emergence or recrudescence within and between States of virulent forms of ethnocentrism, hatred of diversity, the exhumation of buried antagonisms and the obscenity of 'ethnic

cleansing' . . . It is therefore imperative that the internationalization of human rights, and in particular minority rights, is allowed to succeed.[19]

This statement is remarkably reminiscent of Shoghi Effendi's explanation of the parallel processes of order and disorder,[20] the rolling up of an old order and the unfoldment of a new world order.

What these changes bore witness to was the complete failure of the strategy of ignoring minority rights and responding to them only in the same manner as to majorities. We have therefore moved full circle, from collective rights, to individual rights and back to the understanding of the need for collective rights or at least for a collective dimension to individual rights. The purely individualistic reading of human rights is increasingly being considered as being 'inadequate to address fully the needs of communities and ensure that human rights abuses do not present threats to international peace and security'.[21] The irony of history is that it has largely been the reappearance of the problem of minorities in the Balkans that has, once again, called for a reassessment of some kind of minority provision, one that had perhaps been too eagerly and swiftly cast away. But what is this required equilibrium between individual and collective rights to look like? What insights can the Bahá'í writings shed on the matter? It is to the complex dynamics of this loaded question that section three will attempt a response. But before that the merits of a human rights approach to conflict resolution will be examined.

Universal Human Rights as an Approach to Conflict Resolution?

The Correlation Between Conflict Resolution and Peace

The United Nations Charter and the Universal Declaration of Human Rights were the two documents that brought the term 'human rights' into popular usage, both making the fundamental connection between peace and human rights. The Charter of the

United Nations makes this connection in its first Article (1.3) when it establishes as one of the purposes of the United Nations, 'To achieve international cooperation . . . in promoting and encouraging respect for human rights and for fundamental freedoms for all without distinction as to race, sex, language, or religion.' This is also echoed in the preamble of the Universal Declaration of Human Rights:

> . . . recognition of the inherent dignity and of the equal and inalienable rights of all members of the human family is the foundation of freedom, justice and peace in the world . . . it is essential, if man is not to be compelled to have recourse, as a last resort, to rebellion against tyranny and oppression, that human rights be protected by the rule of law.

The Bahá'í International Community echoes the fact that in these documents 'formal recognition has been given to respect for social justice as a correlative of the establishment of world peace'.[22] It further emphasizes that 'human rights must be recognized and protected internationally if peace, social progress and economic prosperity are to be established'.[23]

What is the Connection Between Peace and Human Rights?

Human rights is thus recognized as a key basis on which to establish peace. The following reasons can be given for a fundamental recognition of the connection between conflict resolution and human rights.

- Lasting peace necessitates a comprehensive understanding of the causes of conflict which, without exception, stem from actual or perceived abuses of human rights. The sense of injustice is particularly heightened in cases of abuse against minorities, owing to the perpetual structural discrimination involved in continued infringements against such groups, leading to a collective and accumulated resentment. Human rights serves as a powerful basis and language on which to begin to communicate about lasting resolutions to conflict.

- Human rights is needed within the processes of conflict resolution, peace-keeping, peace-building, peace-making and the maintenance of peace. In short, it is indispensable to the healthy running of a dynamic and peaceful society.

- True 'peace' encompasses respect for human rights.

- Human rights is included within the realization of justice and the oneness of humanity. The oneness of humanity is a prerequisite to unity and therefore to peace.

With the Bahá'í definition of peace encompassing much more than even a permanent end to war, the contribution of human rights is crucial to this enhanced understanding of peace. In fact, the Bahá'í International Community presents universal human rights as an absolute imperative to justice, the establishment of the oneness of humanity and to unity. With human rights serving as one of the prerequisites to equality and unity, human rights itself becomes a fundamental project in the pursuit of peace. The Bahá'í International Community presents the following statement of Bahá'u'lláh as the 'primary challenge facing civilization': 'The well-being of mankind, its peace and security, are unattainable unless and until its unity is firmly established.'[24] Through what other language, if not that of rights, can equality begin to be entrenched in national and international laws, in foreign policy, relations between both states and individuals, the national psyche and legal institutions? Through what other means is unity going to be founded in the legal and political realm? Human rights serves as the framework within which all such reforms can be pursued.

The role of human rights in conflict resolution stems from the fact that it traces such conflicts back to basics, to the roots of resentment which in turn led to the active pursuit of incompatible ends. Any means of conflict resolution which ignores this method of looking at the essence of differences will ultimately fail to address fundamental issues and therefore fail to lead to lasting peace. By emphasizing human rights, fundamental human needs[25] enshrined in inviolable language and upheld through the law can be addressed. Through human rights language we are able to extend equal dignity to all parties to the conflict, whilst not compromising the accepted limits on their freedoms and the abuse of power. Both rights and the limits of tolerance for infringing on the rights of others are simultaneously given credit. Such a linkage encourages the pursuit of a comprehensive picture of the conflict, whilst also pointing towards the basis on which to explore a means out of the existing deadlock.

Human Rights and Peace: What Kind of 'Peace'?

The correlation of human rights with peace is not automatic or constant. As the most immediate path to peace is the preservation of the status quo, then the interests of human rights and peace will sometimes clash.

> Though the improvement of human rights situations in some countries and regions may be a necessary component in the movement towards more stable international relations, the ultimate aim of the human rights movement in the world is not to be an instrument for peace and stability but to promote and protect human rights and fundamental freedoms. This means that sometimes, in order to achieve improvements in the field of human rights, states may have to be ready to risk a certain deterioration of inter-state relations.[26]

The ambitions of human rights are more profound than a mere concern with stability and the short-term absence of war. It calls for no less than a deepened sense of justice, which guarantees the rights of every single individual. The relationship is a complex one. Whittaker explains:

> The imbroglio over Bosnia has shown that the promotion and protection of human rights is an undertaking of vast complexity and uncertainty. Indeed even a human rights orientation on the national and international spheres does not ease the difficulty of decisions regarding possible humanitarian intervention. The contest for power in former Yugoslavia has exploded into an

> unmanageable situation where what are thought to be significant ethnic differences have become justifying criteria for obsessive struggle. The United Nations has been faced with the problem of trying to translate Resolutions, Conventions and Declarations about human rights into practice. Over expectation has meant that international action is almost certainly falling well short of target.[27]

The problem of minorities and conflict stems from the basic needs of security, recognition and justice, which are ideals that find place in human rights documents. Enduring antagonistic perceptions, conditioned by experience and fear, lead to hostilities that breed greater hostilities and, therefore, entrenched conflict.

A Bahá'í Reading of Minorities, Conflict and Human Rights?

The basic dimensions of a Bahá'í response to these challenges can be presented in the five tier set of questions outlined below.

- Human rights and the oneness of humankind
- The oneness of humankind and unity, which is a prerequisite to peace
- The enforcement of human rights
- Minorities and human rights
- World order and the realization of human rights, and peace

Human Rights and the Oneness of Humankind

Whilst human rights, in themselves, are valued in Bahá'í thinking, their main context comes through their association with the central tenet of the oneness of humanity. Like other religions and beliefs, human rights are primarily valued owing to the

Bahá'í belief about the spiritual essence or divine light reflected in every human being. From this follows many of 'Abdu'l-Bahá's assertions about the need for human dignity, equal treatment and legal guarantees. A selection of such writings of 'Abdu'l-Bahá are given below:

> Bahá'u'lláh taught that an equal standard of human rights must be recognized and adopted. In the estimation of God all men are equal; there is no distinction or preferment for any soul in the dominion of His justice and equity.[28]

> All men are of one family; the crown of humanity rests on the head of every human being.[29]

> The Law must reign, and not the individual; thus will the world become a place of beauty and true brotherhood will be realized.[30]

> All men are equal before the law, which must reign absolutely . . . Kings must rule with wisdom and justice; prince, peer and peasant alike have equal rights to just treatment, there must be no favour shown to individuals. A judge must be no 'respecter of persons', but administer the law with strict impartiality in every case brought before him.[31]

> When perfect justice reigns in every country of the Eastern and Western World, then will the earth become a place of beauty. The dignity and equality of every servant of God will be acknowledged; the ideal of the solidarity of the human race, the true brotherhood of man, will be realized; and the glorious light of the Sun of Truth will illumine the souls of all men.[32]

It can already be seen from the selection of Bahá'í writings above that human rights, justice and the oneness of humanity are intertwined. This interrelationship has been made even more explicit through the numerous statements of the Bahá'í International Community (BIC), the non-governmental (NGO) representation of the international Bahá'í community at the United Nations and other international fora. The BIC boldly asserted in 1993 that,

> The concept of human rights should be anchored in the principle of the oneness of humankind . . . The basis for a commitment to human rights is recognition of the oneness of humanity . . . To accept the oneness of humanity is to embrace the variations that characterize human society, and to desire for every individual the opportunity to develop and express his or her unique capacities and inherent talents. Recognition of the oneness of humanity gives rise to an elevated concept of human rights, one that includes the assurance of dignity for each person and the realization of each individual's innate potential. This view differs markedly from an approach to human rights that is limited to preventing interference with the individual's freedom of action.[33]

Also in 1993 the BIC explained that, in the Bahá'í perspective, such a belief in the organic oneness of humanity provides the foundation for the realization of the ideals asserted in documents such as the Universal Declaration of Human Rights (1948).[34] A statement from 1995 goes some way towards defining the oneness of humankind. Whilst acknowledging that the term is mistakenly perceived to be 'deceptively simple' in popular usage, it argues that the concept fundamentally challenges the conflict that has so permeated our world through such avenues as 'the adversarial structure of civil government, the advocacy principle informing most of civil law, a glorification of the struggle between classes and other social groups, or the competitive spirit dominating so much of modern life'.[35] A thorough understanding of the oneness of humanity would challenge all these hidden conflicts, and contribute in no small measure to conflict resolution in everyday life.

All these assertions are a reflection of Bahá'u'lláh's pronouncements about world interdependence and that of Shoghi Effendi that 'in a world of inter-dependent peoples and nations the advantage of the part is best to be reached by the advantage of the whole'.[36] This essential interconnectedness can be visualized in the following manner:

> . . . since the body of humankind is one and indivisible, each member of the human race is born into the world as a trust of the

> whole. This relationship between the individual and the collective constitutes the moral foundation of most of the human rights which the instruments of the United Nations are attempting to define.[37]

From such thinking also follows explicit understandings about the role of responsibilities relating to human rights. Such responsibility is that which is 'devolving upon every person, as a divinely-created being, to recognize the essential oneness of the human race and to promote the human rights of others with this motivation'.[38] This empowering model sets out a very positive context for the assertion of human rights. Human rights assertions, by definition, most often stem from those whose rights have been transgressed. This individualistic fight for rights from the dispossessed, or in the name of the dispossessed, depicts the scenario in which human rights are proclaimed in our current international clime. The re-contextualization of human rights by the BIC, however, potentially releases a new context for individuals and communities to assert the rights of others, drawing upon their fundamental belief in the oneness of humanity and realizing the ideal of unity and peace. As the BIC argues:

> It seems to us essential to broaden the conceptual framework for addressing human rights problems *from an adversarial paradigm* – pitting the government against the individual citizen – *to a cooperative* one, where we consider relations among all human beings as members of one community. In this context, everyone has an essential role to play in implementing fundamental human rights. When individuals assume responsibility for ensuring each other's human rights the foundation for unity will be firmly established.[39]

Human Rights, Oneness and Unity: Prerequisites to Peace

'World unity requires universal respect for human rights.'[40] This section began with the bold and categorical statement from the BIC regarding the absolute indispensability of universal human rights to unity. Previous sections in this essay have already reviewed another equally categorical Bahá'í belief: that unity is a prerequisite to peace.[41] It therefore follows that universal respect for human rights is essential to the quest for conflict resolution and peace.

One way in which Bahá'ís can strive towards peace, therefore, is to promote the international thrust towards nurturing a culture of human rights. Numerous United Nations experts have called for a universal quest for human rights education, establishing an ingrained respect for human rights values worldwide. The BIC supported such efforts in acknowledging that:

> Rooted as it is in the recognition of the organic oneness of mankind, a 'universal culture of human rights' would form the very foundation for a world in which all could feel safe and secure – a world in which a violation of the rights of one would be felt as a violation of the rights of all.[42]

It also hinted at the depth to which such education must reach, in referring to its need to reach 'hearts' and 'minds' in instilling a 'keen, emotionally grounded awareness of the fundamental unity of humankind'.[43]

The Enforcement of Human Rights

The Bahá'í International Community takes a very strong stance on the importance of a united response to violations of human rights. It states that:

> Human rights enforcement at the international level needs to be handled in a manner similar to the treatment of military aggression under a collective security regime. The violation of human rights in one state must be considered the concern of all, and enforcement mechanisms must provide for a unified response on the part of the entire international community.[44]

In recent years there have been numerous disastrous demonstrations of 'dithering' in the face of genocide and cold deliberate considerations of self-interest whilst championing universal human values. These have gone a long way towards making the wisdom of the above statement evident to the growing multitude of victims and disturbed bystanders.

In the above statement an obvious linkage is drawn between aggression and human rights violations. What is particularly significant, is that the Office of Public Information extrapolated Bahá'u'lláh's vision for united responses to military aggression by states[45] to a similar response in enforcing human rights. What is clear is that both violations are unacceptable from a Bahá'í position and a strong united response is regarded as both necessary and just. The significance of the comparability of encroachments on human rights to that of military violations against other states is that of the centrality and sacredness being attached to individual human beings as ultimately a comparable goal to that of the sovereign right of a state to non-intervention in its domestic affairs. Perhaps the significance of the latter, itself, lies in its role in facilitating the nurturing of the rights of the individuals and communities that exist within it. Another dimension is that of the 'sovereignty' that in time, Bahá'ís believe, will come to be assigned to institutions of a world federal commonwealth. Since 'a right is only valid and effective when upheld by an independent sovereignty',[46] it follows that what is being assumed is that 'a world sovereignty is required'.[47] This theme will be touched upon below in the section 'World Order, Human Rights and Peace'.

Minorities and Human Rights

Several remarkably vivid analogies are given in BIC statements regarding the absolutely crucial necessity of engaging all means in the preservation of minority communities. One example is the following:

> Since the body of humankind is one and indivisible, each member of the race is born into the world as a trust of the whole . . . The principle of collective trusteeship creates also the right of every person to expect that those cultural conditions essential to his or her identity enjoy the protection of national and

> international law. Much like the role played by the gene pool in the biological life of humankind and its environment, the immense wealth of cultural diversity achieved over thousands of years is vital to the social and economic development of a human race experiencing its collective coming of age. It represents a heritage that must be permitted to bear its fruit in a global civilization . . . cultures must be enabled to interact with one another in ever-changing patterns of civilization, free of manipulation for partisan political ends.[48]

The BIC draws attention to 'the great urgency' with which the question of minorities needs to be addressed through a reassessment of the 'shared beliefs, attitudes and behaviours' of both individuals and governments.[49] Responsibility for the realization of minority rights, it insists,

> . . . falls on both majorities and minorities. Majorities have a special responsibility, for the sake of justice, to bring about the social and political adjustments which will enable minorities to exercise, to the fullest extent possible, their common and fundamental rights. Minorities, on the other hand, have a moral responsibility to respond honourably to genuine efforts by majorities and . . . respect their duties to the society at large . . . Both must view minority issues in the context of an increasingly interdependent world. In such a world, the advantage of the part is best served by ensuring the advantage of the whole; likewise, the whole cannot flourish when parts are oppressed or deprived.[50]

The BIC refers to the legal, spiritual and moral influences needed in such responses and shares the Bahá'í maxim that 'if any discrimination at all is to be tolerated, it should be in favour of the minority'[51] and argues further that:

> Minorities and majorities must embrace an expansive view of world society that sees all human beings as members of one human family, united in their fundamental aspirations, yet enriched by the *precious variation* in human thought, language, religion and culture. The development of such a universal and

> unshakable consciousness of the oneness of mankind is essential if the rights of minorities are to be fully realized.[52]

In the same way that the BIC re-contextualized assertions for human rights into a universal quest for equal rights stemming from the oneness of humanity, it similarly asserts that the concept of the oneness of humanity revolutionizes the call for minority rights and puts it into a more positive mould.

> We believe that the recognition of the fundamental oneness of humankind and the interdependence of all peoples is the foundation for true social equality and for respect of the fundamental human rights of all people, including persons belonging to minorities. Efforts to protect the rights of minorities which are inspired only by the desire to avoid or suppress conflict between minority groups or between minority groups and the dominant group in society are doomed to failure. The principle of the oneness of humanity provides not only a more constructive and far-reaching approach for ensuring minority rights but also a creative basis for the resolution of long-standing tensions and the construction of a new world-embracing civilization.[53]

This context of oneness, the BIC maintains, is critical to neutralizing the highly-charged, long-standing conflicts that have entrenched polarized positions relating to minority abuses.

> Unity in diversity is at once a vision for the future and a principle to guide the world community in its response to these challenges. Not only must this principle come to animate relations among the nations of the planet, but it must also be applied within both local and national communities if they are to prosper and endure. The unifying, salutary effects of applying this principle to the redesign and development of communities the world over, would be incalculable, while the consequences of failing to respond appropriately to the challenges of an ever-contracting world will surely prove disastrous.[54]

World Order, Human Rights and Peace

Many commentators lament the ineffectiveness of the human rights machinery to realize their implementation at the local, national and international levels. Though even the professed pursuit of the ideals such as those of the Universal Declaration of Human Rights by the great majority of states marks progress in itself, observers at the treaty and non-treaty bodies of the United Nations, journalists and current affairs commentators all daily perceive the numerous occasions on which practice in reality falls drastically short of stated commitment. This critical margin marks the difference between accepting that human rights standards are just idealized markers that are unreachable or standards to which every human being and community is by nature entitled. The BIC believes that:

> Our inherited scheme of rights has become jeopardized through the loss of real sovereignty by the national state a world sovereignty is required. The whole conception of right has undergone change. A right formerly was a defence against an invasion; a right today is a sharing of social status among mankind. Moral and social law can for the first time in human experience blend and unify when humanity as a whole becomes subject to the same law.[55]

Within this scheme of thinking, 'The true destiny of the national state is to build the bridge from local autonomy to world unity'[56] and, in turn, this will be of significant consequence to the ability of the human rights machinery to substantially and effectively address conflict. In fact, such a world commonwealth will have the realization of human rights and minority rights as its fundamental *raison d'être*.

> The order herein affirmed implies the establishment of a world commonwealth uniting all nations, races, creeds and classes and safeguarding the autonomy of its state members and the personal freedom and initiative of the individuals that compose them. The commonwealth would consist of a world legislature functioning

> as trustees of the whole of mankind and enacting the laws required to regulate the life, satisfy the needs and adjust the relationships of all races and peoples. Its world executive, backed by an international Force, would carry out the laws and decisions decreed by the world legislature, and safeguard the organic unity of the whole commonwealth. Its world tribunal would adjudicate and render final and compulsory verdict in any and all disputes arising between the various elements constituting the universal system.[57]

Within such a perspective, therefore, the whole of the human rights system and international law in general is perceived as being in

> . . . a transitional period leading towards a new world legal order in which the individual will be called upon to play a more important role as a subject of international rights, responsibilities and duties. Humanity is rapidly approaching a new order, a world commonwealth, which calls for sufficient flexibility to respond to the growing and ever-changing needs of modern society . . . This will allow humankind to go beyond the inner limitations of the structure of present-day society.[58]

Many scholars have pointed out this principal tension between the processes required by the realization of human rights ideals and the path pursued for the entrenchment of national sovereignty. The two paths are regularly at odds with one another, as vividly demonstrated in relation to the problem of humanitarian intervention by Zarrín Caldwell.[59] The BIC response rests on the belief that the nation state needs to step aside somewhat and allow the space for effective international developments such as human rights to set root.

> Historically the nation represented a great moral victory, a definite and important stage in human progress . . . The national state has reached the limits of its development as an independent, self-directed social body . . . Conceived of as an end in itself, the national state has come to be a denial of the oneness of mankind,

> the source of general disruption opposed to the true interests of its people . . . [60]

The irony of the situation seems to be that we need to build upwards to a truly international system in order to preserve downwards, to entities such as minorities who cannot be adequately catered for under the present system.

Conclusion

In this light it can be seen that, although human rights have emerged to play a much greater role in international relations than previously envisaged, their previous incarnation as minority rights was initially only upheld by governments in order to maintain their sovereignty and preserve the territorial integrity of their increasingly heterogeneous communities. Its negative and defensive beginnings in attempts to prevent conflict were later reset in a more positive mould – that of the ideals of universal human rights. It is therefore not surprising to observe that the period that lent greatest impetus to the main-streaming of human rights in international politics coincided with the period of greatest political flux immediately after the second world war. Human rights emerged as a relief to pressures of emerging internal conflicts or transborder disputes that could once again destabilize the newly-established and fragile peace that had emerged on the ashes of war.

However, whilst it may theoretically be appreciated that the processes of human rights are indeed highly relevant in attempting to address situations of conflict, the serious challenges that came to the fore after the end of the cold war have not yet been adequately successful to instil confidence in their current framework and procedures. This article has attempted to chart the historical motivation for the unfolding of international concern for human rights in general and minority rights in particular. In studying the statements of the Bahá'í International Community, it has also attempted to outline a Bahá'í understanding of where to go from here and point towards what other attitudinal and systemic changes are demanded before the true relevance of human rights values in resolving minority–majority conflict can be realized.

Bibliography

'Abdu'l-Bahá. *Paris Talks*. London: Bahá'í Publishing Trust, 1967.

— *The Promulgation of Universal Peace*. Wilmette, IL: Bahá'í Publishing Trust, 1982.

Bahá'í International Community. *A Bahá'í Declaration of Human Obligations and Rights*. Presented to the first session of the United Nations Commission on Human Rights, Lake Success, New York, USA, February 1947, BIC Document no. 47–0200.

— *Creating a Universal Culture of Human Rights*. Statement to the 45th session of the United Nations Commission on Human Rights, Agenda item 11: Further promotion and encouragement of human rights and fundamental freedoms, including the question of the programme and methods of work of the Commission; alternative approaches and ways and means within the United Nations system for improving the effective enjoyment of human rights and fundamental freedoms; national institutions for the promotion and protection of human rights, Geneva, Switzerland, 15 February 1989, BIC Document no. 89–0215.

— *Obstacles to Progress in Human Rights*. Statement to the United Nations World Conference on Human Rights, Agenda item 9: General debate on the progress made in the field of human rights since the adoption of the Universal Declaration of Human Rights and on the identification of obstacles to further progress in this area, and ways in which they can be overcome, Vienna, Austria, 14–25 June 1993, BIC Document no. 93–0609.

— *The Prosperity of Humankind*. A statement prepared by the Bahá'í International Community Office of Public Information, Haifa, first distributed at the United Nations World Summit on Social Development, Copenhagen, Denmark; Haifa, Israel, 3 March 1995. BIC Document no. 95–0303; also *The Prosperity of Humankind*. London: Bahá'í Publishing Trust, 1995.

— *Protection of Minorities*. Oral statement to the 42nd session of the

United Nations Sub-Commission on Prevention of Discrimination and Protection of Minorities, Agenda item 18: Protection of minorities, Geneva, Switzerland, 15 August 1990, BIC Document no. 90–0815.

— *Protection of Minorities*. Statement to the 46th session of the United Nations Commission on Human Rights, Item 20 of the provisional agenda: Report of the Sub-Commission on Prevention of Discrimination and Protection of Minorities at its 41st session, Geneva, Switzerland, UN Document E/CN.4/1990/NGO/6, January-February 1990, BIC Document no. 90–0127.

— *Protection of Minorities*. Written statement to the United Nations Sub-Commission on Prevention of Discrimination and Protection of Minorities, Geneva, Switzerland, UN Document E/CN.4/Sub.2/1994/NGO/1, August 1994, BIC Document no. 94–0821.

— *Right and Responsibility to Promote Human Rights*. Written comment on the Draft Declaration on the Right and Responsibility of Individuals, Groups and Organs of Society to Promote and Protect Universally Recognized Human Rights and Fundamental Freedoms submitted to the 50th session of the Commission on Human Rights in response to an invitation from Ibrahima Fall, Assistant Secretary-General for Human Rights, issued in accordance with resolution 1993/92 of the Commission on Human Rights, Geneva, Switzerland, 3 December 1993, sections A and C, BIC Document no. 93–1203.

— *Rights of Minorities*. Submitted to the 51st session of the United Nations Commission on Human Rights, Geneva, Switzerland, 31 January 1995, BIC Document no. 95–0131.

— *Rights of Minorities, Comments on the Draft Declaration*. Oral statement presented to the 48th session of the United Nations Commission on Human Rights, Agenda item 18: The rights of persons belonging to national, ethnic, religious, and linguistic minorities, Geneva, Switzerland, February 1992, BIC Document no. 92–0207.

— *Sustainable Communities in an Integrating World*. A statement presented to the United Nations Conference on Human Settlements (Habitat II), Istanbul, Turkey, 3–14 June 1996, BIC Document no. 96–0530.

— *Turning Point for All Nations, A Statement of the Bahá'í International*

Community on the Occasion of the 50th Anniversary of the United Nations, BIC Document no. 95–1001. New York: Bahá'í International Community United Nations Office, 1995.

— *The United Nations Decade for Human Rights Education.* Written statement on the United Nations Decade for Human Rights Education, submitted to the UN Commission on Human Rights, Geneva, March 1996, BIC Document no. 96–0315.

Bahá'u'lláh. *Gleanings from the Writings of Bahá'u'lláh.* Wilmette, IL: Bahá'í Publishing Trust, 1983.

Burton, John. *Conflict: Resolution and Provention.* New York: St Martin's Press, 1990.

Caldwell, Zarrín T. 'Humanitarian Intervention in a Global Society', in Charles O. Lerche (ed.). *Toward the Most Great Justice: Elements of Justice in the New World Order.* London: Bahá'í Publishing Trust, 1996.

Evans, Malcolm D. *Religious Liberty and International Law in Europe.* Cambridge: Cambridge University Press, 1997.

Forsythe, David P. *Human Rights and World Politics.* London: University of Nebraska Press, 2nd edn. 1989.

Müllerson, Rein. *Fifty Years of the United Nations: Peace and Human Rights in the UN Agenda*, in Robert Blackburn and James Busuttil (eds.). *Human Rights for the 21st Century.* London: Pinter, 1997.

— *Human Rights Diplomacy.* London: Routledge, 1997.

Robinson, J. et al. *Were the Minorities Treaties a Failure?* New York: Antin Press Inc., 1943.

Shoghi Effendi. *The World Order of Bahá'u'lláh.* Wilmette, IL: Bahá'í Publishing Trust, 1991.

Thornberry, Patrick. *International Law and the Rights of Minorities.* Oxford: Oxford University Press, 1991.

— 'The UN Declaration on the Rights of Persons Belonging to National or Ethnic, Religious and Linguistic Minorities: Background, Analysis, Observations, and an Update', in Phillips and Rosas (eds.). *Universal Minority Rights.* London: Abo Akademi University, Institute for Human Rights and London Minority Rights Group International, 1995.

UN Document E/CN.4/52

Whittaker, David J. *United Nations in Action.* London: University College London Press, 1995.

Notes

1. Address to the 8th Plenary Session of the Peace Conference of 1919, cited by Robinson et al., *Were the Minorities Treaties a Failure?* p. 21.
2. Thornberry, *International Law and the Rights of Minorities*, pp. 40–1.
3. Müllerson, *Fifty Years of the United Nations*, chapter on 'Human Rights for the 21st Century', p. 143.
4. Forsythe, *Human Rights and World Politics*, pp. 8–9.
5. For more details see Evans, *Religious Liberty and International Law in Europe*, pp. 104–24.
6. Latvia and Lithuania were not obliged to make a formal minorities declaration but did have to agree to be subject to the mechanisms of the minorities system. This was because of their objection to making such declarations. For details see ibid. p. 141.
7. Finland made a declaration in 1921 to preserve the Swedish language, culture and traditions of the population under League supervision.
8. Evans, *Religious Liberty and International Law in Europe,* p. 157. Petitions submitted to the League included those from Albania, Armenia, Lithuania and Poland.
9. Advisory Opinion of 6 April 1935 on Minority Schools in Albania, P.C.I.J., Ser. A/B, no. 64, p. 17. Quoted in Thornberry, 'UN Declaration on the Rights of Persons', p. 16; chapter in Phillips and Rosa (eds.), *Universal Minority Rights.*
10. Forsythe, *Human Rights and World Politics*, pp. 8–9.
11. Evans, *Religious Liberty and International Law in Europe*, p. 144.
12. UN Document E/CN.4/52 section V. Emphasis added.
13. Bahá'í International Community, *Turning Point for All Nations*, p. 2. BIC Document no. 95–1001.
14. ibid. pp. 2–3.
15. Müllerson, *Human Rights Diplomacy*, p. 7.
16. ibid.
17. ibid.
18. ibid. pp. 4–5.
19. Thornberry, 'UN Declaration on the Rights of Persons', p. 11.
20. Shoghi Effendi, *World Order*, p. 161.
21. Evans, *Religious Liberty and International Law in Europe*, p. 375.
22. Bahá'í International Community, *Prosperity of Humankind*, p. 11. BIC Document no. 95–0303.

23. Bahá'í International Community, *Turning Point for All Nations*, p. 16. BIC Document no. 95–1001.
24. Bahá'u'lláh, quoted in Bahá'í International Community, *Right and Responsibility to Promote Human Rights*, section A. BIC Document no. 93–1203.
25. See Burton, *Conflict: Resolution and Provention.*
26. Müllerson, *Human Rights Diplomacy*, p. 5.
27. Whittaker, *United Nations in Action*, p. 186.
28. 'Abdu'l-Bahá, *Promulgation*, p. 182.
29. 'Abdu'l-Bahá, *Paris Talks*, p. 138.
30. ibid. p. 132.
31. ibid. p. 154.
32. ibid. p. 155.
33. Bahá'í International Community, *Right and Responsibility to Promote Human Rights*, section A. BIC Document no. 93–1203.
34. Bahá'í International Community, *Obstacles to Progress in Human Rights*. BIC Document no. 93–0609.
35. Bahá'í International Community, *Prosperity of Humankind*, p. 6. BIC Document no. 95–0303.
36. Shoghi Effendi, *World Order*, p. 198.
37. Bahá'í International Community, *Turning Point for All Nations*, p. 4. BIC Document no. 95–1001.
38. Bahá'í International Community, *Right and Responsibility to Promote Human Rights*, section C. BIC Document no. 93–1203.
39. ibid. Emphasis added.
40. ibid. section A.
41. Bahá'u'lláh states, 'The well-being of mankind, its peace and security, are unattainable unless and until its unity is firmly established.' (Bahá'u'lláh, *Gleanings*, p. 286)
42. Bahá'í International Community, *Creating a Universal Culture of Human Rights*. BIC Document no. 89–0215.
43. Bahá'í International Community, *United Nations Decade for Human Rights Education*. BIC Document no. 96–0315.
44. Bahá'í International Community, *Turning Point for All Nations*, pp. 16–17. BIC Document no. 95–1001.
45. Bahá'u'lláh states, 'Should any king take up arms against another, all should unitedly arise and prevent him . . . This will ensure the peace and composure of every people, government and nation.' (Bahá'u'lláh, *Gleanings*, p. 249)
46. Bahá'í International Community, *Bahá'í Declaration of Human Obligations and Rights*, section III. BIC Document no. 47–0200.

47. ibid.
48. Bahá'í International Community, *Prosperity of Humankind*, pp. 12–13. BIC Document no. 95–0303.
49. Bahá'í International Community, *Rights of Minorities* (1995). BIC Document no. 95–0131.
50. Bahá'í International Community, *Protection of Minorities* (written statement). BIC Document no. 94–0821.
51. ibid.
52. Bahá'í International Community, *Rights of Minorities* (1992). BIC Document no. 92–0207. Emphasis added.
53. Bahá'í International Community, *Protection of Minorities* (oral statement). BIC Document no. 90–0815.
54. Bahá'í International Community, *Sustainable Communities in an Integrating World*, pp. 4–5. BIC Document no. 96–0530.
55. Bahá'í International Community, *Bahá'í Declaration of Human Obligations and Rights*, section III. BIC Document no. 47–0200.
56. ibid.
57. ibid. section IV.
58. Bahá'í International Community, *Protection of Minorities*, BIC Document no. 90–0127.
59. Caldwell, 'Humanitarian Intervention in a Global Society', in Lerche (ed.), *Toward the Most Great Justice*, pp. 187–203.
60. Bahá'í International Community, *Bahá'í Declaration of Human Obligations and Rights*, section II. BIC Document no. 47–0200.

6

Reforming the United Nations: Issues and Options

Olivia Lopez

Introduction

The question of UN structural reform has been the subject of extensive debate and controversy among experts and between the major powers. While providing a rich source of creative, innovative ideas about the future role of the world's international institutions, discussions on the UN and its affiliated agencies have reflected the broadly-held view that it is necessary to transform an antiquated institution to reflect the international community's contemporary political realities.

The issue of reform emerged not long after the creation of the UN, as its original purpose and objectives were directly linked to the post-war political climate and its particular needs. The political dominance of a powerful minority was considered necessary for the preservation of peace and the prevention of war. The emergence of Third World countries as independent states brought increased diversity and new national aspirations to a transforming world order. Significant changes in the distribution of political and economic power, the development in transnational, non-governmental forces and new global threats to peace, prosperity and the environment have drastically altered the priorities and needs of the world in the 21st century. The notion that the UN is no longer able to adequately respond to the many demands placed upon it has been widely confirmed as a result of the organization's various interventions and operations over the past decade.

The aim of this article is to identify and put in perspective the reforms that are necessary to maintain the relevance of the UN in an era of rapid change, where the forces of globalization are transforming the nature of the relations between nation states. The various reforms considered here primarily reflect concerns among many that the UN is no longer an efficient institution operating in a consensual way to safeguard the interests of the international community. The principal focus of this piece will thus be on the General Assembly and the Security Council, as the main legislative, executive and managerial organs of the UN.

In addition to examining a broad spectrum of viewpoints on UN reform, this article considers the views expressed by the Bahá'í International Community, comprised of members of the progressive world religion the Bahá'í Faith. Among the motivations for this paper has been the forward-looking Bahá'í perspective on the modernization of our global structures in the context of an emerging world order.

The UN's Critics

Although criticism of the United Nations is abundant and widespread, the most frequently encountered critiques are those which pertain to the deficiencies and flaws in the institution's structure and organization.

UN reform is inevitable. Expressions of universal dissatisfaction with its performance have increasingly made the UN a preoccupation of leaders of major states. International organizations in general have acquired increased political influence and significance in the affairs of governments. Protests against the realist approaches of western countries, which have often contradicted the spirit and the letter of the Charter, testify to the faults of an organization which itself has often reflected undemocratic practices and conduct. The present UN has been described as 'a minority of governments determined to retain control while preaching democracy to the majority'.[1] The initial aim of the UN – the preservation of international peace and security by a few great powers – has become the principal cause of division between a powerful few, preserving their advantageous positions, and the majority seeking a world community. Nobel laureate and writer Alexander Solzhenitsyn has described the United Nations as

> . . . a United Governments Organization which, thanks to the venal prejudice of the majority of its members, jealously guards the liberty of certain nations and neglects the liberty of others . . . Failing to investigate private grievances, groans, cries and entreaties of simple, humble individuals, insects too tiny for such a large organization to concern itself with; and which having produced the Universal Declaration of Human Rights has failed to make endorsement of it an obligatory condition of membership, and thus . . . let ordinary people at the mercy of governments not of their choosing.[2]

The issues which currently preoccupy every elected leader and the international community as a whole – poverty, hunger, unemployment, environmental degradation, ethnic and religious tensions – highlight the need to modernize the framework for global governance.

Maurice Bertrand, in his report for the UN Joint Inspection Unit, claims that the UN system was never set up to manage problems of global dimensions. Global conferences have functioned as a new framework for eliciting agreement on urgent problems while embracing a wide variety of global actors. *Ad hoc* conferences have responded to the failures of UN organs to develop procedures for identifying and solving new problems as a matter of routine. Such conferences have been considered symptoms of the changes in the underlying structure of power, of new perceptions of global problems and their solutions and the need to diminish the breach between knowledge, organization and the real world. Global conferences on the environment, population and women's issues have been a form of adaptation of the UN. Its polycentric organization is not able to coordinate the necessary economic and social activities. Although the Economic and Social Council had been intended to manage the system, it has failed to coordinate activities of specialized agencies. The General Assembly lacks the authority to instruct UN agencies, which it tends not to consult in any event. Hence the lack of coherent management and the need for separate funds, or programmes such as UNCTAD, which are born as a result of polycentrism and become causes for an even further polycentric UN.

The Bertrand Report, whose primary objective was to determine the sources of UN mismanagement and disorganization, has provided an in-depth analysis of the fundamental flaws of the institution. The most evident and inimical fault of the UN system is the lack of a common philosophy, vision and approach. Although the General Assembly has adopted 'an integrated approach to development', for the UN as a whole, this dictum has remained 'an empty formula'.[3] The absence of a unified concept of development and the lack of a common methodology for projects have made goals uncertain and procedures inadequate. The numerous criticisms of UN inefficiency stem from the fragmentation and duplication of roles, functions and policies, which are all reflections of the lack of a common, united outlook. Each organization, i.e. FAO, ILO, UNIDO or UNESCO, has its own methods, theories of development and priorities to be pursued, leaving very little room for consensus.

The 'sectoral approach' of the UN has intensified the fragmentation of aid, further complicating it for 'aid-receiving' countries as well. The various agencies, which make up 30 bodies, often offer divergent and contradictory recommendations. The sectoralized, decentralized and fragmented structures of the UN are the main reason for its failure to adapt to the solution of development problems, hence the urgent need to reconsider the structure of the United Nations. Evidence of the UN's inadequate performance in the realm of development is apparent in a recent UNDP evaluation.

> The concept of rural development as a process of far-reaching political, economic, social transformation of agrarian society, and

> of agrarian society as the core of the Third World national development, rarely emerges . . . the UN has reconciled itself to acting as a social safety net rather than aiming to influence the causes of development . . . and if this persists, the holes in the net will grow larger as the System won't be able to keep up. UNDP lacks a clearly focused policy guideline for rural development. UN policy is loose and general. The resident representative of the UNDP is compelled to rely on his own resources to produce a degree of internal agency programme consistency.[4]

Bertrand traces the UN's inadequate and 'ill-adapted goals' to three fundamental fallacies which have served as the basis for UN operations. The first is that the maintenance of peace can be brought about in the modern world through a single institution. The second is that the development of poorer zones can be brought about by a sectoral and non-integrated approach. The third is that negotiations to improve or alter world consensus can be conducted without prior definition of negotiation structures accepted by all participants. The correction of each of these fallacies implies fundamental structural changes to the main organs of the UN. The deficient nature and organization of the UN 'family' of agencies and programmes, as a place for responding to disasters, is also evident through its ineffective mandates. In Bertrand's view, the UN has deteriorated to a nearly irrelevant actor of marginal importance in world politics. Nevertheless, the UN with its 'family' is still the only consistent intergovernmental network for disasters and global crises.

The diminished role of the United Nations is partially attributable to its financial crisis. States such as Australia, Singapore and Great Britain have left individual UN organizations such as UNESCO because they regarded their membership as 'a waste of money'.[5] The 'inefficient universalism'[6] of the UN is known to drain the resources of small states and encourage the wealthy ones to seek alternative solutions. The main cause for the UN's deficiency in funds is the disproportionate imbalance of financial burdens. Of the UN regular budget, the US provides 25 per cent. The US, Japan and Germany alone finance 53 per cent of the peacekeeping budget, of which the US contributes 32 per cent.[7]

There has also been no effective system of penalties for failure to pay assessed amounts on time. The loss of voting rights in the General Assembly has proved an insufficient threat. Lack of finances has also been attributed to the UN's insufficient commitment to issues and programmes, as well as the system's structure, which gives the greatest donor no more control than the smallest. Contributions from states are tiny in relation to GNP. The failure of wealthier states to donate such insignificant sums to the most important intergovernmental institution illustrates the sort of importance states attribute to the UN as an investment. The financial troubles of the UN derive from its lack of political influence, not money.

Further reasons for the UN's diminished funds are likely linked with the emergence of NGOs and INGOs, whose productivity and effectiveness have increasingly elicited greater support and interest from governments. Also, the UN's disregard of global actors such as multinational corporations and INGOs has made the system incomplete and often misinformed. Former UN General Secretary Boutros-Boutros Ghali believed that

> . . . new development models should specifically recognize the role of organizations of civil society in giving voice to the people. Grassroots people's movements should be strengthened and supported. They are the best chance to engage people fully in the betterment of their own lives . . . NGOs are a basic form of popular representation in the present day world. Their participation in international organizations is, in a way, a guarantee of the political legitimacy of those international organizations.[8]

The aloofness of the UN towards NGOs has been described as

> . . . the UN's most insuperable credibility gap . . . these corporations are creating multi-lateralism while we (UN) are still playing with what it might, in a properly ordered world, mean. There is a role for governments, but it is only by working with and through the market approach that we can discover the market imperfections which need to be addressed . . . the government-oriented bias of most UN activity is one reason why the driving

> impulses of the new multi-lateralism are coming from outside the global frameworks . . . the test for global organizations will be to make the most of them.[9]

Despite the numerous faults and inadequacies of the institutions and structure of the United Nations, some acknowledge the fact that the UN has suffered from excessively high expectations and a constantly expanding mandate, approved by member states without concern for its feasibility nor the political will to give the organization the necessary financial resources. Blanchard, director of the ILO, recognized the 'basic weakness of the UN' in its 'tendency to take on too many issues with too scant resources and to approach these issues as part of an ideological or political confrontation'.[10] There has been general agreement on the need to limit the number of issues to the most vital and also on the need for member governments to take the lead in reform, as the bureaucracy will not reform itself.

The Security Council

The areas of the UN which this paper focuses on as being most urgently in need of reform have elicited a variety of proposals. They have also been identified by Evan Luard as the four 'failed' hopes for the United Nations to surpass the League of Nations. The first hope was to establish an international armed force. The second was to grant the Security Council much greater authority. The third goal was to create an effective voting system, which would not paralyse the workings of the organization. The last unrealized hope was to secure universal membership.

The UN has no military force at its disposal; the veto and under-representation of the Security Council has prevented it from assuming a position of important global authority. The veto power has also been the principal cause for the system's paralysis. Finally, universal membership could not be completely secured as it fell under the jurisdiction of a veto-wielding Security Council. Perhaps the most reproached aspect of the Security Council, the power of the veto, was created for a specific purpose. This purpose, however, served the needs and circumstances of a particular time which, no one will deny, has since drastically changed. The veto power was initially considered a 'safety valve', which would serve to prevent dissension among its members and the possibility for war between the 'Great Powers'. Without the veto, the Organization risked being destroyed.

The present reality demonstrates the failure of the five 'Great Powers' to maintain world peace and security in the context of the global economy and common ecology. The emergence of Asian economies, the independence and importance of India, the request for UN membership of communist China, the re-admission of Germany, Japan and Italy to the society of nations, the rise of regional groups, have all altered the distribution of political and economic power and, thus, created new priorities for global cooperation. The Security Council has marginal relevance for development, trade and ecological problems, which have acquired overwhelming political importance. In the opinion of F. H. Hinsley,

> What we have done is to exchange a system which might or might not have worked for one which cannot work, and that instead of limiting the sovereignty of states we have actually extended the sovereignty of the Great Powers, the only states whose sovereignty is still a formidable reality in the modern world . . . the five permanent members of the Security Council in 1945 accounted for two-thirds of the population of the world. The end of the Cold War, reunification of Germany, the collapse of the Soviet Union, the emergence of economic powers like Japan, the demand by Third World countries for fairer representation in the Security Council, and the rise of ethnic conflict – all imply that the 1945 settlement, exemplified in the Security Council, must be rethought . . .[11]

The fact that the Security Council is not an accurate reflection of UN membership, nor even an accurate reflection of the current distribution of power between states, undermines the legitimacy of its decisions and contributes to its criticism. Some, such as Ramesh Thakur, have advocated the more equitable 'geographical representation', 'although the principle of equitable geographical representation has been brought into disrepute, it is essential to the philosophy of the organization and adds to its legitimacy'.[12] Any proposed change reflecting the political realities of the 21st century rather than of 1945 will enhance the legitimacy of the UN's decisions. Also, the fact that the five permanent members of the Security Council are all nuclear powers creates the perception that the possession of nuclear weapons confers power and status.

Despite the universal scope of its twin objectives of peace and security, the Security Council and its individual members have not always acted in the interests of the world community. During the cold war 'the super powers' combined weight on the veto was formidable . . . the Soviet Union and the US comprised an unholy alliance of formidable dimensions'.[13] The Council is nevertheless dependent on the political wills and preferences of the members, especially the permanent members, which continue to pursue particularistic national interests. Thus the independent responsibility of the Council is subordinated to power politics. This fact presents grave potential danger when one considers the actual implied powers of the Council. The Security Council alone was given the responsibility for the maintenance of international peace and security, with the associated executive, legislative and judicial powers. It enjoys the power to determine the nature of a dispute, to undertake territorial administrations, to establish a non-enforcement force, to authorize its use of force irrespective of the host state's intentions. And the scope of the implied power of the Council may continue to expand, as it submits to no superior authority.

Despite the vastness of its powers, the Security Council has nevertheless on numerous occasions proved itself incapable of taking decisive action or of resolving international conflicts. Its resolutions have been increasingly defied or ignored by states for which the UN presents no real threat. The Security Council has also proved powerless to generate sufficient support and influence to ensure that its decisions are respected, even when taken unanimously. Thus the process of 'peaceful settlement of disputes' prescribed in the Charter is often disregarded.

Richard Butler has publicized how the Security Council has been blatantly bypassed, defied and abused by the international community.[14] In its military actions against Milosevic, NATO bypassed the Council, as Russian and Chinese vetoes would have surely obstructed military intervention. Saddam Hussein defied the Security Council by disobeying UN disarmament resolutions, breaking all of Iraq's non-proliferation undertakings and lying to the UN. The fact that Russia was a strong supporter of Iraq inevitably led treaty violations to be judged by the Council on narrow, subjective political grounds. North Korea also continues nuclear weapons development in contravention of its obligations under the non-proliferation treaty. The Council has also been abused by China, who prevented peacekeeping operations in Guatemala and Macedonia for the mere reason that these countries had dealt with Taiwan. These incidents have profoundly questioned the Council's ability to function as a credible guardian of international peace and security. The Council's inadequate responses are related to the divisive and conflicting interests of its permanent members. China and Russia have often prevented the Council from acting with a single unified vision. During the cold war the Soviet Union misused the veto 60 times over a period of ten years, rejecting admission of new members and candidates for Secretary General. The US attitude to the veto is that it has been 'a blow to the prestige of the UN'. It has disrupted the work of the Security Council, blocked the admission of peace-loving nations and prevented peaceful settlement of disputes. 'It has embittered great power relations, confused and delayed the process of negotiation and has compelled members of the UN to seek out alternative methods of coping with problems.'[15] The Secretary General in 1986 made a special report of his disappointments with the Security Council, criticizing its 'unwillingness to take seriously collective security "measures" provided by the Charter, the impact of the unanimity rule, its inability to follow up resolutions and its acceptance of resolutions as substitute for action'.[16] The veto power was also blamed in reports prepared for the UN's 50th anniversary.

> Much of the disappointment about the UN performance on global security issues between 1945–1989 was mostly due to gridlock in the Security Council as a by-product of bi-polarity and East-West

> stand-off . . . And again in Bosnia, Rwanda and Somalia the UN was seen as unable to restore normal conditions . . .[17]

Since the creation of the UN, over one hundred major conflicts have left over 20 million dead.[18] The UN was powerless to deal with many of these crises owing to the vetoes cast in the Council, amounting to 279.[19] Richard Gott has also affirmed that 'of all the organs of the UN none has shown greater discrepancy between promise and performance than the Security Council'.[20]

The reality is that despite successive disappointments in the role of the United Nations, particularly the Security Council, it remains the only possible arbiter for international disputes and a forum for global consultation. The potential benefit and contributions an inspired intergovernmental institution could provide to the development and advancement of mankind are too important and necessary to remain complacent with the present structures, which prevent the realization of the UN's initial purposes and actual responsibilities.

Reform Proposals for the Security Council

The spectrum of proposed reforms for the organs of the UN is wide-ranging in terms of practicability and their intended time frame for implementation. I will elaborate on the most influential and pertinent reforms for the present and examine arguments both in favour and against.

Perhaps the most frequent proposals concern the size and composition of the Security Council, deriving from the need to give its decisions more broad-based support and legitimacy. It is argued that although a larger Council might be less efficient, its increased authority and legitimacy would make it more effective. The review of the Open-ended Working Group on Equitable Representation concluded that in view of the substantial increase in UN membership, especially of developing countries, the Security Council should be expanded. Its working methods are also in need of review in order to strengthen its capacity to improve its effectiveness and overall legitimacy.[21] Among the alternatives for membership are: a rotating membership, entailing periodically rotating seats shared by two members; extended membership, where seats could be held for consecutive terms without re-election; flexible membership, which would re-determine every ten years new permanent members. The creation of a second group of non-permanent members without the veto power would expand the Council to a 'two-tier structure'.[22]

The addition of Japan and Germany to the Council has been frequently debated, as the most likely future members. However, the inclusion of Germany would contradict the principle of equitable geographical representation, which is fundamental to the United Nations. The addition of two- to three-year seats to the Council for 'middle-range' powers has been proposed in the interest of a more accurate representation of the actual political reality. Criteria for categorizing countries would depend on financial contributions, population and provision of troops and funds for peacekeeping. The redistribution of the existing permanent seats has also been suggested but without realistic expectations, since the current permanent members would have to consent to any structural reform for its implementation. Selection of permanent and non-permanent members on a regional basis has been advocated for more equal representation of the south with that of the north. Some working groups have suggested the creation of an 'inner cabinet' in addition to the Security Council, which would include representatives of Confucian and Islamic cultures and help in drafting resolutions.[23] Bertrand has proposed the creation of an Economic Security Council, with permanent seats for states or regions of major economic importance. Such an organ would function as a ministerial body, rather than as part of the UN's diplomatic organization, and would include Germany and Japan. An Economic Security Council would serve as a world economic forum and would be largely free from political issues, thus able to focus on development.

Underlying the many and diverse proposals for executive reform are urgent and profound concerns shared by the major critics and governments involved. It is strongly felt that only through structural reform will the Security Council be enabled to respond effectively to new global challenges such as economic development, population growth and environmental issues. Transparency of the Council must also be improved upon for other member states, regional organizations and NGOs to influence UN deliberations and replace the restricted Council bargaining and private decision-making. Finally, the most deeply felt argument for Security Council reform is the need for a more just representation of states. UN democracy will remain unachieved as the majority of the world's countries remain excluded from Security Council decision-making. Some of the most intractable problems in the world today, such as poverty, lack of education, a feeling of disaffection reflecting a lack of empowerment, are too often crudely perceived through the largely western perspective of the Council as 'ethnic warfare' or 'tribal hostility'. Hence the failures of many UN peacekeeping operations.

Security Council Right of Veto

Regarding the power of the veto, often described as the greatest weakness of the Security Council, several critics have advocated its abolishment. Most, however, have considered abolition or modification of the veto power politically impractical and even imprudent. Granting the veto to new permanent members such as Germany or Japan would not be widely supported, as it would contribute further to the north/south imbalance. A political declaration calling on the permanent members to narrow the range of issues to which the veto applies has been considered one plausible way of restricting its use. The reinforcement of the distinction between substantive and procedural issues, where vetoes of only the former are permitted, would also restrict its use and abuse. A longer term reform suggests the eventual transfer of peacekeeping functions to the General Assembly. 'Uniting for Peace Resolution' was a suggestion that UN members be able to take collective action against aggression if the General Assembly approved it by a two-thirds vote, regardless of a Security Council veto.[24] Other suggestions include the non-application of the veto to the election of the Secretary-General or to the admission of new UN member states. Requiring the negative votes of more than one veto power to block an action or granting a 'regional veto' by which negative votes from all members from a particular region would constitute a veto have also been suggested as alternatives. A system of weighted voting, as used in the IMF and World Bank, could be a possible, though more complex option.

Less optimistically, several experts insist that the removal of the veto is not a realistic proposal. The veto protects the self-interests of the permanent members; therefore, it would not be in their individual or collective interests to renounce it. Removal of the veto would require an amendment to the Charter – which requires the support of all permanent members. The power of the veto does offer some advantages: it guarantees some measure of control over the number of operations the UN engages in; the possession of the veto by a small number of powerful states also redresses the imbalance that these states face in the General Assembly, as a result of the strict equality in the distribution of votes, which bears no relation to effective power. Removal of the veto might also lead to a loss of interest in the UN from permanent members.

Regardless of the possible benefits or disadvantages of the veto, history shows that it has been abused by the permanent members in defence of self-interest or for ideological reasons. The abuse of veto power has often exposed the political confrontations between member states more concerned with securing their own national victories than with securing international peace. The urgency of the need to reform the veto has emerged in the efforts of individual member states to create systems of collective defence free from the crippling effects of the veto. Some have criticized these pacts of states as 'designed to by-pass the UN'[25] but they are actually designed to circumvent the frustrating situation in the UN as a result of the veto impasse. Further evidence of an unproductive Security Council is the recognized fact that the General Assembly has displaced the Council as a forum for managing international political issues.

The most thoughtful, compelling and possibly most radical proposals for reform of the Security Council have been elaborated by Clark and Sohn in the 'Clark-Sohn plan'.[26] Clark and Sohn envision the eventual replacement of the Security Council by an Executive Council consisting of 17 representatives elected by the General Assembly. They advocate limited use of the veto to only specific areas, leaving issues such as arms' regulations, enforcement action and UN membership free from the threat of the veto. The veto power of the current permanent members would be replaced by a 12/17 majority vote. The Council would constitute an 'executive arm', subordinate to the Assembly.

In a report of the President of the US to the San Francisco Conference founding the UN, it was declared that 'the cornerstone of world security is the unity of those nations which formed the core of the grand alliance against the Axis'.[27] Presently, the veto power has served to undermine any unity among the members of the Council. The resulting stagnation has prevented important and often urgent consensual decisions, essential to the preservation of the originally envisioned 'world security'.

The Bahá'í International Community, as early as 1955, advocated the gradual elimination of the concept of 'permanent membership' for Security Council members and questioned the sustainability of the 'veto power'. These features went some way towards undermining the credibility of the Security Council at a time when the UN was acquiring an increasingly global character. A redefinition of the concept of collective security, based on a more democratic and representative Security Council, could become an important factor for uniting the member states.

A majority of the non-permanent member states vest modest hopes in any significant transformation of the Security Council. Delegates at the 1994 Pontignamo Conference on Aspects of UN Reform agreed on the improbability of the permanent Five to consent to weakening their own positions.[28]

Pre-conditions for Reform and Recommendations

In light of the radical nature of structural reforms, several preconditions have been recommended for their successful realization: the need to build up general popular support for the UN, the need to lower expectations of the UN and thus the demand for UN intervention. More specific conditions include the definition of the task before discussing the means, the production of clear mandates, the provision of adequate resources to fulfil them and the creation of a peacekeeping fund. The Council should aim to promote substantive negotiations and not merely pass resolutions. The Security Council needs to be publicly recognized by governments and draw world attention. One way of achieving greater influence and respect among governments would be to invite foreign and prime ministers to Council meetings. The Council also needs to develop a policy of consistent principles and recognized rules of international behaviour and judgements on issues such as intervention and secession. Conditions more directly related to the reform process assert that any structural changes will have to be incremental to avoid opposition. The current permanent members will have to perceive any changes as conducive to the continuing effectiveness of the UN. The permanent members will have to believe that all changes will be for the overall advantage.

Non-aligned countries will need to see the new collective security arrangements as a means of reducing dominance of the west on the Security Council. The non-aligned will also have to be satisfied that a reformed Security Council will meet their security needs as or more effectively than the present Security Council. Above all, however, the successful activity of the Security Council depends on two major conditions: the harmony between the Council and the Secretary General and the willingness of members to serve the Council's original purpose of preserving world peace, rather than pursuing their national interests.

Among other recommendations for improved decision-making of the Security Council have been two formal proposals and two suggestions that the Council request advisory opinions of the International Court of Justice. The Council has neither adopted nor followed them. Concerning decisions on the question of competence, the Council has preferred implicit to explicit decisions, dealing with questions of competence by itself, without using the Court as an adviser.[29] Article 99 of the Charter grants the Secretary General the right to bring to the attention of the Security Council situations threatening peace and security. Consultation of the Council with the other organs of the UN would increase UN democracy and further legitimize the Council's decision-making power.

Measures which would promote wider participation, more transparent decision-making and improve the availability of information include the following: *regional briefings*, to improve relations and information flow between the Security Council and the General Assembly. Regular and institutionalized briefing sessions for regional groups would ensure that issues or conflicts are treated as they arise and not when the Council chooses, i.e. Rwanda. The closed nature of the Security Council's decision-making process prevents any substantial influence of the General Assembly on the Council. Some member states such as Colombia have proposed measures for controlling the constitutionality of Security Council decisions. The need for a coherent system for the verification of legality emerges in light of the experience that UN organs have often proved contradictory.[30] *Consultation with specially affected countries* would allow countries which are affected by measures under consideration in the Security Council to participate in informal consultations and raise their concerns. *In-camera hearings* should be open to any state wishing to express its views on important matters before the Council in a non-public setting.

The prevailing view concerning Security Council reform, however, is that any new arrangements should be regarded as necessarily transitional. Thus a reform package would have to include an agreed time frame for future review.

Proposals for Reform of the General Assembly

Among the most frequently expressed criticisms of the United Nations structure is the restricted authority of the General Assembly. Article 12 of the Charter forbids the Assembly from making any recommendation on any situation or subject with which the Security Council is already dealing in accordance with its own functions. Similarly it cannot make decisions binding on members of the United Nations. The Assembly's influence is limited to the power of appointment and is constantly challenged by the Security Council. Political influence of the General Assembly on the Council is almost non-existent.

> The limited powers and influence of the General Assembly has rendered the UN . . . a quasi-dependent international actor, reflecting changes elsewhere in the international system, rather than initiating changes by its existence and undertakings . . . The UN has even defeated Charter expectations and made it impossible for the UN to carry out its intended role . . . although the Charter was never intended to transform the structure of international society, it did embody a commitment to create a flexible instrument of collective action that would be readapted to the dominant trends of international life.[31]

The structure of the UN has thus enabled member states to use it as an instrument of confrontation and political rivalry.

The UN's deficient powers with respect to the world community of states undermines its claims to international authority. It has been generally acknowledged that greater authority of the United Nations is impeded by the following: sovereign equality in the General Assembly, permanent membership of 'antiquated World War II Powers' in the Council and the failure to confer UN status to regional/trans-national actors.[32] The persistence of the present structure of the United Nations will assure that its role continues to be marginal, maintaining the pre-eminence of principal sovereign states and traditional modes of diplomatic interaction. The British ambassador to the UN has even gone as far as to say that

> . . . the whole organization has become obsessed by political and economic problems, where the West finds itself in a small and embattled minority, the question of apartheid in South Africa, the Arab/Israeli conflict and the North/South 'dialogue' being among the most vivid examples . . . small wonder that the US has become impatient with an organization that complicates rather than ameliorates disputes, contains a parliamentary majority bent on pillorying it and, expects the US to pay up to twenty five percent of the cost of a system in which the largest donor can exercise no more control than the smallest.[33]

Contentious and divisive issues will remain a constant in international politics but they need not be aggravated by inadequate and unjust structures.

Voting and Representation

The absence in the General Assembly of an effective voting structure founded on universal consensus prevents it from enjoying effective control and influence. A voting system of representation based on one vote for each member state is inequitable as it fails to recognize the importance of states' relative populations and economic influence. This is especially relevant as the number of newly independent small states has risen and could collectively represent a majority. The requirement of unanimity for resolutions often prevents the discussion of many important issues which fail to be raised for lack of unanimous support. Several proposals for various methods of determining the 'legal weight' of individual states have been expressed, taking into consideration population, geographical representation and financial contributions to the UN. The present situation potentially allows for the control of the Assembly by several small states. Such outcomes, owing to the Assembly's voting system, created much cynicism among member states. The original intention of some leaders for the UN was to allow universal membership of the world's countries. 'We hope that eventually every nation on earth will be a fully qualified and loyal member of this organization.'[34]

The Future of the General Assembly

Proposals for the long-term future of the General Assembly have alluded to its potential as a global parliament. Variations include the creation of an assembly of parliamentarians in addition to an assembly of government representatives. The United World Federalists have suggested a bicameral Assembly, where one camera would have representation in relation to population. Making the General Assembly a legislature with direct election has also been proposed as a means to increasing its responsibility and accountability. Some critics have envisioned the eventual role of the Assembly as supranational with increased governing powers. These would be legitimized by greater openness to external consultants for self-evaluation, such as an 'NGO council', incorporating information and opinions of organizations of civil society, and substantially enhanced relations with the Security Council. A more dramatic structural reorganization of the General Assembly includes the creation of three separate chambers: the Prince chamber, consisting of government representatives; the Merchant chamber, including multinational, transnational and local economic actors, the IMF and the World Bank; and the Citizen chamber, comprising an equal representation of men and women. Marc Nerfin bravely advocated that the 'first responsibility is to invent and explore new institutional paths to make the UN the instrument we need . . . the UN is a project which as the only embryo of a planetary organization belongs to all of us members of the human species.'[35]

The Management Crisis

The enormous difficulties coordinating UN activities and what some have called its 'management crisis' have incited a profusion of proposals for improving upon the internal organization of the United Nations. Sir Robert Jackson refers to the UN as

> . . . probably the most complex organization in the world . . . The evidence suggests that governments do not, and also that the machine is incapable of intelligently controlling itself . . . it is so organized that managerial direction is impossible . . . the machine as a whole has become unmanageable in the strictest sense of the word. As a result, it is becoming slower and more unwieldy, like some prehistoric monster . . . most of the periodic drives for reform have been ad hoc responses to crises (generally financial), aimed at bringing UN agencies/bodies under some sort of political control . . . Pleas for readable, relevant documents, flexible forward-planning, monitoring of programmes, transparent budgeting and greater accountability reflect the frustrations of states dealing with the ungovernable and incomprehensible.[36]

Although analysts and experts such as Jackson and Bertrand have formulated compelling and innovative proposals for structural reform, the general tendency has been to modify reforms to fit institutional moulds. The fear of radical reforms and their potentially destabilizing effects has thus prevented any substantial changes and improvements of the organization of the UN. Time and experience have shown, however, that minor repairs and modifications cannot prevent the deterioration of a system and the more hopeless the state of a structure, the more daunting it will be to embark upon its reform.

Presently the United Nations comprises three different, complex aggregates of intergovernmental organizations: the Economic and Social Council, the General Assembly and a Trade and Development board, each with its own group of subsidiary bodies. The resulting conditions of such organizations are of extreme fragmentation of effort and resources and lack of coordination and definition of priorities. The distribution of objectives among independent bodies causes the repetition of general debates and creates an overall 'state of confusion'.[37]

The extreme decentralized organization of the United Nations has elicited appeals for the reconvergence of all UN agencies and structures (i.e. UNDP, WFP, UNICEF and UNESCO). Bertrand has suggested the creation of an interdisciplinary central secretariat including economic, sociological, technological and other specialists to replace the various dispersed sectoral secretariats. Consolidation of the various secretariats would greatly contribute to more effective coordination. Closer relations and consultation between the levels from resident representatives, programmes and regional offices to UN headquarters would also help establish concrete and consistent policies and methods. Structural reform would radically modify the prevailing polycentric autonomy of the UN, the main cause of misuse of finances. There is overall consensus on the benefits of the consolidation of offices, departments and programmes for improved UN performance and efficiency.

Development for Peace

All agencies and programmes of the UN should be united by a common vision/priority for 'regional development'. Among Bertrand's more far-reaching proposals is the need to replace the UN's traditional 'peacekeeping' objectives with joint ventures in regional/economic development as a means for peace. Common endeavours, involving efforts of those providing as well as receiving aid, are much more likely to have beneficial and lasting results without the stigma of charity. A focus on development has also been advocated by former Secretary General Boutros-Boutros Ghali in his report *Agenda for Development*:

> While peace provides the most secure context for lasting development, it is recognized that the root causes of political conflicts are economic and social . . . living standards and conditions are all factors to be taken into account in the quest for true peace and security . . . only sustained efforts to resolve underlying socio-economic, cultural and humanitarian problems can place an achieved peace on a durable foundation . . .[38]

Interdependence, globalization and democratization have generated new global needs which surpass traditional notions of security to a more human/individual conception of security, requiring conditions of stability and democracy for realizing sustainable development.

The principles and values upheld in the Charter and the Universal Declaration of Human Rights have prompted groups such as the Bahá'í International Community to advocate the raising of minimum requirements for membership. Respect and commitment to basic human rights, such as freedom of expression and democratic elections should be preconditions for states intending to join. Similarly there should be consequences for member states that violate these standards.

Innovative Suggested Reforms of the UN

In an innovative spirit, many suggestions for new kinds of institutions have emerged. A 'World Commission'[39] would help establish new policies and items for open negotiation through an integrated approach to world problems. An 'Inspection Commission'[40] would be created for the protection of nations and individuals against possible human rights abuses. Bertrand has recommended the creation of a high-level commission or council to identify world problems, functioning as an 'early warning centre'. Such a commission would provide the intellectual leadership presently lacking in the UN.[41] The proposal for a 'Second Assembly', composed of representatives from INGOs, indicates the need to incorporate their valuable expertise and influence. A 'World Development Authority' would ensure funds for development projects in the form of grants in aid and interest free loans. A 'World Equity Tribunal'[42] would also help the enforcement of international law and serve as an organ of mediation and conciliation.

The eventual evolution of the IMF to a Global Central Bank would enable it to better manage the global economy, its capital markets and eventually serve as a lender of last resort for the world. Requests for the World Bank and IMF to decentralize their operations, expand representation of Third World countries and base their cooperation on a more equitable partnership are founded on the need to reduce the world's economic and social inequalities. As is the case now, the IMF and World Bank are independent institutions from the UN, largely run by the industrialized west, which has at times prevented them from successfully managing the debt crisis and other Third World economic problems.[43] Economic instability, fluctuating exchange rates and the liberalization of capital markets have necessitated greater measures for protection from the uncertain effects of economic interdependence. A global system of taxation has also been suggested, if only in general terms, as a means for reducing the great economic disparities of the world. Such a system would ameliorate the negative effects of capital flight and provide a pool of resources for global use. Its goal would be to achieve a system of automatic collection of revenue, possibly through a progressive international income tax.[44] Potentially taxable items include international trade, military expenditures, exports of arms, natural resource exploitation, etc. Such a system of universal and automatic contribution would also help establish a greater sense of global responsibility towards development, ecology and the global commons.

UN Finances

Universal taxation could also be a source of revenue for the United Nations, which still lacks any sort of economic independence. Several strategies for UN funding have been devised and considered as a consequence of the critical state of its finances. Explanations for the financial crisis of the UN invariably relate to its lack of political influence, which has been partially attributed to a lack of confidence in the UN, as a result of the inadequate voting system of the General Assembly. Some experts have suggested that payment assessments be reconsidered and based on gross national income rather than per capita income. The introduction of penalties for countries failing to pay for political reasons and incentives for early payment would help regularize income. The UN should also not disregard voluntary financial contributions and mechanisms for their encouragement, such as increased engagement with the press and the public. A powerful budgetary committee would help impose discipline and coherence on spending demands and expenditures. Such an organ could fulfil a very important role, given that major contributing states have withdrawn donations as a result of perceived weaknesses on the part of the UN to keep costs under control and, more generally, manage financial resources efficiently. One suggestion of the Bahá'í International Community for a more cost-efficient UN has been to implement the use of a single common language. The adoption of one universal auxiliary language and common script, such as English, instead of the current six official UN languages would significantly reduce costs, simplify bureaucratic procedures and ultimately create a greater spirit of unity. More generally, the Bahá'ís have been supportive of proposals to give the UN a degree of financial independence as a way of giving it a larger measure of political independence and accountability.

UN Military Forces

The creation of an international police force has often been referred to as the only means to ensure genuine world peace. Such a force, comprised of soldiers from the entire world, would support the peacekeeping operations of the UN and add credibility to resolutions of the Security Council. The command and control of such a force would reside with the Secretary-General under the authority of the Security Council. Immediate steps towards the establishment of a fully armed force would entail the institutionalization of present *ad hoc* military arrangements. Brian Urquhart has also advocated an efficient 'rapid response force', equipped by member states and instantly available for preventing genocidal horrors, as in Rwanda.

> The UN has been marginalized in combat since 1945, it will continue to be so, unless its members can agree on some basis for effective international control of the wars that ravage the poorest countries.[45]

The creation of an international force, as propagated by the Bahá'í International Community, would also serve as a vital step towards global disarmament and the ultimate ban on all weapons of mass destruction. Indeed, the Bahá'í teachings speak about the need to 'make Force the servant of Justice',[46] suggesting the existence of a hierarchy of ethical principles, with justice occupying centre stage. The original idea of the Charter was

> . . . that the collective security system of the UN would provide the sense of security and mutual confidence which would allow disarmament and arms control to proceed under the auspices of the Security Council . . . However the UN has yet to create a new world order where every state derives its security from the collective strength of the whole . . . the UN reflects the fears, disorders and rivalries of the world.[47]

Clark and Sohn envisaged universal and complete disarmament as a fundamental premise for world peace. According to them, disarmament could be achieved through a 12-year plan of equal percentage reductions, leaving a world police force as the principal military power, under UN authority. Clark and Sohn, in *World Peace through World Law*, emphasize the importance of the universal adoption of measures for peace and their statement in constitutional and statutory form. Consequently they have proposed revision of the UN Charter, to precede and give legal authority to the adoption of universal and complete disarmament. Bertrand has likewise supported 'constitutional reform' as the only means to reinstate the organization in its legitimate role.[48]

The Charter

Structural reform often implies revision of the United Nations Charter, as several proposed changes could only become effective through its formal amendment. A change in the permanent membership of the Security Council or a grant of increased authority to the General Assembly would require formal amendment to the Charter. The Charter should thus be regarded as a flexible instrument, adaptable to changing needs and circumstances. The potential complications and difficulties involving Charter revision, such as the 'Pandora's box effect', have inclined many to place it in the medium/long-term perspective. However, the requirement of a two-thirds majority of the Assembly and the power of permanent members to veto constitutional changes have stifled most hopes for Charter reform. Attempts to expand the power of the General Assembly, the International Court or the Secretary-General have often been described as 'anti-constitutional' or 'anti-Charter', as the Charter has assigned the maintenance of 'international peace and security' to the Security Council only. Despite the apparent rigidity of the Charter, the Open-ended Working Group on UN Reform in 1995 concluded that prospects for reform are excellent: 'The Permanent Five are in agreement on a range of issues for the first time, the North-South conflict has subsided and many structures have shown themselves to be increasingly flexible and adaptable for new purposes.'[49]

New Objectives

The 21st century will continue to witness the emergence of globally defined problems and issues with a strong international or global component. The recent interventions and peacekeeping operations of the UN in Africa and Central Europe were sufficient to prove the tremendous deficiencies of an organization, at best capable of partially fulfilling purposes defined 50 years before. The prevailing opinion among UN critics and officials is for the need to redefine the objectives of the United Nations in light of the demands and constraints of the emerging world order. The concept of security has also required a new definition, as Great Power conflict no longer represents a threat to world peace. The current priorities for the maintenance of a stable international society extend over a very wide range from population growth, energy depletion, immigration, refugees and extreme poverty.

David Steele has identified three problem areas whose successful management would only be possible through a collective, institutional approach. The global economy is in increasingly greater need of management and safety nets. The UN with its various bodies, i.e. World Bank, IMF, UNCTAD and the WTO offer the best hope for better managing the global economy and addressing global inequalities. The situation of Third World debt is as much a political as an economic problem but its resolution has been largely left to the World Bank and the IMF, whose particular interests and narrow focus have prevented a more successful management of the debt crisis. Rural/regional development has been advocated by Bertrand as the new common vision and objective for the UN. Collective efforts from western industrialized powers and developing countries would also strengthen the sense of unity between the two groups and encourage multilateral negotiations. Organs of the UN such as UNITAR (UN Institute of Training and Research) are potential centres for the research and resolution of socio-economic problems. Finally, and perhaps most urgently, is the problem of disarmament, for which the UN is the most likely and appropriate forum. The United Nations, through its extended family of agencies and programmes, could provide regional support and supervision for the process of disarmament and arms limitation. Regional approaches have been strongly supported over global ones as the 'incentives for regional arms are largely the by-products of regional factors . . . [And as they] reflect better the specific conditions and characteristics of the regions concerned than arrangements derived through global approaches.'[50]

Consequently the question rises whether the United Nations is properly equipped to meet these new challenges. And it has nevertheless become apparent that the UN's and Security Council's existing rules and procedures are unsuitable for the resolution of ecological and demographic problems. Several thinkers have been quick to identify the obsolescence and inadequacy of the Westphalia system, based on national sovereignty.[51] Westphalian institutions, based on sovereign equality, where states cooperate and act primarily out of self-interest, can no longer realistically respond to common global problems. 'If the UN and its regional organizations fail to rise to the tasks ahead, they are in danger of becoming irrelevant . . . and there are dangerous signs to this effect.'[52]

> As far as disarmament, peace and security, monetary policy and international trade are concerned – to mention only a few of many fields involved – major moves have been, and continue to be, initiated outside the framework of the UN. There would appear to be a gap of some sort between felt needs and the system's ability to meet them; an indication, no doubt, that the international agencies are lagging behind the pace of change in the world.[53]

Prospects for Reform

Despite the volume of comprehensive and far-reaching proposals for structural reforms for the United Nations, some, including Bertrand, have acknowledged that these have 'no chance at all of being implemented now' and could be considered only in a context of a break with the past. 'Improving the system is impossible, there are too many interests involved . . . trying a halfway-house would produce the worst of all worlds.'[54] Other opinions suggest waiting for clearer results of the present economic and social changes under way before defining the structure of new universal organizations. The general consensus, however, is that it will be inevitably difficult to reform an organization so long as its leading members insist on defying it when national interests are at stake. As long as states fail to accept the sacrifice of sovereignty, the United Nations will continue to be powerless. Although some critics have argued that a reformed, impartial and just UN is an idealistic hope owing to the realist nature of states, they must realize that certain conditions must first be established to make the transition possible and long-term reform attainable.

A few more general requirements include starting a programme of thorough research on reform and for the expansion of UN problem-solving capabilities and technical expertise and the adoption of multilateral negotiations and measures for rebuilding confidence among members, especially between north and south. The implementation of reforms must be such that superpowers perceive them as supportive of their own interests and not as threats to their status. Such a view can only thrive once all member states realize that each one's survival is directly related to the fulfilment of universal interests. National interests can no longer be defined independently of the international system. Any reform is destined to fail unless it is supported by a profound commitment of all member states and it recognizes the changing nature and needs of our progressive international system.

It is difficult to imagine the survival of the UN without a revolutionary change of the *status quo*. The UN remains the greatest potential forum for governments to cooperate, raise concerns, request aid and collectively seek solutions to global problems.

The very nature of the tasks which lie before the United Nations suggests the need for maximizing internal order and organization. However, an inherent danger in large-scale organization is that its natural tendency for order prevails at the expense of creative freedom. Order and freedom are both essential elements for large organizations: the freedom of small, autonomous and practical units with the order and clarity of global principles and the recognition of the unity of mankind. A system which is able to provide practical help to the individual level is essential for the present crusade against misery and human degradation. Trust and loyalty can only grow from the smaller units to the larger units and the UN has yet to earn these from the vast majorities of the peoples of the world. According to Schumacher's philosophy, 'the present structure of large-scale enterprise in spite of heavy taxation and endless proliferation of legislation is not conducive to the public welfare'.[55]

Propitiously, the United Nations under Kofi Annan has been instilled with a spirit of reform. In many ways, the UN has made progress towards more practical methods and increased freedom. Besides internal structural changes and a new results-based budgeting system, the UN has increased its contact and relations with civil society via 'The Global Compact', a principles-based framework for engaging the private sector with the United Nations. The Security Council has succeeded in attaining more openness and transparency by holding an open session on the subject of the International Criminal Court and increasing its consultation with non-members. The Monterrey Conference on Financing and Development was a significant development towards a more global and united approach, as it brought together international financial institutions with representatives from diverse parts of civil society.

The overall result of recent, modest but significant reforms and developments has been to increase the 'unity of purpose' of the United Nations, as well as highlight the essential commitment and will of member states and support of international society. The United Nations is the most promising hope for the achievement of world peace, human progress and universal prosperity but it depends on the will of our leaders, representatives and people of the world.

Bibliography

Annan, Kofi. *Renewing the UN: A Program for Reform.* New York: UN Department of Public Information, 1997.

Bahá'í International Community. *Turning Point for All Nations, A Statement of the Bahá'í International Community on the Occasion of the 50th Anniversary of the United Nations.* New York: Bahá'í International Community United Nations Office, 1995.

Bedjaoui, Mohammed. *The New World Order and the Security Council.* The Hague: Kluwer Academic Publishers, 1994.

Beigbeder, Yves. *The Internal Management of United Nations Organizations: The Long Quest for Reform.* New York: St Martin's Press, 1996.

— *Management Problems in UN Organizations: Reform or Decline?* London: Frances Pinter, 1987.

Bertrand, Maurice. 'Some Reflections on Reform of the UN'. Joint Inspection Unit, UN, Geneva 1985.

Bourantonis, D. and M. Evriviades. *The United Nations of the Twenty-First Century: Peace, Security and Development.* The Hague: Kluwer Law International, 1996.

Butler, Richard. 'Reforming the U.N.', *Foreign Affairs,* vol. 78, no. 5, September/October 1999.

Childers, Erskine. *Challenges to the United Nations: Building a Safer World.* New York: St Martin's Press, 1995.

Commission on Global Governance. *Our Global Neighbourhood.* New York: Oxford University Press, 1995.

Ferenz, Benjamin. *New Legal Foundations for Global Survival: Security through the Security Council.* New York: Oceana Publications, 1994.

Ghali, Boutros-Boutros. *Agenda for Development.* New York: UN Department of Public Information, 1995.

— *An Agenda for Peace: Peace-making and Peace-keeping.* Report of the Secretary-General Pursuant to the Statement Adopted by the Summit Meeting of the Security Council, 31 January 1992. New York: United Nations.

Gordenker, Leon. *The United Nations in International Politics.* Princeton, NJ: Princeton University Press, 1971.

Hinsley, F. H. *Power and the Pursuit of Peace: Theory and Practice in the History of Relations between States.* Cambridge: University Press, 1963.

Hiscocks, R. *The Security Council: A Study in Adolescence*. New York: Free Press, 1973.

Jackson, Sir Robert. *A Study of the Capacity of the UN Development System*. Geneva: United Nations, UNDP/5, 1969.

Jacobson, Harold K. *Networks of Interdependence: International Organizations and the Global Political System*, New York: Knopf, 1984.

Kahng, T. J. *Law, Politics, and the Security Council*. The Hague: Martinus Nijhoff, 1964.

Kaufmann, Johan. *United Nations Decision-Making*. Alphen aan den Rijn: Sijthoff and Noordhoff, 1980.

Lister, Fred. *Decision-making Strategies for International Organizations: The IMF Model*. Denver, CO: University of Denver, 1984.

Luard, Evan. *The UN: How it Works and What it Does*. Basingstoke: Macmillan Press, 1994.

Renniger, John P. *The Future Role of the United Nations in an Interdependent World*. The Hague: Martinus Nijhoff, 1989.

Righter, Rosemary. *Utopia Lost: The United Nations and World Order*. United States: Twentieth Century Fund Inc., 1995.

Roberts, A. and B. Kingsbury. *United Nations, Divided World*. New York: Oxford University Press, 1988.

Schumacher, E.F. *Small is Beautiful: Economics as if People Mattered*. London: Vintage Press, 1993.

Shoghi Effendi. *The World Order of Bahá'u'lláh*. Wilmette, IL: Bahá'í Publishing Trust, 1991.

Sohn, Louis B. and Grenville Clark. *World Peace through World Law*. Cambridge, MA: Harvard University Press, 1966.

Stassen, Harold. *UN: A Working Paper for Restructuring*. Minneapolis: Lerner Publications, 1994.

Steele, David. *The Reform of the United Nations*. Kent: Croom Helm Ltd., 1987.

Strange, Susan. 'The Westfailure System'. *Review of International Studies*, vol. 25, 1999.

Streeten, Paul. *Global Governance for Human Development*. New York: Human Development Report Office, 1992.

Thakur, Ramesh. 'Reforming the UN: An Encouraging Start Under Annan', in *International Herald Tribune*, Friday, 19 July 2002.

UNDP. *Human Development Report: Global Governance for the Twenty-first Century*. New York: UN Department of Public Information, 1994.

Urquhart, Brian. *For a UN Volunteer Military Force.* New York: *New York Review of Books*, 10 June 1994.

Williams, Douglas. *The Specialized Agencies and the UN: The System in Crisis.* London: Hurst in association with the David Davies Memorial Institute of International Studies, 1987.

The World Commission on Environment and Development. *Our Common Future.* Oxford: Oxford University Press, 1987.

Notes

1. Childers, *Challenges to the United Nations.*
2. Quoted in ibid.
3. Bertrand, 'Some Reflections on Reform of the UN'.
4. Steele, *The Reform of the United Nations.*
5. Righter, *Utopia Lost.*
6. ibid.
7. Taylor, Daws and Adamczick-Gerteis, *Documents of United Nations Reform.*
8. Quoted in Childers, *Challenges to the United Nations.*
9. Righter, *Utopia Lost.*
10. Quoted in Childers, *Challenges to the United Nations.*
11. Hinsley, *Power and the Pursuit of Peace.*
12. Beigbeder, *Internal Management of the United Nations Organizations.*
13. Renniger, *Future Role of the United Nations in an Interdependent World.*
14. Butler, 'Reforming the U.N.' *Foreign Affairs*, vol. 78, no. 5, Sept./Oct. 1999.
15. Erskine, *Challenges to the U.N.*
16. Bourantonis and Evriviade, *United Nations of the Twenty-First Century.*
17. ibid.
18. ibid.
19. Ghali, *Agenda for Peace.*
20. Quoted in Beigbeder, *Internal Management of the United Nations Organizations.*
21. ibid.

22. ibid.
23. Taylor, Daws and Adamczick-Gerteis, 'Review of the Open-ended Working Group on Equitable Representation' in *Documents on Reform of the United Nations*.
24. Childers, *Challenges to the United Nations*.
25. ibid.
26. Sohn and Clark, *World Peace through World Law*.
27. ibid.
28. ibid.
29. Kahng, *Law, Politics, and the Security Council*.
30. Bedjaoui, *New World Order and the Security Council*.
31. Gordenker, *United Nations in International Politics*.
32. ibid.
33. Renniger, *Future Role of the United Nations in an Interdependent World*.
34. Harry S. Truman, quoted in Childers, *Challenges to the United Nations*.
35. Quoted in Beigbeder, *Management Problems in UN Organizations*.
36. Jackson, *Study of the Capacity of the UN Development System*.
37. Bertrand, 'Some Reflections on Reform of the UN'.
38. Ghali, *Agenda for Development*.
39. Renniger, *Future Role of the United Nations in an Interdependent World*.
40. Sohn and Clark, *World Peace through World Law*.
41. Renniger, *Future Role of the United Nations in an Interdependent World*.
42. ibid.
43. For a thorough discussion of these issues see Stiglitz, *Globalization and its Discontents*.
44. Streeten, *Global Governance for Human Development*.
45. Urquhart, *For a UN Volunteer Military Force*.
46. Shoghi Effendi, *World Order*, p. 204.
47. Roberts and Kingsbury, *United Nations, Divided World*.
48. ibid.
49. Quoted in Taylor, Daws and Adamczick-Gerteis, *Review of the Open-ended Working Group on Equitable Representation*.
50. Bourantonis and Evriviades, *United Nations of the Twenty-First Century, Peace, Security and Development*.
51. Strange, 'The Westfailure System', *Review of International Studies*, vol. 25, 1999.

52. Bourantonis and Evriviades, *United Nations of the Twenty-First Century, Peace, Security and Development.*
53. From an address of the Director-General of ILO, in Renniger, *Future Role of the United Nations in an Interdependent World.*
54. Righter, *Utopia Lost.*
55. Schumacher, *Small is Beautiful.*

7

Bahá'u'lláh's Concept of Collective Security in Historical and Theoretical Perspective[1]

Ariane Sabet

As long ago as 1956 political scientist Inis Claude stated that the concept of collective security 'has largely lost its clarity and specificity'.[2] Today the notion is applied to such varied instruments as alliances, *ad hoc* coalitions, balance of power arrangements and peacekeeping operations. However, none of these mechanisms completely fulfils the conditions and standards of a true collective security system. Such a system would have to be based on the principle of the indivisibility of peace and would require this principle to be universally applied through clearly defined and permanently established procedures and institutions.

This paper attempts to situate Bahá'u'lláh's concept of collective security, as outlined in His letter to Queen Victoria, in the context of the evolving theory and practice of security in international relations. Specifically, the characteristics of the Bahá'í notion of collective security are explored and analysed, using a typology developed by Inis Claude.

Introduction

Collective security is a loosely defined term. Strictly speaking, collective security describes a universal or nearly universal state system that comes to the aid of an attacked member and punishes any aggressor state, according to the principle of 'one for all, all for one' – the musketeers' credo – elevating it from the personal to the nation state level.

Collective security might also be described as a 'Policy by an association of nations to maintain international peace through a league or confederation that would oppose by united action violations of the peace by an aggressor'.[3] Thus the term collective security is mainly used to refer to an international agreement that obliges its members to assist another in the event of an attack perpetrated by one of its member states. Whereas an alliance envisages the 'duty of assistance' in case of attack by a non-member[4] – and the pact may even envision a specific adversary – the sanction in a system of 'collective security' would take place against a member of the system itself.[5] As regards the structure and membership of contemporary international organizations, NATO corresponds to the first and the UN to the second of these types of agreements.

It is the aim of collective security to prevent war or quickly end war, a goal it shares with systems of deterrence. However, in the case of collective security, a stable world order is not created by fear of atomic annihilation or exclusively by a system of balance of power but by the great majority of states working together to maintain peace.[6] Such an arrangement requires an institutional framework in which diplomatic, economic and military measures can be coordinated. It may evolve out of an initially informal, even spontaneous arrangement, to become a fully institutionalized set of procedures. One may also think of collective security as a 'half-way house'[7] between anarchy and a world government. It is a more useful and politically more easily achievable instrument than the former but not as far-reaching or controversial as the latter. Seen from this perspective, the history of collective security is also the history of the development of international organization as a whole.

It is the purpose of this paper to explore and analyse Bahá'u'lláh's concept of collective security as outlined in His Tablet to Queen Victoria and the Súriy-i-Mulúk and elaborated in the writings of 'Abdu'l-Bahá and Shoghi Effendi, within the framework defined in Inis Claude's academic study of the subject. Claude's typology of collective security, despite its age, still represents one of the most comprehensive models in this relatively underdeveloped field. An overview of collective security visions and realities are sketched and Bahá'u'lláh's prescriptions located, analysed and assessed according to the chronology and theory of collective security.

Collective Security – An Ideal Type

According to Claude's idea of collective security, the system should have the following seven characteristics:

1) Use of force is outlawed
2) Collective security is guaranteed
3) Collective force serves as deterrent or sanction
4) Automatism
5) Anonymity of the aggressor
6) Determination of guilt
7) Permanence and generality of the system

The system builds on the axiom that wars can – and should – be prevented. The use of force as in Immanuel Kant's idea of a *foedus pacificum* is outlawed. Every single state should be able to rely on the collective security guarantee. The military superiority of peace-loving nations serves as a deterrent or, in case of an attack, as a means for sanction. Such military predominance can only be guaranteed through arms reduction of all states. The institutionalized global force further needs to have the right to intervene in case of an attack. The intended deterrence can only remain effective if collective action against aggression is swift, impartial and absolutely certain, not allowing any ifs, ands or buts.[8]

According to Claude, the counteraction should not discriminate between major powers and small states and should not take traditional friendships into account. This principle of the 'anonymity' of the aggressor amounts to a blanket condemnation of aggression.[9] The determination of guilt necessitates an appropriate institutional framework based on a legal definition of aggression. Finally, collective security, rather than being the result of *ad hoc* reactions to specific situations, should be permanently anchored in the institutions of world order.

Subjective and Objective Conditions

A collective security system cannot be created in a vacuum. Moreover, there are a number of critical subjective and objective preconditions. The subjective preconditions refer to certain principles, among which is the belief that humans are in essence good and can act rationally. By contrast, the use of violence is seen as irrational and immoral. Furthermore, peoples and their governments must be ready to take on global responsibility and believe in a world community that transcends the nation state, a community in which the welfare of humanity as a whole is perceived as being congruent with their national interest. This results in a third premise: the indivisibility of peace. Each attack on a part of the world must be understood as an attack on one's own security.

Table 1: Subjective Conditions for Collective Security
1) Belief in the goodness of man and in his rationality
2) Belief in a world community
3) Belief in the indivisibility of peace
4) Belief in collective guarantees
5) Belief in the impartiality of the system
6) Belief in the status quo

Two other prerequisites are derived from confidence in the system itself. First, the participating states must be convinced of the security guarantee offered by the system. This belief is strengthened by the 'automatic' and institutionalized nature of the process. Equally important is confidence in the impartiality of the system, based on the existence of universal norms and a high degree of honesty and objectivity in the decision-making process. Furthermore, it should be appreciated from the outset that collective security is designed as a means for the re-establishment of the *status quo ante*. That is, with the successful completion of collective action, the territorial integrity, as well as the original political situation, is reinstated. Collective security, as conceived by Claude, is therefore, not a means for transformation or change.

While the subjective attitude of humanity to such a system is important, there are also objective conditions favouring its establishment. These do not depend so much on the perception of the member states as on structural conditions. For example, collective security can be more easily implemented in a state system without major power blocs.

Table 2: Objective Conditions for Collective Security

1) Power diffusion
2) Universal membership
3) Legality of concepts, procedures, institutions
4) Building up transnational sovereignty

Ideally, all nation states would need to participate in a system of collective security but at the very least the support of the majority of states, including the major powers, is necessary. In order to function efficiently, the system should be grounded in legal concepts and procedures, safeguarded by impartial institutions. These concepts must be formulated in such a way that they are generally and universally applicable, in view of the fact that the weakness of such a system – in contrast to an alliance treaty or pact – is that the potential aggressor is unknown; thus the system cannot prepare itself for the actions of a specific state. Finally, collective security, the 'half-way house', is a step towards a world order not limited by national sovereignty.

Criticisms

While the idea of collective security has an appeal for some, it is also criticized by others on the basis of enforceability, usefulness and desirability. It is regarded by some as a more useful instrument than a balance of power system, yet less revolutionary than a world government. While for some critics collective security goes too far, for others it does not go far enough. For example, it is distasteful to pacifists, since it not only tolerates violence against an aggressor nation but also regards such violence as an integral part of the concept. In addition, collective security is based – so the criticism goes – on a concept of negative peace which outlaws war without paying enough regard to elements of positive peace such as the reduction of structural violence.[10]

A different criticism is levelled at the shortcomings and loopholes of practical implementation. What is an act of aggression and how should an aggressor state be defined?

The question also arises how a military force greater than that of any single state may be achieved. Does the concept of superiority still apply in a nuclear age and, if so, how can the system of collective security function if the aggressor is a nuclear state? Also, since the vast majority of conflicts in the world today are intra-state, one may ask to what extent a system based on interstate conflict can be relevant.

The belief in the *status quo* poses yet another problem. Are all forms of government or specific individuals exercising power 'worthy' of being reinstated or should that right be reserved only for largely democratic governments? More generally, is the *status quo* always desirable and what would happen to groups seeking self-determination?

Furthermore, the subjective premises discussed above suggest a dilemma. If, as has been shown, the success of collective security depends on trust as an underlying principle, how can governments trust the system before it has been put to the test and shown to be effective? The greatest scepticism, however, derives from the experiences of collective security to date. After the ambivalent results of the League of Nations era, the system was once more included in the UN Charter but until today, no UN military force exists. The view that the idea of collective security has failed is reinforced when the current situation, with its multiple conflicts, is contrasted with the eager enthusiasm with which the concept was greeted at the end of World War One. Even though the Gulf War of 1991 highlighted the scope of possibilities of a united Security Council and a large coalition of states, the hesitant, unassertive behaviour of the UN during the conflict in the former Yugoslavia and the unilateral actions of the US in Iraq in 2003 caused the temporary softening of scepticism to harden yet again. From the relative failure of the implementation of collective security emerged the practice of collective self-defence. The renewed interest in security alliances after the end of the cold war underscores this tendency.

Historical Overview

To better understand and situate Bahá'u'lláh's letters to the kings, with their clear aim of institutionalizing common actions against aggressor states, a brief overview of 1) the political realities in the world at the time of Bahá'u'lláh and 2) a review of early drafts and proposals for collective security may be helpful.

Political Realities at the Time of Bahá'u'lláh (1817–92)

What were the power relations in the world at the time of Bahá'u'lláh's call for collective security? Which nations were predominant? What were the relationships among them and to what extent did they influence the notion of security?

The world at mid-19th century can be broadly divided into the following zones:

1) Europe, whose sphere of influence included also the colonies;

2) the Middle East, viewing itself as a centre of political activity. The Ottoman Empire, despite acting as an interface between the first two geographic zones, is, from the beginning of the 19th century, beginning to disintegrate;

3) the United States, becoming increasingly independent of Europe, is developing into a new power factor; in addition to territorial expansion beyond its borders, intervention on the American continent is taking place according to the Monroe Doctrine formulated in 1823;[11]

4) Latin America, searching for ways to cut the cord from Spain and where several new states are being established;

5) Japan and China, both strategically important areas in the Far East but forced to open themselves to western influence; whereas Japan survives the forced opening in the 1850s relatively well, China finds itself, since the Opium Wars, in a state of decline and becomes increasingly vulnerable to demands for concession on the part of the European powers.

Political determining factors were the intellectual currents of liberalism, nationalism and the socialist movement. The colonialism of the 16th to 18th centuries developed in the 19th century into imperialism, which had an increasing influence on the politics of the European Powers from 1880 onward. The pursuit of security and the military behaviour of the Powers were also characterized by navalism. The best-known representative, A. T. Mahan, emphasized the significance of a paramount naval power for the supremacy of a war-waging nation.[12] Neither the workers' movement nor pacifism were ultimately able to influence the imperial politics of the Great Powers.

The nucleus of European politics was grouped around five states and their respective areas of influence: France, Russia, Great Britain, Austria and Prussia. In the 19th century Europe's power system witnessed a transition from Russia to France owing to Russia's defeat in the Crimean War and the successful mediation of France which appeared as arbitrator at the peace negotiations in Paris in 1856. In 1862 Prussian designs for hegemony began under Bismarckian *realpolitik*. The fear of Prussian-German dominance, the rapprochement of Prussia with Russia and Italy provoked the Franco-Prussian War. The defeat of isolated France caused a transition of power to the new nation state of Germany. Italy established itself within the European state system. After portraying himself as a liberal and supporter of the Italian unification movement, Pope Pius IX adopted a reactionary stance. Fear of losing secular power led to controversial papal decisions, such as the Syllabus of Errors (1864) and the Doctrine of Papal Infallibility (1870).

How did these interlocking factors influence the understanding of security? In order to strengthen the position of the state and guarantee themselves increasing security, 19th century governments resorted to a variety of tried and true methods, among which figured alliances and pacts, family ties, ideological linkages, trade and conferencing.

An example of the alliance method was the Bismarckian alliance policy, the effects of which lasted well into the 20th century. Another important example was the Holy Alliance, suggested by Russia in 1815, and which at first joined Austria and Prussia but which later included all European rulers except England's King George III, the Sultan and the Pope. The Holy Alliance was based on a vague covenant between throne and altar for the application of Christian principles in international diplomacy and envisioned in the congress accord the establishment of a conference system. The Holy Alliance became the basis for the Dreikaiserbund (the League of the Three Emperors), established informally in 1872 and in legal form in 1881. It was renewed in 1884 but fell apart in 1887.

The alliances themselves produced counter-reactions. In 1833–4 the Quadruple Alliance was formed as a countermeasure against the reactionary Holy Alliance. Great Britain became the reservoir of liberal thinking and ideas. Spain, Portugal and France joined what was understood to be the liberal bloc. After the Crimean War, France and Russia formed an Entente in 1856, which ended with France's support of Poland's national aspirations. An increase in alliance activity took place after 1871. Next to the League of the Three Emperors, Germany concluded a Dual Alliance with Austria in 1879, joined by Italy in 1882. In the same year Germany and Romania formed an alliance. The reinsurance treaty between Germany and Russia negotiated in 1887 was in conflict with the Dual Alliance and added to tensions. The long period of peace – also a consequence of the elaborate alliance system – could not be sustained in the long run. Bismarck's wish to achieve lasting security against France did not work out. Moreover, the ongoing Austro-Russian rivalry flared again.

The second classic form of safeguarding territorial security was to contrive to have family members in positions of power.

This was achieved either by placing relatives in key positions or by arranging marriages. Such a tie was created by the marriage of Clotilde, daughter of King Victor Emmanuel of Italy, with a cousin of Napoleon III. Queen Victoria, through her many relatives, had close family ties with many dynasties in Europe.

Ideological commonalities linked nations together in collective action and influenced some alliance-building.[13] But the ideological development and the influence of the form of government on a potential alliance partner could not always be foreseen. Thus Bismarck's design to permanently isolate France turned out to be a miscalculation and in 1904 the Entente Cordiale between Great Britain and France was concluded.

Another form of striving for security can be seen in imperialist policies and in claims to parts of the Ottoman Empire. However, any designs in that direction also meant possible confrontation with the nation whose influence one sought to curtail. Alongside the need for political security was also the aspiration for economic security and independence. This led to attempts to secure new markets and room for emigrants, as well as a number of trade agreements made in the 19th century.[14]

Yet another form of security management stemmed from the conference system. Peace was sought through the holding of periodic joint conferences and by a Permanent Court of Arbitration established in 1899.

Early Drafts and Proposals for Collective Security

The history of collective security up to the 20th century is one of drafts and visionary proposals aimed at finding the means to establish peaceful coexistence between nations, as well as provide for the security of states. Attempts to create a system with elements of collective security can be traced back to the early 14th century. *De recuperatione terrae sanctae* ('On the Recovery of the Holy Land') by Pierre Dubois, published in 1306, addressed the establishment of a federation of Christian nations with the aim of recapturing the sites, revered by the followers of Christ, in the Holy Land. Conflicts arising within the federation were to be solved through a court of justice.[15] Despite the obvious weakness posed by the fact that this system was based not on universality but on a coalition against the 'infidels', its significance lies in its emphasis on the nonviolent settlement of disputes among the members of the coalition.

The idea of collective security developing only out of a threat from non-member states was clear in the project of Bohemian King George Podiebrad in 1461 proposing a European confederation.[16] This peace plan, developed 150 years after that of Dubois, aimed at the creation of a defence pact among Bohemia, France and Venice against a possible Ottoman invasion. Article 21 of the pact provided members with a guarantee of security and established the nonviolent resolution of conflicts. The primary organs of the pact were to be a Court of Justice and a General Assembly. Members that did not abide by the decisions of the Court of Justice would face sanctions. The scope of the institutions, as well as the correlation between the ideas of peace and security and the concepts of law and justice, are the most notable features of this proposal.

Major changes took place in the 16th century with the emergence of the nation state, European expansionism, New World discoveries and the rise of intellectual movements such as the Renaissance, humanism and the Reformation, all of which exerted a profound influence on collective security projects. Erasmus, for instance, posed the question of peace among European Powers in *Querela pacis*. However, it was only the 17th century and the impact of the 30 Years War which saw concrete suggestions advanced for international organizations and security mechanisms. The two defining yet contradictory themes were those of tolerance, on the one hand, and the common crusade against the Ottomans on the other. The traditional Guarantor of Security and Peace, a proposed universal monarchy put forward by Dante between 1310 and 1313, was contrasted with the idea of a 'Christian republic'.[17] The most widely-known drafts were penned by the abbot Emiré de Crucé (1623), the Duke of Sully (1638) and William Penn (1692).[18]

Crucé, in *Le nouveau Cynée*[19] (*The New Cyneas*, 1623), first tabled a peace plan with a universal organizational structure. A permanent gathering of all states, a federation of nations with its seat in Venice, would be given the responsibility for the nonviolent resolution of conflict. Those states that did not obey by majority-based decision would be forced to do so. Within the organization, Crucé provided an inclusive structure which extended from the Pope, the Sultan and the Prussian king over various other emperors and kings to the Mogul ruler. Aside from its universal reach, the economic and socio-political principles of the 'New Cyneas' were clearly innovative, as it advocated free trade and had the stated goal of strengthening the position of traders and artisans.[20] Crucé was criticized on two fronts: first, he was accused of not being serious about his image of the world as a *cité commune à tous* but was merely presenting it as a mind game;[21] second, pacifists criticized him for not completely banning war as a political tool, since he not only sanctioned the use of force by the federation of nations but also advocated war against pirates and 'uncultured' peoples.[22]

The '*Grand Design*', *Drafted by the Duke of Sully* (1560–1641) was written in 1635 but only published in 1662, after his death. The Duke of Sully was a confidant of King Henri IV of France until the king's assassination in 1610 and Henri is given credit by Sully as the author of the project. This 'great plan' aimed at the redistribution of Europe into 15 states of more or less equal strength. Six were to be hereditary monarchies,[23] five were to be elected monarchies[24] and the remaining four, republics.[25] These measures were primarily aimed at limiting the power of the Habsburgs. However, the amalgamation into a federal 'Christian republic' served the aim of safeguarding European civilization and justifying a crusade against the Muslim Ottomans. A General Council and Senate were proposed as the principal institutions of the system. The greater power of large states would be reflected in their having a larger number of representatives.[26] To secure the undertaking, a general tax was to be levied and an international military force established. The Grand Design put forward the idea of an equilibrium among Christian nations to be ensured through an appropriate representation of the Churches, namely Catholic, Lutheran and Reformed.[27] Sully said little about the mandates of these institutions, his main concern being the international military force.[28] His critics were principally concerned about the validity of the deliberate use of war for the remodelling of Europe.

William Penn (1644–1718), founder of Pennsylvania, presented his peace plan for Europe in 1693 in the midst of the war of Britain against France. In his 'Essay Towards the Present and Future Peace of Europe', Penn, a Quaker, put the religious idea of peace in the centre of his argument. Owing to the brevity of the document and its religious foundation, Penn was accused of naivety. He suggested a 'European Diet', i.e. a European representative parliament which would decide upon contested issues and in which the German Reich would play the leading role. In Articles IV and V of his essay Penn outlined the grounds for military action, in effect, proposing a modern security concept. He stated that if a member state refused to accept or wait for a verdict or used armed force, then all the other member governments should unite and enforce the decision and the aggrieved party should be compensated.[29]

In the 18th century Abbé de St Pierre developed his ideas for ensuring peace, gradually attracting both the interest and ridicule of well-known contemporaries. St Pierre laboured throughout his life on his *Projet pour rendre la paix perpétuelle en Europe* (1712), excerpts of which were compiled by Rousseau. St Pierre proposed an 'authentic federation' of sovereigns, who would hold an ongoing Congress.[30]

> . . . the federation must embrace all the important powers in its membership; it must have a legislative body, with powers to pass laws and ordinances binding upon all its members; it must have a coercive force capable of compelling every state to obey its common resolves whether in the way of command or of prohibition; finally, it must be strong and firm enough to make it impossible for any member to withdraw at his own pleasure the moment he conceives his private interest to clash with that of the whole body.[31]

Among the institutions of the federation was a court of arbitration, whose decisions were to be considered binding. Violations of the federation charter were to be punished by a ' ban of Europe' and a declaration 'as a public enemy' and, in extreme cases, by military measures against the miscreant former ally until the latter surrendered and corrected his injustices.[32] St Pierre's project promoted the re-establishment of the *status quo*.[33] To limit the danger of religious confrontations he advocated the study of religion and regarded the Golden Rule as an expression of the commonalities among faiths.[34]

St Pierre's idea of a lasting peace arrangement, which later led to his being considered the father of collective security, was met with great scepticism. Voltaire branded him 'abbé de Saint-Pierre d'Utopie'.[35] Of all St Pierre's philosophical contemporaries, the only one to pay serious attention to the *Projet* was Rousseau, who saw in its implementation great advantages for the European sovereigns and for their peoples.[36] However, even he, after having published parts of St Pierre's outline in an *Extrait* in 1761, considered that St Pierre's ideas belonged to the realm of Utopia and were of no real practical use.[37]

Although both Bentham and Kant wrote in the latter years of the 18th century, the extent of their influence is such that they are often identified more with the 19th century.[38] Jeremy Bentham's 'A Plan for a Universal and Perpetual Peace' (1787), published in 1843, focused on two basic proposals:

> 1.The reduction and fixation of the force of the several nations that compose the European system; 2. The emancipation of the distant dependencies of each state. Each of these propositions has its distinct advantages; but neither of them, it will appear, would completely answer the purpose without the other.[39]

He pleaded explicitly for the abolition of secret diplomacy[40] and connected internal and external political interests. Bentham, known as the founder of utilitarianism, stated that war has deleterious effects on both security and prosperity:

> . . . war is, in this way, just as unfavourable to opulence as in the other. In the present mode of carrying on war – a mode which it is in no man's power to depart from, security is in proportion to opulence. Just so far then as war is, by its direct effects,

> unfavourable to opulence – just so far is it unfavourable to security.[41]

Bentham also suggested the establishment of a congress or parliament, as well as a tribunal.[42]

The comparatively limited attention that was paid to Bentham's peace plan may be explained by the earlier publication – although written later – of Immanuel Kant's *On Perpetual Peace* in 1795. Kant chose the form of a peace agreement in order to present his views of a world peace structure.[43] In his proposal he identified the difference between a peace agreement and cessation of hostilities and pleaded for state sovereignty. He considered a republican constitution desirable, since the citizen – deciding on policy – would be unwilling to commit himself to war. Kant's peace proposal also included a league of nations – *foedus pacificum* – which would bring an end to war altogether, not only to a specific war, as is the case with most peace treaties. Kant's league of nations, based on international law and the free acceptance of certain norms and laws, 'holds back the stream of those hostile passions which fear the law'.[44] In the first supplement, Kant makes a remarkable statement concerning the 'Guarantee for perpetual peace'[45] in which he outlines formal and subjective preconditions for peaceful coexistence. In the third article, entitled 'The Law of World Citizenship Shall Be Limited to Conditions of Universal Hospitality', he rejects the legitimacy of great power imperialism.

Central to the development of the concept of collective security is the final sentence of Kant's article, in which he describes the interdependence of the world community and its implications for international law, pointing to the indivisibility of peace:

> Since the narrower or wider community of the peoples of the earth has developed so far that a violation of rights in one place is felt throughout the world, the idea of a law of world citizenship is no high-flown or exaggerated notion. It is a supplement to the unwritten code of the civil and international law, indispensable for the maintenance of the public human rights and hence also of perpetual peace. One cannot flatter oneself into believing one

can approach this peace except under the condition outlined here.[46]

Kant's proposal is complex, expressing as it does both philosophical and practical conditions for peace: the primacy of law, attention to the practical demands of implementation of any undertaking, the clear exposition of the philosophical foundations of his understanding of human nature, the form of state and government, and the relationship between morals and politics – all give this comparatively short work a timeless relevance and put a stamp on subsequent proposals and organizational developments.

These early proposals were never implemented, even to a limited extent, and their aims were insufficient for a system of collective security. Their principal shortcoming lay in their restricted universality, limited as they were to the European continent. Nevertheless, they were important precursors for later conceptions of collective security and for the structure of future international organizations. The later 19th century saw more practical manifestations than theoretical applications of international organization, such as the Congress of Vienna and initial forms of international organizations in the non-military field (e.g. seafaring and the postal system).

The 20th Century: Collective Security within the League of Nations and the United Nations

The traumatic experience of World War One led to the first attempts at putting the vision of an international peace organization into practice. Notwithstanding the fact that the era of the League of Nations (1919–38) was born out of the vision of America's President Woodrow Wilson, the US Senate never ratified the Covenant of the League of Nations. The power and influence of the short-lived League suffered greatly from this continued absence of one of the Great Powers.

The fact that the League of Nations emerged from the blood and trauma of war led to its founding agreement being focused on the prevention of war. Fully a third of the Covenant's 24

Articles related to collective security. These fell into four categories: general instructions about collective security, disarmament, peaceful settlement of conflict and sanctions.

Articles 10, 11 and 19 were in the first group. Peace was described as indivisible but security measures were limited to non-member aggressor states. Article 11 was both a pact of non-aggression and also one of mutual support in the case of external aggression. Although Article 19 was originally supposed to clarify the possibility of peaceful change, French concerns about a strong Germany led to dominance of the idea of the *status quo*. Articles 8 and 9 addressed disarmament[47] and Article 15 foresaw the political settlement of disputes to be decided by the Council or the Assembly.[48]

This section had two major weaknesses: on the one hand collective action required the unanimous agreement of all member states; on the other, war was still considered a legal mechanism. Article 16 institutionalized economic, moral and military sanctions.[49] While the latter two were not binding, economic sanctions were to be imposed automatically.

Commentators' views of collective security and its implementation in the League of Nations vary from valuing it as the first attempt at such a system to regretting the absence of 'punch' in its set-up and implementation. The Covenant itself is criticized for its vague language: terms such as 'aggression' and 'aggressor state' were undefined, while others, such as 'civil war', were non-existent. War continued to be a means of conflict management in certain cases and the peaceful resolution of disputes was not obligatory. Military sanctions were not always imposed and even economic ones were not automatic in their practical application. Finally, the effectiveness of the League of Nations was seen as limited by the continuing existence of regional arrangements.[50]

The League of Nations tried, in several instances, to actually carry out its responsibilities in the field of collective security and it was successful in cases where the warring parties were relatively small and the disputed issues limited in scope.[51] The conflict between Italy and Abyssinia, however, is considered one of the great failures of the League. Although economic sanctions were imposed against Italy, not much was put in the way of the aggression of a Great Power.[52] Moreover, Italy was not 'morally' punished by being excluded from the League.

Cooperation between France and Great Britain, needed for the required unanimity in both executive organs, did not always occur and this further added to the vulnerability of the League system.

Table 3: Comparison of Claude's Ideal of Collective Security with the League of Nations

Claude's Ideal	**League of Nations**
1) Outlawing of force	Only limited; Arts. 10, 12, 13, 15
2) Guarantee of collective security	Limited; no integration of national military forces; Art. 16
3) Collective power as deterrent/sanction	Disarmament only theoretical
4) Automatism	Provided for in Arts. 2(1), 16(1), (2), (4)
5) Anonymity of aggressor	Advantage of the Great Powers
6) Identification of guilt	Not clearly defined
7) Permanence and generality of system	No permanent military force, although an organization with permanent secretariat

A devastating world war also gave birth to the United Nations. However, in contrast to the brief gestation of the League of Nations, the Allies after World War Two took considerably more time to draft the UN Charter. From the very first Article the Charter puts questions of peace and security in the spotlight. The focus here is on the prevention of conflicts and their resolution through peaceful means.

When applying the seven test categories of Claude's system of collective security to the UN system, it is evident that the Charter seeks to avoid the use of force and prefers nonviolent means for the management of conflicts.[53] Articles 106, 107[54] and 51 (which institutionalizes the right to self-defence), however, weaken the prohibition of the use of force. Nevertheless, these exceptions are reserved for specific cases.[55]

Regarding obligations towards the attacked state, the UN Charter not only endorses the idea of common defence but also clearly identifies specific measures to be taken in the case of a threat to peace (Art. 39 (24)). It also foresees the establishment of a collective military force (Arts. 43–5) and identifies a planning and command structure for collective measures (Arts. 45–7).[56] The plans under Chapter 7, which refer to 'Action with respect to threats to the peace, breaches of the peace, and acts of aggression' are much more developed than those of the League of Nations. As a result of problems that could ensue from the veto right of the permanent Security Council members,[57] Article 43, on the establishment of a UN military force, has not yet been realized.[58] An additional weakness lies in the fact that the regions still have the right to provide for alternative security arrangements, which may hinder a more universal process in the United Nations.[59]

Effective deterrence requires disarmament on the one hand and a strong collective military force on the other. In comparison to the League of Nations, the question of disarmament is weakly addressed in the UN Charter. The Military Staff Committee is given only a consulting function in the 'regulation of armaments and possible disarmament' under the supervision of the Security Council.[60] The question of strength or military superiority of a UN army thus depends on the will of each nation to commit troops.

Despite the fact that any war against a member state of the League of Nations was considered a threat to all members, the UN uses a cumbersome three-stage process. First, the Security Council must consult about the crisis and may at this point take only provisional measures;[61] following this, peaceful, and later military sanctions can be imposed.[62] The system does not contain any automatism with regard to military engagement but rather engages in a process of conflict management based on the consensus of the permanent members of the Security Council. Theoretically, the United Nations is obliged to take steps against every aggressor state. A permanent member, though, can cast a veto for its own gain – or in favour of a power bloc, as often occurred during the cold war. Thus the anonymity of the aggressor and/or victim is not truly realized. Since the Charter does not provide for a clear definition of the term 'aggression', the identification of a crisis is left to the Security Council and is thus hindered by political considerations.

The UN is an institutionalized international organization without a permanent mechanism of collective security. As there is no standing military force at the UN's disposal, it has been constrained to patch one together on an *ad hoc* basis. However, the potential for effectiveness of such a non-permanent system, in rare cases when the political will and a readiness to deal collectively are present, has been proved in the Gulf War against Iraq in 1991.

Table 4: Comparison of Claude's Ideal of Collective Security with the UN

Claude's Ideal	**UN**
1) Outlawing of force	Yes but weakened by Art. 51 (right to self-defence)
2) Guarantee of collective security	Provided in Art. 43 but not put into practice. Veto, regional security structures
3) Collective power as deterrent/sanction	Few measures for disarmament
4) Automatism	No; decision in the Security Council
5) Anonymity of aggressor	Advantage of the permanent Security Council members and their allies
6) Identification of guilt	Unclear definition of aggression; preference to political criteria
7) Permanence and generality of system	Measures are planned but have not been implemented

To make up for the inherent weaknesses described above, the UN has put considerable effort into assisting the processes of conflict prevention and resolution through diplomatic activities for the express purpose of avoiding or limiting the escalation of conflict.

Moreover, in a number of situations it has advocated and supervised the violence-free resolution of conflicts and mandated economic and diplomatic sanctions as leverage.

Collective Security in the Bahá'í Writings

The heart of Bahá'u'lláh's concept of collective security is described in a passage in His letter to Queen Victoria. Written in 1868 in Arabic and sent to the Queen 'through the post',[63] the letter is one of several Tablets Bahá'u'lláh addressed to the kings and rulers of His time.[64] It is the only message of Bahá'u'lláh to a ruler which is reputed to have been received positively by the addressee.[65] In this series of weighty messages, written over the course of His exile in Constantinople, Adrianople and 'Akká between 1863 and about 1873,[66] Bahá'u'lláh clearly announced His claim to be a Manifestation of God and called on the rulers to govern justly, to reconcile their differences and to establish a peaceful order. Stylistically, the letters follow the tradition of 'Mirrors for Princes', as used by numerous authors in the east and the west over centuries to bring ethical issues and virtues to the attention of a ruler. However, Bahá'u'lláh went further by including commentaries on the institutions of society and the intended results. Whereas some of His exhortations were aimed directly at the rulers themselves, He used these Tablets as a means of addressing a wider range of people and issues beyond the individual to whom the message was originally addressed.[67]

On the specific issue of collective security, Bahá'u'lláh stated in the Tablet to Queen Victoria:

> Be united, O kings of the earth, for thereby will the tempest of discord be stilled amongst you, and your peoples find rest, if ye be of them that comprehend. Should any one amongst you take up arms against another, rise ye all against him, for this is naught but manifest justice.[68]

In another passage He reiterated the central idea of collective security:

> Should any king take up arms against another, all should unitedly arise and prevent him. If this be done, the nations of the world will no longer require any armaments, except for the purpose of preserving the security of their realms and of maintaining internal order within their territories. This will ensure the peace and composure of every people, government and nation.[69]

Bahá'u'lláh's statements, along with the explanatory comments made later by 'Abdu'l-Bahá and Shoghi Effendi, constitute the indispensable framework of such a system, with the specific structure and organization left to be determined by the nations in future. The general characteristics of the system are as follows:

- The system should combine 'strength' and 'elasticity'.[70] More precisely, 'strength involving the use of an adequate force to ensure the efficacy of the proposed system, and elasticity to enable the machinery that has been devised to meet the legitimate needs and aspirations of its aggrieved upholders'.[71]

- The establishment of such a system should take place within the framework of a 'vast, an all-embracing assemblage of men'[72] in which representatives of the nations should consult about measures and instruments of the foundation of peace. Such a gathering should result in a 'binding treaty and . . . a covenant, the provisions of which shall be sound, inviolable and definite', regulating fundamental questions, such as the exact determination of borders and the size of national armaments.[73] Institutions to be added – possibly at a later stage – are a world parliament, a tribunal with power to make binding decisions and a world government.[74]

- This scheme of collective security also presupposes the unity of the rulers, especially of the Great Powers.[75]

These passages emphasize the prohibition of the use of force, the first principle of collective security as outlined by Claude. Bahá'u'lláh confirms this idea elsewhere in His writings by, for example, explicitly declaring as obsolete the concept of holy war.[76] This system also fulfils the collective security guarantee to the attacked state. Not only is the principle 'one for all, all for one' implicitly contained in the address to the 'kings of the earth' but also the nations making up the world community as a whole are obliged to impose sanctions against the aggressor nation.

Moreover, the necessity of general, simultaneous and multilateral disarmament is emphasized,[77] the provisions of which should be laid down in a comprehensive international agreement and federal treaty.[78] Unilateral disarmament is regarded as counterproductive.[79] A minimum of weapons for internal order and defence purposes continues to be granted[80] but it is anticipated that in the future advanced technologies would be used for peaceful purposes, thus effecting a conversion of 'weapons of war . . . into instruments of reconstruction'.[81]

The fourth element of collective security refers to the automatic triggering of measures in the event of an attack. As with the League of Nations and United Nations systems, it is not clear exactly what such an automatism would look like in the Bahá'í proposal. While Bahá'u'lláh's plan for a collective security system rests on international institutions (world parliament, international tribunal and world court), it is not clearly specified which organ would exercise which decision-making function. It is also not clearly spelled out whether military troops would be deployed immediately in each case or whether preference should be given to non-military means for ending a conflict.

As the path proposed by Bahá'u'lláh for a collective security system should be characterized by both 'elasticity' and 'strength', it is possible that the automatism referred to by Bahá'u'lláh may be a process of urgent and immediate consultation on the part of representatives of a number of institutions.

Of further importance is the fact that in the Bahá'í teachings collective security represents only one element in the establishment of an enduring peace. Particularly significant in this regard is the fundamental principle of the unity of humanity. The acceptance of this basic principle is the primary, subjective condition enabling the system of collective security to function. The importance of this general consciousness of unity was emphasized by the Universal House of Justice in a message written in 1985:

> Two points bear emphasizing in all these issues. One is that the abolition of war is not simply a matter of signing treaties and protocols; it is a complex task requiring a new level of commitment to resolving issues not customarily associated with the pursuit of peace. Based on political agreements alone, the idea of collective security is a chimera. The other point is that the primary challenge in dealing with issues of peace is to raise the context to the level of principle, as distinct from pure pragmatism. For, in essence, peace stems from an inner state supported by a spiritual or moral attitude, and it is chiefly in evoking this attitude that the possibility of enduring solutions can be found.[82]

The notion in Bahá'u'lláh's system of the anonymity of the aggressor and victim state respectively – releasing the nations from their traditional friendships or 'blocs' in favour of an encompassing security system – represents the greatest contrast to the dominant concept of national security in 19th century Europe. Particularly in its waning years, both old and new alliances gained importance, with traditional friendships and family ties playing an important role in defending against assaults and soliciting support in the event of attack. The idea of an alliance system for balance of power purposes had an initially stabilizing but later destabilizing effect upon international relations prior to World War One. Bahá'u'lláh's proposal for a world community – articulated before Bismarck's alliance policy (*Bündnispolitik*) was put into effect – wholly replaces the previous notion of friendly ties and alliances based on such familiar commonalities as religion, race, past history of cooperation or family ties. Furthermore, the model of collective security contained in Bahá'u'lláh's Tablet to Queen Victoria does not equate the anonymity of victim and aggressor state with indifference. Rather, the community of nations must evolve from its traditional understanding of friendship to a far more encompassing network of interdependent relationships based on the principle of unity of the human family. In Bahá'u'lláh's model, the systematic encouragement of friendly relationships aimed at the consolidation of human unity should be supported and pursued in order for peace to be achieved in any form. While adhering to the anonymity principle, in this model existing friendships are not necessarily viewed as a hindrance but as a helpful stepping stone towards a system of collective security.

The Bahá'í model deals with the question of assigning guilt in two ways. First, definitions of aggression may be laid out in the binding treaty. The contents of the pact have been deliberately left open and are to be specified by the international institutions yet to be established, one example being the definition of aggression.[83] Moreover, the functions of the international tribunal and the world parliament – also sketched only in brief in Bahá'u'lláh's model – remain to be clearly delineated. The importance of precise determination of borders suggested for the Covenant implies that it may have to include strong measures for dealing with inter-state conflict. The importance of implementing a process of consultation or talks with regard to specifying an aggressor party, as mentioned by Bahá'u'lláh, leads to the inference that each incident may, in future, be examined on a case-by-case basis.

As concerns the last point of Claude's typology, the permanence and generality of the system, it can be assumed that such permanence would be assured by the terms of the treaty.[84] Moreover, there should be further development towards the realization of a world commonwealth in order to motivate the nations to make the necessary commitments to the establishment of an international force,[85] thereby ensuring a mechanism to safeguard the permanence and applicability of the system as a whole. Thus the system proposed by Bahá'u'lláh to the rulers of His time includes all the key components of a functional collective security mechanism.

Table 5: Comparison of Claude's Ideal with Bahá'u'lláh's Concept

Claude's Ideal	**Bahá'í Model**
1) Outlawing of force	Yes
2) Guarantee of collective security	Established in treaty
3) Collective power as deterrent/sanction	Disarmament
4) Automatism	Automatism (of consultation; of military measures)
5) Anonymity of aggressor	Idea of world unity stronger than traditional friendships
6) Identification/Assignation of guilt	Aggression defined as armed attack (inter-state); identification of guilt institutionalized (Court)
7) Permanence and generality of system	Permanence and generality; adapted to each case. Safeguards of permanence can be laid down in treaty.

Subjective Preconditions

The motives underlying the implementation of collective security are at least as important as the formal criteria for the system. These subjective preconditions originate, fundamentally, in the worldview and consciousness of human beings. Equally important is human trust that actions and measures being taken are realistic and reliable. Thus the strength of the system is dependent on human conviction with regard to its purpose and confidence in its ultimate effectiveness. Both are required.

Thus it is clear that the preconditions for a 'world community' and the 'indivisibility of peace' are key elements in Bahá'u'lláh's teachings. His statement that 'It is not his to boast who loveth his country, but it is his who loveth the world'[86] emphasizes the vital importance of the principle of the oneness of the human family. As a consequence of this deep conviction, a new understanding of identity is fostered which allows the individual – or the nation

– to continue to identify closely with one's ethnic group or nation and at the same time to see these forms of solidarity as being secondary to allegiance to the world community.

The nation was the single most important principle of community in the state system of the late 19th century. Nationalism has its roots in 18th century absolutism, which gave rise to the modern nation state. Since the beginning of the 19th century, the identity of European ethnic groups has been realized increasingly in movements to satisfy national aspirations. The German and Italian nation states were results of this integrative movement. The greatness of one's own nation was proclaimed and its supremacy advocated. As the century unfolded, moderate forms of nationalism turned, under the influence of social Darwinism, into overtly chauvinistic movements. Adding fuel to the fire, racist[87] and anti-Semitic[88] tendencies were used to advance this agenda.

Imperialism was another tendency highlighting the contrast between Bahá'u'lláh's proposal and the European Great Power policy. The feeling of superiority over other peoples and nations and the myth of the 'civilizing' mission of the European nations, intensified by racist and nationalistic concepts, were used to justify colonialism, which was, in turn, bolstered by economic arguments to increase export markets and by internal political pressure to expand the territory for migration and to take advantage of the decline in unemployment.

Colonialism also played a vital role in security politics. Acquiring new colonies, generally extending a country's sphere of influence, resulted in continual changes in the European balance of power. Peace ended up being 'divisible': the advantage of one's own state and the striving to increase one's power prevailed over thoughts of the common good.

Claude proposes as a precondition belief in the essential goodness of human beings and in their capacity for rationally motivated activity. These ideas were in contrast with those of Darwin, social-Darwinists, racists and Marxist-materialists, whose quite different views of a mechanistic, externally driven human nature were being developed and increasingly spread. The opposite end of the spectrum was still occupied by remnants of the Renaissance, with their belief in the innate rationalism of humans. In comparison, the Bahá'í model offers a more complex, developmental view of human nature. While acknowledging human goodness and potential, the Bahá'í model also recognizes the need for proper education and divine guidance in order to realize the human capacity for constructive, moral behaviour.[89]

Claude correctly assesses the belief in a collective guarantee and in the nonpartisanship of the system as being circular. Trust in the system is imperative if it is to function. Bahá'u'lláh's model has the potential to win the trust of states, since the responsibility for developing the agreement lies with the governments and its clauses are binding on those who formulate it.

One of the most controversial elements of collective security is the manner in which it deals with the *status quo.* A collective security system is responsible to the *status quo* and the whole system is geared towards its restoration. The question arises, logically, whether the *status quo* itself represents justice. Since the restoration of the *status quo* is concerned with the territorial integrity of the state, the support of its sovereignty and a rightful government, one may well ask whether that government is, in fact, rightful in the first place. Another question with regard to the *status quo* concerns how state borders are identified and what role self-determination should play in that identification.

In the decisions taken at the Congress of Vienna of 1815, the third great European peace conference, a two-dimensional understanding of the *status quo* can be discerned. The *fait accompli* was accepted in many cases; i.e. a decision was taken against the *status quo* and against restoration of the territorial positions of 1789. But as for the reinstatement of governments, the principle of the *status quo* was only selectively applied.[90] These principles were used as instruments within the prevailing security concept of the balance of power.[91] States were often less concerned with increasing their own power and far more with preventing an increase in the power of others. Basic trends such as nationalism and liberalism were ignored at the Congress. At the same time, a period of conferences was begun with the Vienna Congress that strongly influenced the political climate until 1870.

Bahá'u'lláh's proposal was being articulated just as the last traces of the concert of Europe, not formally functioning since 1825, were withering away. The Bahá'í model presumes a treaty that would far surpass the 'fairest fruits' of contemporary European diplomacy. The proposed treaty would be elaborated at and accepted by an 'all-embracing assemblage'[92] and would contain guarantees of territorial integrity which would help to stabilize and maintain the *status quo*. In order to achieve this, the borders of states must be clearly defined by a non-partisan international commission, which should make suggestions for unsolved border issues and thus prepare a final settlement, addressing all claims for self-determination.[93]

The question of the legitimacy of a government is less clearly defined. 'Abdu'l-Bahá saw in the 'covenant of eternal friendship' the most important components and the required superstructure for the establishment of peace.[94] In such a system the precise form of government is secondary, although the Bahá'í writings express support for the fundamentals of democracy.[95] However, it follows that whatever the structure, governments should not be 'tyrannical' and that any government – no matter what its type – acting against the provisions of the pact must either comply or be replaced.[96]

In His system for collective security, Bahá'u'lláh presents the idea that the kind of world order that must be aimed for and developed is one in which the *status quo* will become, in fact, desirable and attractive. The Bahá'í peace system is dynamic, taking for granted an understanding of organic growth processes and containing provisions for peaceful change. For instance, it is possible that the world parliament and the international tribunal will discuss questions of ethnic and national self-determination. However, while acknowledging the legitimacy of ethnic and national feeling and aspirations, Bahá'u'lláh's teachings aim to promote a higher, world-embracing identity. The ramifications of the provisions of the Congress of Vienna and the dissatisfaction of some nations led to the constant quest for revision of the conditions. The possibility of peaceful change and the institutional support represents an improvement in the Bahá'í model.

Table 6: Subjective Preconditions for Collective Security

Claude's Ideal	**19th Century Ideas**	**Bahá'u'lláh's Model**
1) Belief in the goodness of man and his rational abilities	Images of man: 1) Man is good 2) Man is selfish 3) Some human beings (ethnic groups, races, classes, gender) are more or less valuable	Complex view of human nature: essentially good but requiring guidance and education
2) Belief in a world community	Over-emphasis on nation, culture and race	Global consciousness of the organic unity of the world
3) Belief in the indivisibility of peace	Peace is divisible	That which benefits one is to benefit the whole and vice versa
4) Belief in collective guarantees	Preference for alliances/friendships	Should be established on the basis of a treaty
5) Belief in the non-partisanship of the system	Preference for alliances/friendships	Testing of individual cases by consultation within institutions
6) Belief in the *status quo*	Principle of *status quo* is being applied when convenient.	Fixing of state boundaries by international commission; mechanisms for peaceful co-existence and change; idea of a just world order; replacement of aggressor government

Objective Conditions

Claude's typology assumes four objective conditions for collective security. The first applies to the world situation, the remaining three to the functioning of the security model.

A decentralized distribution of power is important for the implementation of collective security. A predominance by super-powers or power blocs, as in bipolar systems, makes an efficient application of collective security more difficult. The centralization of power undermines a fair application of the system, both in the decision-making process – e.g. the composition and objectives of an armed force – and in the concrete application of security measures. This problem was manifested in the UN decision-making process during the cold war.

In making the well-being of the nation dependent upon the well-being of the world's people as a whole, it can be seen that Bahá'u'lláh's proposal is in stark contrast with the *zeitgeist.* In His teachings, the legitimate form of love for one's nation is a 'sane and intelligent patriotism',[97] clearly distinguishing it from nationalism and chauvinism. Despite this universalistic worldview, however, He recognized the leading role of the Great Powers to whom He addressed the Tablets. What He proposed to them was not simply another alliance but a true collective security system, although Bahá'u'lláh is careful not to denounce the alliance system *per se* and acknowledges the temporary stabilizing factor of Bismarck's action.[98]

Bahá'u'lláh avoids discussion about which type of government is to be preferred. Instead, He offers general praise for representative as well as monarchical elements of government. This confirms the impression of the subordination of institution-oriented ethics to result-oriented ethics in Bahá'u'lláh's model.

The three other objective conditions – universal membership, legality of the system and the development of institutions with transnational sovereignty – are premises that are also present in Bahá'u'lláh's model. Universal membership, especially the participation of the Great Powers, is seen as a precondition for the functioning of the model, to be established and implemented by all nations with full legality and legitimacy. The procedures to be used in implementing it are to be guided by the Articles laid out in the treaty itself. Moreover, the Bahá'í writings point out the necessity for a future world government.[99] Thus the system of collective security foresees the eventual transformation of combined troops into an international police force at the service of the entire world community.

Conclusions

Summary

Bahá'u'lláh's design for the concerted action of governments against an attacker state is noteworthy in several aspects. First, earlier proposals emerged primarily from western thinkers; Bahá'u'lláh presents a design for a collective security system not only from an eastern thinker but infused with a universal world-view, going far beyond the largely Eurocentric earlier models.

Second, Bahá'u'lláh's proposal fills a vacuum in the history of ideas as well as providing a scenario for the practical implementation of collective security. Time seems to have stopped at Kant's *Zum ewigen Frieden.* New projects make reference to Kant's milestone in peace philosophy but attract less attention.

Third, Bahá'u'lláh's blueprint for collective security creates a new category of war prevention and peace creation. His call marks a significant transition from the purely utopian, often religiously-motivated wishful thinking of earlier visionaries to the practical realities of human implementation and serves as a bridge linking the history of ideas of the 18th century to the 21st century world of international organization.

How does Bahá'u'lláh's model stand up under the criticism directed at collective security? First, the system envisages obligatory and not optional decisions of the arbitration tribunal. Thus all states are encompassed by the system. Second, the model envisions multilateral disarmament or arms reduction of all states, giving intervention by the international military force a far greater chance of success. Third, Bahá'u'lláh defines aggression as military aggression, giving some clarity to the concept. Fourth, Bahá'u'lláh's system of collective security provides for the prior determination of borders of all countries. This might have the consequence of turning the vast majority of current intractable civil conflicts into inter-state conflicts, rendering them more amenable to the application of collective security measures.

The procedure in cases of civil war is still open for discussion. It may be assumed, however, that the determination of borders would be one of a number of ways in which the concepts of collective security might be applied successfully to internal conflicts. Others might include attention to such issues as the appreciation and integration of minorities, gender bias and economic disparity.[100]

The strength of the Bahá'í model lies also in its relevance to the subjective preconditions that engender confidence in a collective security mechanism. The problem of circularity may be addressed before the implementation of the system by focusing on the subjective requirements.

One of the unusual elements of Bahá'u'lláh's proposal is the broad discretion left to the governments of the world as to the manner of establishing a collective security system. It does not impose a single valid path but leaves it to the assembly of political leaders to decide the details of the undertaking. This attitude of non-imposition of a specific set of procedures distinguishes Bahá'u'lláh's concept from those that preceded it.

Historically, the time seemed favourable for Bahá'u'lláh's call. The states He addressed in His letters were not only powerful but also connected by an intricate existing web of alliances, interests and family ties. Nevertheless, His idea seemed premature and difficult to comprehend and implement at that time. However, World War One caused a change of consciousness, one important element of which was the concept of collective security as an indispensable element of a peaceful world order. In contrast to many historians who regarded it as an abject failure, Shoghi Effendi commented, in 1936, that the League of Nations experiment of collective security represented a step in the right direction.[101] Even though the criticisms of certain aspects of the League were fully justified, the fact that the League members had 'for the most part, agreed to impose collectively sanctions on the condemned aggressor, and should have succeeded in carrying out, to a very great measure, their decision, is no doubt an event without parallel in human history'.[102]

To date, neither an assemblage of leaders – as Bahá'u'lláh had postulated – nor a worldwide consultation on the determination of borders has taken place. However, the institutionalization of the UN and collective action in crisis situations demonstrate the first attempts to implement elements of such a system. Yet the challenge of the concept of collective security remains, as:

> . . . it offends the most pacific and the most bellicose of men; it challenges neutralism and isolationism as well as militarism and imperialism; it clashes with the views of the most conservative supporters of national sovereignty and the most liberal proponents of democratic control in foreign policy; it demands alike the dissolution of ancient national hatreds and the willingness to abandon traditional national friendships.[103]

Outlook: A Broader Concept of Security

Over the past decade, the need for a broader concept of security has been realized. 'Human security' encompasses economics; nutrition; health; the environment; and individual, community and political elements of security; and opens up the field to aspects and needs of security that were earlier considered of secondary importance at best.[104]

Similarly, Bahá'u'lláh's security concept addresses numerous non-military issues and encompasses different security mechanisms. Security, on the institutional level, entails new behavioural norms, laws, institutions and intentions and clearly articulated goals, framed within the model of a 'new world order' and aiming at providing international stability. The result of this system is not only the strengthening of the subjective sense of individual security but the overcoming of estrangement between peoples and nations, enabling them to work together towards the realization of a closer-knit world community. With the notion of security inextricably linked to justice as well as to peace, the energy and resources of the human community may be released for the constructive solution of its many remaining challenges.[105]

Bibliography

'Abdu'l-Bahá. *Paris Talks.* London: Bahá'í Publishing Trust, 1967.

— *The Secret of Divine Civilization.* Wilmette, IL: Bahá'í Publishing Trust, 1990.

'Abdu'l-Bahá in Canada. Ontario: Bahá'í Distribution Canada, 1962.

Bahá'í International Community. *Rights of Minorities*. Submitted to the 51st session of the United Nations Commission on Human Rights, Geneva, Switzerland, 31 January 1995, BIC Document no. 95–0131.

— *Turning Point for All Nations: A Statement of the Bahá'í International Community on the Occasion of the 50th Anniversary of the United Nations*. New York: Bahá'í International Community United Nations Office, 1995.

Bahá'u'lláh. *Gleanings from the Writings of Bahá'u'lláh*. Wilmette, IL: Bahá'í Publishing Trust, 1983.

— *The Summons of the Lord of Hosts: Tablets of Bahá'u'lláh*. Haifa: Bahá'í World Centre, 2002.

— *Tablets of Bahá'u'lláh*. Wilmette, IL: Bahá'í Publishing Trust, 1988.

Bentham, J. 'A Plan for an Universal and Perpetual Peace'. <http://www.la.utexas.edu/research/poltheory/bentham/pil/pil.e04.html>, last accessed 2 July 2003.

Claude, Inis. *Swords into Plowshares*. New York: McGraw-Hill, 4th edn. 1983.

Cole, J. *Modernity and the Millennium. The Genesis of the Bahá'í Faith in the Nineteenth-Century Middle East*. New York: Columbia University Press, 1998.

The Compilation of Compilations. Prepared by the Universal House of Justice 1963–1990. 2 vols. [Sydney]: Bahá'í Publications Australia, 1991.

Fenske, H. A. O. *Geschichte der politischen Ideen*. Frankfurt: Fischer, 1987.

Fischer, D. *Nonmilitary Aspects of Security*. Dartmouth and Aldershot: UNIDIR, 1993.

Galtung, J. 'Violence, Peace and Peace Research'. *Journal of Peace Research*, vol. 6, no. 3, 1969, pp. 167–91.

Hoffmann, S. and D. P. Fidler (eds.). *Rousseau on International Relations*. Oxford: Clarendon Press, 1991.

Kant, I. *On Perpetual Peace*. <http://www.constitution.org/kant/perpeace.htm>, last accessed 6 July 2003.

Ledermann, L. *Les Précurseurs de l'Organisation Internationale*. Neuchâtel: Edition de la Bonnerie, 1945.

Naidu, M. V. *Collective Security and the United Nations: A Definition of the UN Security System*. New York: St Martin's Press, 1975.

Raumer, K. von. *Ewiger Friede: Friedensrufe und Friedenspläne seit der Renaissance*. Freiburg/München: Karl Alber Verlag, 1953.

Rougement, D. *Ecrits sur l'Europe: Oevres complètes de Denis de Rougement*, vol. 1. Paris: Editions de la Différence, 1994.

Shoghi Effendi. *The Advent of Divine Justice*. Wilmette, IL: Bahá'í Publishing Trust, 1990.

— *God Passes By*. Wilmette, IL: Bahá'í Publishing Trust, rev. edn. 1974.

— *The Promised Day is Come*. Wilmette, IL: Bahá'í Publishing Trust, rev. edn. 1980.

— *The World Order of Bahá'u'lláh*. Wilmette, IL: Bahá'í Publishing Trust, 1991.

The Universal House of Justice. *The Promise of World Peace*. London: Bahá'í Publishing Trust, 1985. <http://www.bahai-library.org/published.uhj/world.peace.html>, last accessed July 2003.

— 'Responses of Napoleon III and Queen Victoria'. Memorandum of the Research Department, 6 November 1997. <http://www.bahai-library.org/uhj/napoleon.victoria.html>, last accessed November 1999.

— 'Tablets to the Kings'. Memorandum of the Research Department, 20 November 1989 (revised August 1995).

Notes

1. I would like to express my gratitude to Charles Lerche, Nancy Ackerman and Nasser Danesh for their constructive remarks and suggestions. Needless to say, all the shortcomings in this paper are solely my responsibility.
2. Claude, *Plowshares*, p. 247.
3. *Webster's Third New International Dictionary*, 'Collective Security'.
4. For example, Article 5 of the North Atlantic Treaty.
5. In such a system there is no room for traditional friendship. In case of attack, such a friendship becomes 'neutralized'. Claude, *Plowshares*, p. 250ff.
6. It is conceivable for a balance of power and a collective security system to coexist. The two forms do not mutually exclude one another.

7. Claude, *Plowshares*, p. 246.
8. ibid. p. 249ff.
9. For Claude, the principle of anonymity means that the identity of the aggressor is not predetermined and that the system is applied to all states equally. ibid. p. 255.
10. See Galtung, 'Violence'. It can be argued that the very mission of the UN implies elements of positive peace in its integration of the principles of human rights and development.
11. e.g. Spanish-American War 1898
12. *The Influence of Sea Power upon History* was published in 1890 and *The Influence of Sea Power upon the French Revolution and Empire* in 1892.
13. As in the Holy Alliance, later in the Dreikaiserbund.
14. France concluded the Cobden–Chevalier Treaty with Great Britain in 1860 and other commercial treaties with Belgium, Italy, Spain, Switzerland, the Netherlands, Austria and Portugal.
15. Ledermann, *Précurseurs*, p. 40.
16. The project was presented to Louis XI in Latin in 1463. The French title is *Traité d'alliance et confédération entre le Roy Louis XI, Georges roy de Bohème et la Seigneurie de Venise, pour résister au Turc.* See Rougement, *Ecrits*, vol. 1, p. 529.
17. Raumer, *Ewiger Friede*, p. 62.
18. Further projects were by Comenius (1645) and Goudet (1691).
19. *Le nouveau Cynée ou discours d'Estat représentant les occasions et moyens d'établir une paix générale et la liberté du commerce par tout le monde.*
20. Raumer, *Ewiger Friede*, p. 87.
21. Raumer claims that this criticism was supposed to have been voiced, for example, by Gabriel Naudé, librarian and publicist, a contemporary of Crucé. ibid. p. 88.
22. ibid.
23. France, Spain, Great Britain, Denmark, Sweden and Lombardy
24. The German Reich, the Papal State, Poland, Hungary and Bohemia
25. Venice, Italy, Switzerland and the Netherlands
26. Four representatives for the monarchies, except Hungary and Bohemia, and the Venetian Republic. Two ambassadors would represent other states. Ledermann, *Précurseurs*, p. 87.
27. The Eastern Church, however, would be excluded. Raumer, *Ewiger Friede*, p. 72.

28. Not surprising, considering his occupation as military advisor to Henri IV. Ledermann, *Précurseurs*, p. 87, and Raumer, *Ewiger Friede*, p. 76.
29. See Raumer, *Ewiger Friede*, pp. 326–7.
30. Hoffmann and Fidler, *Rousseau*, p. 67.
31. ibid. p. 68.
32. ibid. p. 70. See also Rousseau, 'Auszug aus dem Plan des Ewigen Friedens des Herrn Abbé de Saint-Pierre' (1756/1761), in Raumer, *Ewiger Friede*, pp. 354–5.
33. In an earlier edition of St Pierre's peace concept the Ottoman Empire, Iran and Ethiopia were present but were later removed. Cole, *Modernity*, pp. 120–1.
34. ibid. p. 121.
35. According to Ledermann, *Précurseurs*, p. 110. To Voltaire is also attributed the following unflattering poem, cited in Rougement, *Ecrits*, vol. 1, p. 427:
    Je vous l'avoue, je formais des souhaits,
    pour que ce beau métier ne s'exerçât jamais,
    Et qu'enfin l'équité fût régner sur la terre,
    l'impracticable paix de l'Abbé de Saint-Pierre.
36. Rousseau, 'Urteil über den ewigen Frieden' (1756/1782), in Raumer, *Ewiger Friede*, p. 369.
37. See Raumer, *Ewiger Friede*, p. 133ff.
38. In between we find more drafts by Bellers, Alberoni, Toze, and de la Harpe. Bellers, *Some Reasons for an European State* (1710); Cardinal Alberoni, *Progetto del Cardinal Alberoni per ridurre l'impero Turcheso all'obedienza dei Prinicipi Christiani e per dividere tra di essi la conquista del medesimo* (1735); Toze, *Die Allgemeine christliche Republik in Europa* (1752); de la Harpe, *Des malheurs de la guerre et des avantages de la paix* (1766). See Ledermann, *Précurseurs*.
39. Bentham, 'A Plan for an Universal and Perpetual Peace'. See also Raumer, *Ewiger Friede*, p. 384.
40. See Raumer, *Ewiger Friede*, pp. 404, 408, 414 and 415.
41. Bentham, 'A Plan for an Universal and Perpetual Peace'. See also ibid. p. 415.
42. Raumer, *Ewiger Friede*, pp. 403, 404.
43. The agreement consists of six preliminary and three definitive articles, two supplements and an appendix. Kant, *On Perpetual Peace*.
44. Kant, *On Perpetual Peace*.
45. ibid.

46. ibid.
47. The only conference on disarmament, held in 1923, ended without concrete results.
48. The disputes regarding Manchuria, Chaco, Leticia and between Russia and Finland were forwarded to the Assembly.
49. A moral sanction consisted of the expulsion of a member state from the League.
50. Article 21, for example, protected the Monroe Doctrine.
51. For example in the conflicts of the Aaland Islands and Leticia and in the Greco-Bulgarian War.
52. Mussolini was also able to continue the war because important products such as oil and coal were exempt from the sanctions.
53. Use of force here is understood as military force and not – as often demanded by developing countries – economic or psychological pressure. Article 2, (4), (3).
54. Article 106 accords the 'Big Five' special privileges in security policy unless Article 43 is implemented. Article 107 contains stipulations for the treatment of enemy states from World War Two, i.e. Germany and Japan. With the admission of both these countries into the UN, this article has become obsolete.
55. The right to self-defence exists when a state has been attacked and a decision by the Security Council is still outstanding.
56. See also Naidu, *Collective Security and the United Nations*, p. 96ff.
57. Veto questions were temporarily pushed into the background at the end of the cold war. For the problem of veto, see ibid.
58. The mere thought of a permanent UN military force was greeted with scepticism from the outset. Telling is the following statement by US President Franklin D. Roosevelt of 15 June 1944: 'We are not thinking of a superstate with its own police forces and other paraphernalia of coercive power. We are seeking effective agreement and arrangements through which the nations would maintain, according to their capacities, adequate forces to meet the needs of preventing war and of making impossible deliberate preparation for war and to have such forces available for joint action when necessary.' (Roosevelt, quoted in Claude, *Plowshares*, p. 69)
59. Articles 51, 106, 107
60. Article 47
61. Articles 39, 40
62. Article 41 and 42
63. 'Abdu'l-Bahá, *Paris Talks*, p. 77.

64. See Bahá'u'lláh, *Summons of the Lord of Hosts.*
65. Queen Victoria is reported to have said: 'If this is of God, it will endure; if not, it can do no harm.' (*Promised Day is Come*, p. 65) Shoghi Effendi, however, pointed out that there is no written source for this statement. From a letter written on behalf of Shoghi Effendi, 21 February 1942, cited in 'Responses of Napoleon III and Queen Victoria', memorandum by the Research Department of the Universal House of Justice, 6 November 1997.
66. For example, to Napoleon III, Pope Pius IX, Tsar Alexander II, Sulṭán 'Abdu'l-Azíz and Náṣiri'd-Dín Sháh.
67. See Shoghi Effendi, *God Passes By*, pp. 211ff.
68. Bahá'u'lláh, 'Letter to Queen Victoria', in *Summons of the Lord of Hosts*, para. 182.
69. Bahá'u'lláh, 'Lawḥ-i-Maqṣúd', in *Tablets*, p. 165.
70. Shoghi Effendi, *World Order*, p. 192.
71. ibid.
72. Bahá'u'lláh, 'Lawḥ-i-Maqṣúd', in *Tablets*, p. 165.
73. 'Abdu'l-Bahá, *Secret of Divine Civilization*, p. 64.
74. Shoghi Effendi, *World Order*, p. 40.
75. 'Such a peace demandeth that the Great Powers should resolve, for the sake of the tranquillity of the peoples of the earth, to be fully reconciled among themselves.' (Bahá'u'lláh, 'Lawḥ-i-Maqṣúd', in *Tablets*, p. 165) See also *Gleanings*, pp. 249–50.
76. Bahá'u'lláh, 'Bishárát', in *Tablets*, p. 21.
77. 'By a general agreement all the governments of the world must disarm simultaneously . . . It will not do if one lays down the arms and the other refuses to do so. The nations of the world must concur with each other . . . Now the question of disarmament must be put into practice by all the nations and not only by one or two.' ('Abdu'l-Bahá, in *Compilation*, vol. 2, no. 1604, p. 172)
78. See 'Abdu'l-Bahá, *Secret of Divine Civilization*, pp. 64–5; also quoted in Shoghi Effendi, *World Order*, p. 37. See also *'Abdu'l-Bahá in Canada*, pp. 50–1.
79. ibid.
80. Bahá'u'lláh, 'Lawḥ-i-Maqṣúd', in *Tablets*, p. 165. See also Bahá'í International Community, *Turning Point*, p. 11.
81. Bahá'u'lláh, 'Bishárát', in *Tablets*, p. 21.
82. The Universal House of Justice, *Promise of World Peace*, p. 15.

83. In Article 1, paragraph 1, the UN Charter mentions as one of the aims of the organization 'the suppression of acts of aggression'. In Article 39 it is specified that the Security Council 'shall determine the existence of any . . . act of aggression and shall make recommendations . . .' It is therefore up to the Security Council members as to what constitutes an act of aggression and what does not.
84. See 'Abdu'l-Bahá, *Secret of Divine Civilization*, p. 64.
85. Shoghi Effendi, *World Order*, p. 203.
86. Bahá'u'lláh, *Gleanings*, p. 95.
87. For example, Gobineau, *Essai sur l'inégalité des races* (1853–5) and Robert Knox, *The Races of Men* (1850).
88. See for example Karl Marx, *Zur Judenfrage* (1844). In France, Alphonse de Toussenel, *Les Juifs, rois de l'époque* (1845) and Edouard Drumont, *La France Juive* (1886). See Fenske, *Geschichte*, pp. 488ff.
89. See for example Bahá'u'lláh, *Gleanings*, pp. 259–60.
90. The Bourbon king returned to Spain, power was restored to the rulers of middle Europe and the Pope. Some German states and the Holy Roman Empire were not revived. Also, Saxony and Denmark had to accept territorial losses.
91. The 'pentarchy' of France, Great Britain, Russia, Austria and Prussia.
92. Bahá'u'lláh, *Gleanings*, p. 249.
93. Bahá'í International Community, *Turning Point*, p. 9.
94. 'Abdu'l-Bahá, in *Compilation*, vol. 2, no. 1604, p. 172.
95. 'Then, whether a government is constitutional or republican, hereditary monarchy or democratic, the rulers will devote their time to the prosperity of their nations, the legislation of just and sane laws and the fostering of closer and more amicable relations with their neighbours . . .' ('Abdu'l-Bahá, in ibid.)
96. 'The fundamental principle underlying this solemn Pact should be so fixed that if any government later violate any one of its provisions, all the governments on earth should arise to reduce it to utter submission, nay the human race as a whole should resolve, with every power at its disposal, to destroy that government.' ('Abdu'l-Bahá, *Secret of Divine Civilization*, p. 65)
97. Shoghi Effendi, *Promised Day is Come*, p. 122.
98. ibid. p. 57. He describes Bismarck as a statesman rightly to be regarded as 'one of the geniuses of his century . . . [a] sagacious statesman, the true founder of his empire, to whose

sagacity Bahá'u'lláh had paid tribute, and to the unwisdom of whose imperial and ungrateful master 'Abdu'l-Bahá had testified'. (ibid. pp. 57–8)

99. A world government is regarded as a long-term goal. From the current UN system to this long-term objective several intermediate stages are envisaged. See Bahá'í International Community, *Turning Point*.

100. 'Outstanding irredentist claims continue to be a major source of conflict and war, highlighting the critical need for general agreements on national boundaries. Such treaties can only be arrived at after consideration of the arbitrary manner in which many nation-states were originally defined and of all outstanding claims of nations and ethnic groups. Rather than relegating such claims to the World Court, we believe it would be best to establish a special International Commission to research all claims affecting international boundaries and then, after careful consideration, to make recommendations for action. The results would serve as an early warning system for growing tension among civil or ethnic groups and assessment of threats in situations benefiting from early preventive diplomacy.' (Bahá'í International Community, *Turning Point*, p. 9)

'If any discrimination is at all to be tolerated, it should be a discrimination not against, but rather in favour of the minority, be it racial or otherwise. Unlike the nations and peoples of the earth, be they of the East or of the West, democratic or authoritarian, communist or capitalist, whether belonging to the Old World or the New, who either ignore, trample upon, or extirpate, the racial, religious, or political minorities within the sphere of their jurisdiction, every organized community enlisted under the banner of Bahá'u'lláh should feel it to be its first and inescapable obligation to nurture, encourage, and safeguard every minority belonging to any faith, race, class, or nation within it. So great and vital is this principle that in such circumstances, as when an equal number of ballots have been cast in an election, or where the qualifications for any office are balanced as between the various races, faiths or nationalities within the community, priority should unhesitatingly be accorded the party representing the minority, and this for no other reason except to stimulate and encourage it, and afford it an opportunity to further the interests of the community.'

(Shoghi Effendi, *Advent of Divine Justice*, p. 35) See also Bahá'í International Community, *Rights of Minorities*)

101. Shoghi Effendi, *World Order*, pp. 191–2.
102. ibid. p. 191. 'For the first time in the history of humanity the system of collective security, foreshadowed by Bahá'u'lláh and explained by 'Abdu'l-Bahá, has been seriously envisaged, discussed and tested. For the first time in history it has been officially recognized and publicly stated that for this system of collective security to be effectively established strength and elasticity are both essential – strength involving the use of an adequate force to ensure the efficacy of the proposed system, and elasticity to enable the machinery that has been devised to meet the legitimate needs and aspirations of its aggrieved upholders. For the first time in human history tentative efforts have been exerted by the nations of the world to assume collective responsibility, and to supplement their verbal pledges by actual preparation for collective action. And again, for the first time in history, a movement of public opinion has manifested itself in support of the verdict which the leaders and representatives of nations have pronounced, and for securing collective action in pursuance of such a decision.' (Shoghi Effendi, *World Order*, pp. 191–2)
103. Claude, *Plowshares*, p. 256.
104. See for example Fischer, *Nonmilitary Aspects*.
105. 'Although originally conceived within the context of a threat of military aggression, the principle of collective security, some argue, may now be applied in an expansive manner to all threats which, although apparently local in nature, are actually the result of the complex breakdown of the present-day global order. These threats include but are not limited to international drug trafficking, food security, and the emergence of new global pandemics.' (Bahá'í International Community, *Turning Point*, p. 11)

8

Conflict and Harmony Among Nations: The Case of International Trade

Shahruz Mohtadi

The 20th century witnessed an increasing internationalization of economic activity and interdependence. Over the last 50 years, world trade has grown much faster than world output and income. As a result, trade has become a larger share of most national economies. Economists applaud the process of internationalization because it integrates economies, promotes competition and yields a more efficient allocation of resources on an international scale. Despite, and in some cases because of the internationalization of economic transactions, we have frequently encountered international economic conflicts. These conflicts arise because 1) each nation strives to acquire a larger share of the gains from trade, 2) each nation tries to protect its domestic industries from foreign competition and 3) each nation wants to maintain its domestic autonomy in policy-making. National policy-makers, business leaders and commentators talk about trade wars rather than military wars.[1] In many cases nations blame their domestic economic problems on the trade policies of other nations. Many people view the world economy as an arena where nations compete for a given amount of goods and services and the goal of every nation is to capture a larger share of the market for them. Nations are then viewed as competing in a game where there are losers and winners.[2]

This essay looks at the application of some of the principles and teachings of the Bahá'í Faith to the resolution of trade conflicts. The essay focuses on and examines the effects of international trade on the welfare of nations. Why do nations engage in trade and what are the reasons that lead to trade conflicts? How have we dealt with these trade conflicts? What principles, rules and standards can be invoked to control the behaviour of nations in the world economy? Can a new trade regime be created that will accommodate conflicts, make better policy choices and control change?

Historical Development of Trade Theory and Policy

During the 17th and 18th centuries the doctrine of mercantilism represented the dominant attitude towards international trade. This was a period of nation-building and the consolidation of power by the newly-formed nations. A central belief of mercantilism was that power and wealth were closely interrelated and legitimate goals of governments. Wealth was necessary for power, and power could be used to obtain wealth.

In this period, gold and silver circulated as money and the quantity of these precious metals held by any nation symbolized that nation's wealth. Given this view of national wealth, exports were viewed as good and imports were seen as bad. If a nation imported more than it exported, then it had to ship gold and silver to foreigners. On the other hand, if a nation exported more than it imported, it would receive gold and silver that not only increased the nation's wealth but could also be used to maintain a large military for the nation. Given that the stock of the world's gold and silver was limited, mercantilist nations viewed themselves as locked into a zero-sum conflict in the international economy.[3] One country's gains came at the expense of other countries, since a trade surplus for one country must be a trade deficit for some other country. Based on this mercantilist thinking, governments imposed taxes and limits on imports and subsidized and encouraged exports.

In late 18th century the doctrine of mercantilism came under attack by some leading political economists. In 1752 David Hume pointed out that it is not the quantity of gold and silver a country holds that matters; rather it is the quantity of goods and services that the gold and silver can buy. People's welfare increases when they consume goods and services and not when they accumulate precious metals. The mercantilists wanted to export as many goods and import as few as possible. This implied that other countries would accumulate all the world's output of goods while the mercantilist nation accumulated all the gold.[4]

The mercantilists were also attacked for their static view of the world economy. To the mercantilists, the world's economic output was of a fixed size. This meant that one nation's gain from trade came at the expense of its trading partners; not all nations could simultaneously enjoy the benefits of international trade. Another economist, Adam Smith, writing in 1776, argued that the world's output is not a fixed quantity. He argued that international trade allows nations to take advantage of specialization and the division of labour, which increase the general level of productivity within a nation and thus increase world output. Smith's dynamic view of trade suggested that both trading partners could simultaneously enjoy higher levels of production and consumption with free trade. Smith's trading principle was the principle of absolute advantage. A nation should specialize in and export those products which it could produce at the lowest cost and import those products which another country could produce at the lowest cost. The resulting increase in the output of both products measures the gains from specialization in production available to be divided between the nations. Adam Smith thus demonstrated that trade is a positive-sum activity rather than a zero-sum one.[5]

But what if a nation is more efficient than its trading partner in the production of all goods? Will the nation benefit by trading with other nations? In 1817 David Ricardo developed the principle of comparative advantage to show that mutually beneficial trade can occur even when one nation is absolutely more efficient in the production of all goods. According to the principle of comparative advantage, even if one nation is less efficient than another in the production of both products, there is still a basis for mutually beneficial trade. The nation should specialize in the production of and export the product in which its absolute disadvantage is smaller, that is the product of its comparative advantage, and import the product in which its absolute disadvantage is greater, that is the commodity of its comparative disadvantage. Trade based on the principle of comparative advantage allows a nation to consume beyond its ability to produce and reach a higher level of national welfare. Furthermore, the whole world gains from trade and each nation is at least as well off with free trade as with no trade.[6]

At the close of the 18th century, world events and the effect of these economists' works moved trade policy away from mercantilism and towards trade liberalization. Throughout much of the second half of the 19th century many countries adopted free trade policies and negotiated bilateral trade agreements. As a result of these agreements, the world economy became much more integrated, with global trade expanding much faster than global output. However, during the late 1800s, trade restrictions were erected in both Britain and the United States. Germany and France were growing and industrializing rapidly, eroding Britain's technological advantage from the Industrial Revolution. During the first decade of the 20th century, the negative effects of these policies on world growth and trade were gaining recognition. Policy-makers laid plans for trade liberalization, but the First World War intervened before any serious liberalization could take place.

After the First World War, industrial countries suffered from persistent unemployment, unstable financial markets and currencies, and new countries erected trade barriers to protect their industries and agriculture. To a large extent this reflected US trade policies, which were traditionally rather protectionist. The US was unwilling to participate in efforts during the 1920s to liberalize and re-establish a more open global economy following the disruption that occurred during the war. As the US economy moved from recession into depression following the 1929 stock market crash, the US Congress adopted the infamous Smoot-Hawley Tariff Act, leading to a rise in average US tariffs from 38 to 52 per cent. This led US trading partners to impose retaliatory trade restrictions. Countries attempted to 'export' their unemployment problems by blocking imports. A domino effect occurred as trade flows were diverted to relatively unprotected markets, forcing down prices, leading to protectionist pressure and thus inducing higher trade barriers.

The negative consequences of the trade policies of the early 1930s inspired the US willingness to pursue the type of international cooperation on trade that it had rejected in the 1920s and to actively support multilateral liberalization efforts. The fear of a repeat also considerably hampered protectionist forces in the post-Second World War period. In 1947 many countries signed the General Agreement on Tariffs and Trade (GATT). This agreement established an international organization in Geneva to assist trade negotiations and work to reduce restrictions on trade. The GATT became the forum for consultation and for negotiations to extend multilateral liberalization and cooperation on trade and related policies.

Since its establishment the GATT has been guided by two principles: reciprocity and non-discrimination. Reciprocity means if a nation gives up something, it gets something in return. Non-discrimination means that trade concessions granted one member are automatically extended to all other members under the most-favoured-nation (MFN) clause. Based on these principles, GATT members have successfully reduced tariffs and other barriers to trade through several rounds of trade negotiations.

In 1995 GATT was replaced with the World Trade Organization (WTO). The Preamble of the agreement establishing the WTO states that member nations should conduct their trade and economic relations with a view to raising the standard of living and expanding the production of and trade in goods and services. This was to be achieved while allowing for the optimal use of the world's resources in accordance with the objective of sustainable development and the preservation and protection of the environment. The basic underlying principle of the WTO is that open markets, non-discrimination and global competition in international trade are conducive to the national welfare of all countries. The essential functions of the WTO are: 1) administering and implementing the multilateral trade agreement, 2) acting as a forum for multilateral trade negotiations, 3) seeking to resolve trade disputes, 4) overseeing national trade policies and 5) cooperating with other international institutions involved in global economic policy-making.[7]

An Analysis of Trade Conflicts

Let us now turn to an analysis of these historical periods of conflict and cooperation in international trade. Conflict arises in international trade when countries perceive that the gains from trade are unevenly distributed between countries or some countries gain at the expense of others. During the mercantilist period, the perception was that if you exported more than you imported this would lead to an accumulation of gold and wealth. As gold and silver lost their importance as a source of wealth, national economic welfare and jobs became the major issues in international trade. Exports lead to economic growth and create jobs, while imports replace domestic production and destroy domestic jobs. Since every country wants to provide more jobs for its people, everyone tries to increase their exports as much as possible, while at the same time limiting imports, which of course costs jobs. The problem, however, is that since one country's exports are another's imports, it is clearly not possible for everyone to have an export surplus but, nonetheless, everyone tries. This is why international trade is often called a 'beggar-thy-neighbour' game whose object is to make yourself better off at your neighbour's expense. Tariffs and quotas have been the major instruments of protectionist policies designed to limit imports while subsidies are the major instrument designed to promote exports.[8]

Trade protectionism can be viewed and analysed with the help of game theory and game-theoretical concepts.[9] The theory of games is the branch of mathematics that analyses situations where actions by decision-makers (players) are interdependent. Outcomes or payoffs depend on how the game is played, that is, the rules of the game, the information available to the players, the strategies available to each player and the way the players form expectations about the actions of the other players. There are two basic games, cooperative and non-cooperative. The first type assumes that the gains from trade are maximized and what is at issue is the distribution of the possible gains across players. Cooperative games also assume that a binding enforcement mechanism exists and that other players can observe defection by players from the cooperative solution. Non-cooperative games emerge in settings where there is no central enforcement mechanism and where there is no presumption that outcomes will be such that no party can be made better off without another party being made worse off.[10] This can be illustrated by a simple example.[11]

Assuming we can use numbers to represent the net trading benefits (i.e. payoffs) perceived by mercantilistically-minded political leaders, suppose two nations, A and B, each gain 10 if they both follow a free trade policy. However, if nation A erects trade barriers (protection) while B opens its markets (free trade), nation A gains 20, while nation B loses 10. If nation A maintains open markets while nation B erects barriers, then nation A loses 10 and nation B gains 20. If both nations erect trade barriers, both lose 5. Nation A asks what its best payoff will be if B maintains open markets. The answer is the erection of trade barriers (that is, with a payoff of 20, compared to 10 if A also maintains open markets). If B erects trade barriers, the preferred policy for A is also to erect barriers. Thus, whichever strategy choice B makes, the erection of barriers yields the higher payoff to A.[12] If nation B reasons in the same manner, it too will erect trade barriers. The dominant strategy for each nation is to protect, since this yields each nation the highest gain no matter what strategy the other nation follows. The game will attain a 'non-cooperative solution', with each nation erecting trade barriers where each loses 5.[13] In their self-interest, both nations pursue a protectionist trade policy, although it would be in their collective interest to follow free trade. Each nation, in trying to pursue its own self-interest, ends up with a lower payoff.[14] The belief that they were involved in this sort of game may account for the protectionist policies adopted by many industrial countries in the early 1930s, when the possibility of increasing employment through unilateral protection was especially appealing. Most nations enacted high tariffs and restrictive quotas on imports. In turn, nations that lost their foreign markets retaliated and imposed their own tariffs and quotas. In the end, no one benefited and international trade collapsed.

One way to resolve this dilemma is for the nations to establish an agreement to refrain from protection. Each nation will be better off if it limits its own freedom of action, provided the other nation limits its freedom of action as well. The various GATT rounds of trade negotiations have been an exercise in solving this dilemma through reductions in trade barriers and more open markets. It is a fact that after every round of trade negotiations in which certain barriers to trade were reduced or eliminated, world output and welfare has increased.[15]

Suppose nations made a prior agreement not to protect. In this case, nation A thinks that it can count on nation B to cooperate. Now if nation A breaks the agreement, it will gain 20 and nation B will lose 10. Of course, a symmetrically identical way of reasoning will also induce nation B to break its agreement. If both think they can get away with cheating, self-interest will make them both cheat (that is, protect) and both lose 5. Trustworthiness thus becomes an essential prerequisite for both nations to gain.

One instrument that can ensure compliance with the agreement and prevent cheating is the establishment of an enforcement mechanism. Under the present system, WTO members have an obligation under international law to comply with the WTO rules but the WTO itself has no means to force countries to honour those obligations. For example, countries do not have recourse to the International Court of Justice for disputes, nor is there a provision to expel members for bad behaviour. Unlike other international bodies, WTO members explicitly did not establish supranational bodies with power to change laws or extract fines or other penalties from member countries.[16] The WTO has two bodies: the Trade Policy Review Board is responsible for making sure that the trade policies of member nations are in accordance with the multilateral trade agreements and the Dispute Settlement Body is responsible for settling trade disputes among the member nations. If two nations are unable to settle their dispute between themselves, they can bring the matter to the Dispute Settlement Body. The Dispute Settlement Body has the authority to establish a panel that prepares a report and makes recommendations. Compensation and retaliation are the two options available to impose costs on the nation that is found in violation of a WTO agreement and is unwilling to implement the panel's findings.[17]

The Effect of Trade on the Distribution of Income

One of the misconceptions about international trade policy is that policy choices pit the interests of one country against those of another. In fact, trade policy primarily affects the distribution of income *within* each country. When governments meet in the international arena, their actions reflect the political situation at home. In each country international trade is almost sure to divide the society into gainers and losers from trade. These groups will then rely on their governments to enact trade policies that are advantageous to them. In order to understand trade policy, we must look at the effect of trade on the domestic distribution of income.

Trade theory asserts that countries should export products that use their abundant factors of production, such as labour or capital, intensively and import products that use their scarce factors of production intensively. Thus if a nation has an abundant supply of labour, it should specialize in the production of goods that use labour intensively and export those goods. This is because labour is relatively cheaper and the country can produce those labour-intensive products at a relatively lower cost than other countries. In other words, the country has a comparative advantage in labour-intensive products. Similarly, a country should import products in which it has a comparative disadvantage.[18]

As trade begins there will be an expansion in industries in which the nation has a comparative advantage and a contraction in the industries in which it has a comparative disadvantage. Workers in the expanding industries will realize an increase in their incomes, while workers working in the contracting industries will see a decrease. Thus if you are a worker in a labour-abundant country, you gain from trade by receiving a higher income. If you are a worker in a labour scarce country, you lose from trade by receiving a lower income.[19] This implies that opening trade leads to changes in the distribution of income, creating incentives for workers in a labour-abundant country to support free trade and for workers in a labour scarce country to resist moves towards free trade.[20]

A corollary of these effects on different groups' incomes is that trade can reduce international differences in how well a worker is paid. Labour tends to lose its high income in countries where it was scarce before trade and tends to gain in countries where it was abundant before trade.[21] In other words, trade will lower the incomes of workers in the high wage countries and raise the incomes of workers in the low wage countries. Thus while trade increases the welfare of the nation as a whole, there will be some who gain from trade and others who will lose. This is why workers in high wage nations generally oppose free trade and lobby their governments for protection.

Another factor that can explain why national governments enact protectionist policies is the distribution of the costs and benefits of free trade. The costs of international trade tend to be concentrated on a relatively small number of producers and their workers who are affected by import competition. The benefits of international trade, on the other hand, come primarily as lower prices for consumers and are spread over a large group, with each individual capturing a small portion of the benefits.

Special-interest groups that represent producers and their well-organized labour unions that stand to lose with free trade therefore dominate trade protection policy. Consumers generally are not organized and their losses are widely dispersed. Thus the affected industries will lobby government officials through campaigning and contributions to vote for protection, while consumers will not find it worthwhile to do so. Politicians wishing to remain in office will adopt protectionist policies. The end result is while some groups may benefit from these policies, the nation as a whole will see a loss in overall welfare.[22]

Thus it is the pursuit of self-interest by the producers, labour unions and elected officials that dominates trade policies. Economic self-interest almost always prevails over a person's concern for the welfare of other groups or the nation as a whole, when a significant part of an individual's income is affected by trade policy. Similarly, nations are interested in how trade agreements will affect their own national welfare rather than the welfare of other nations or the world as a whole. Governments still act as downright protectionists on some occasions and as mercantilists almost as a matter of course. A prominent economist has referred to our present system as 'enlightened mercantilism'. It is mercantilist in that it presumes that each country, acting on its own, would like to subsidize exports and discourage imports. But it is enlightened in that it recognizes that it is destructive if everyone does this.[23]

Bahá'í Principles Related to Trade

The Bahá'í teachings are a source of fundamental spiritual principles relevant to creative processes of social change and there are a number of references in the Bahá'í literature that are directly relevant to the theme of this essay. 'Abdu'l-Bahá stated, for instance, that

> . . . it is apparent that whenever the ties between nations become strengthened and the *exchange of commodities accelerated*, and any economic principle established in one country, it will ultimately affect the other countries and universal benefits will result.[24]

He further stated that the expansion of trade, which increases the people's wealth, is one of the 'vital agencies which would constitute an immediate remedy for society's chronic ills'.[25] Shoghi Effendi, in describing world conditions in 1931, wrote:

> That a narrow and brutal nationalism, which the post-war theory of self-determination has served to reinforce, has been chiefly responsible for the policy of high and prohibitive tariffs, so injurious to the healthy flow of international trade and to the

> mechanism of international finance, is a fact which few would venture to dispute.[26]

In the previous sections we have seen that the underlying cause of trade conflicts was the perception of trade as a zero-sum game. Clearly this erroneous perception needs to be changed if we want to promote an open trading regime. The most fundamental change in attitudes amongst the peoples of the world must be the concept of world citizenship. Bahá'u'lláh wrote:

> It is not for him to pride himself who loveth his own country, but rather for him who loveth the whole world. The earth is but one country, and mankind its citizens.[27]

According to the Universal House of Justice, the international executive body of the Bahá'í Faith:

> Acceptance of the oneness of mankind is the first fundamental prerequisite for reorganization and administration of the world as one country, the home of humankind.[28]

> Unbridled nationalism, as distinguished from a sane and legitimate patriotism, must give way to a wider loyalty, to the love of humanity as a whole . . . The concept of world citizenship is a direct result of the contraction of the world into a single neighbourhood through scientific advances and of the indisputable interdependence of nations. Love of all the world's peoples does not exclude love of one's country. *The advantage of the part in a world society is best served by promoting the advantage of the whole.*[29]

Elaborating on this theme, in one of its statements the Bahá'í International Community's Office of Public Information stressed that:

> Only through the dawning consciousness that they constitute a single people will the inhabitants of the planet be enabled to turn away from the patterns of conflict that have dominated social

> organization in the past and begin to learn the ways of collaboration and conciliation.[30]

As previously demonstrated, one way to resolve the trade dilemma is for the nations to cooperate and refrain from protection. In negotiating trade agreements, nations should consider the welfare of all nations rather than individual national welfare. Bahá'u'lláh, in a letter to the leaders of countries with elected representative governments, stated:

> Take ye counsel together, and let your concern be only for that which profiteth mankind, and bettereth the condition thereof, if ye be of them that scan heedfully. Regard the whole world as the human body which, though at its creation whole and perfect, hath been afflicted, through various causes, with grave disorders and maladies.[31]

Reciprocity is a fundamental spiritual principle that has been promoted by all the religions of the world.[32] 'Abdu'l-Bahá has stated that 'All economic problems may be solved by the application of the *Science* of the Love of God'.[33] Howard Colby Ives comments:

> That is to say: if the Rule called golden . . . were actually applied to the world's economic problems, which if not solved bid fair to destroy us, and the love of God, the sort of love which makes a home life happy, were used as a *scientific* measurement to regulate our international and national affairs; to settle all relations between labour and capital, between rich and poor; to regulate all coinage and commerce, can there be any doubt that the results would be far more conducive to human welfare than our present policies have produced?[34]

Bahá'u'lláh states the Golden Rule as:

> O Son of Being! Ascribe not to any soul that which thou wouldst not have ascribed to thee, and say not that which thou doest not. This is My command unto thee, do thou observe it.[35]

To apply this rule to trade means that a nation should treat other nations as it would want other nations to treat it. Thus if a nation desires to export its products without any barriers, then it should not erect any import barriers. Following the Golden Rule would then place us in the upper left cell of the trade war matrix with a higher payoff for both countries. Expanding this rule on a non-discriminatory basis, that is to all nations, will result in even larger welfare gains for each nation and the world as a whole.

An agreement is worthwhile if the parties trust each other that the terms of the agreement will be honoured. Bahá'u'lláh states:

> The fourth Ṭaráz concerneth trustworthiness. Verily it is the door of security for all that dwell on earth and a token of glory on the part of the All-Merciful. He who partaketh thereof hath indeed partaken of the treasures of wealth and prosperity. Trustworthiness is the greatest portal leading unto the tranquillity and security of the people. In truth the stability of every affair hath depended and doth depend on it. All the domains of power, of grandeur and of wealth are illumined by its light.[36]

With regard to commerce in general, Bahá'u'lláh states: 'Commerce is as a heaven, whose sun is trustworthiness and whose moon is truthfulness.'[37]

The process by which any decision is made or any agreement reached within the Bahá'í Faith is what Bahá'u'lláh refers to as consultation.

> . . . this process . . . is far beyond the patterns of negotiation and compromise that tend to characterize the present-day discussion of human affairs . . . Debate, propaganda, the adversarial method, the entire apparatus of partisanship that have long been such familiar features of collective action are all fundamentally harmful to its purpose; that is, arriving at a consensus about the truth of a given situation and the wisest choice of action among the options open at any given moment.[38]

In the Bahá'í process of consultation, individual parties try to rise above their personal self-interest in order to function as members of a body with its own interests and goals. More importantly, once a decision has been reached, all parties must abide by it.

To ensure compliance with the terms of the agreement, a supranational institution, similar to the WTO, must be created. Another function of this institution would be to settle trade disputes. A key feature of this new trade agreement should be that if a trade dispute occurs between two member nations and a nation is found in violation of the agreement, all other nations should ensure that the offender is subject to really credible sanctions as determined by the institution. This will reduce the probability of cheating by the member nations and prevent nations from following competitive 'beggar-thy-neighbour' policies.[39]

In summary, the Bahá'í teachings on world order provide spiritual as well as practical approaches to the resolution of trade conflicts and the promotion of trade among nations. The spiritual principles of unity, love, reciprocity, trust and cooperation are the *sine qua non* of any decision to establish a new international trade regime that will accommodate conflicts and promote harmony among all nations.

Conclusion

As we begin the new millennium, we have a very different pattern of international trade. A growing percentage of world trade is now in trade in services such as telecommunications, banking, insurance and transportation. Furthermore, a substantial percentage of trade in goods now occurs between foreign affiliates of the same companies. There are very few products that are exclusively made in a particular country. Many workers are employed in domestic industries owned by foreign companies. In the future, there will be fewer national products or technologies, fewer national companies, fewer national industries, and in some cases, fewer national economies.[40] We are moving towards a truly global economy and a 'borderless' world, yet our current political system is still based on nation states. But nations can no longer afford to pursue independent trade policies without taking into consideration their effects on the welfare of other nations. The welfare of their own people depends on the welfare of other nations. Trade must be viewed as a win-win game where the prosperity of others enhances one's own prosperity.

The vision is a world commonwealth as described by Shoghi Effendi, 'in which all nations, races, creeds and classes are closely and permanently united'.[41] Within this commonwealth, 'the economic resources of the world will be organized, its sources of raw materials will be tapped and fully utilized, its markets will be coordinated and developed, and the distribution of its products will be equitably regulated'.[42] And specifically, 'economic barriers and restrictions will be completely abolished'.[43]

Bibliography

'Abdu'l-Bahá. *The Secret of Divine Civilization.* Wilmette, IL: Bahá'í Publishing Trust, 1990.

— *Selections from the Writings of 'Abdu'l-Bahá.* Haifa: Bahá'í World Centre, 1978.

Bahá'í International Community. *The Prosperity of Humankind.* London: Bahá'í Publishing Trust, 1995.

Bahá'u'lláh. *Gleanings from the Writings of Bahá'u'lláh.* Wilmette, IL: Bahá'í Publishing Trust, 1983.

— *The Hidden Words.* Wilmette, IL: Bahá'í Publishing Trust, 1990.

— *Tablets of Bahá'u'lláh.* Wilmette, IL: Bahá'í Publishing Trust, 1988.

The Compilation of Compilations. Prepared by the Universal House of Justice 1963–1990. 2 vols. [Sydney]: Bahá'í Publications Australia, 1991.

The Economist. 'The beef over bananas'. 6 March 1999.

Fieleke, Norman S. 'The Uruguay Round of Trade Negotiations: An Overview'. *New England Economic Review,* Federal Reserve Bank of Boston, May–June 1995.

Hoekman, Bernard and Michel Kostecki. *The Political Economy of the World Trading System: From GATT to WTO.* Oxford: Oxford University Press, 1995.

Ives, Howard Colby. *Portals to Freedom.* London: George Ronald, 1967.

Krugman, Paul. 'The Illusion of Conflict in International Trade'.

Peace Economics, Peace Science, and Public Policy, vol. 2, no. 2, Winter 1995.

— 'The Move Toward Free Trade Zones', in *Policy Implications of Trade and Currency Zones: A Symposium*. Jackson Hole: Federal Reserve Bank of Kansas City, 1991.

— and Maurice Obstfeld. *International Economics*. New York: Addison Wesley, 1997.

Lindert, Peter H. and Thomas A. Pugel. *International Economics*. Boston: Irwin, 1996.

Mankiw, N. Gregory. *Principles of Economics*. New York: The Dryden Press, 1998.

Neumann, John von and Oscar Morgenstern. *The Theory of Games and Economic Behavior*. Princeton, NJ: Princeton University Press, 1944.

Rost, H. T. D. *The Golden Rule: A Universal Ethic*. Oxford: George Ronald, 1986.

Schott, Jeffrey, assisted by Johanna W. Burman. *The Uruguay Round: An Assessment*. Washington DC: Institute for International Economics, 1994.

— (ed.). *The World Trading System: Challenges Ahead*. Washington DC: Institute for International Economics, 1996.

Shoghi Effendi. *The World Order of Bahá'u'lláh*. Wilmette, IL: Bahá'í Publishing Trust, 1991.

The Universal House of Justice. *The Promise of World Peace*. London: Bahá'í Publishing Trust, 1985.

Yarbrough, Beth V. and Robert M. Yarbrough. *The World Economy, Trade and Finance*. New York: The Dryden Press, 1997.

Notes

1. It is interesting to note the titles of some of the popular books on this topic: *Head to Head: The Coming Battle Among America, Japan, and Europe* by Lester Thurow; *A Cold Peace: America, Japan, Germany and the Struggle for Supremacy* by Jeffrey Garten; *The Silent War* by Ira Magaziner and Mark Patinkin. See Krugman, 'The Illusion of Conflict in International Trade' and see 'The beef

over bananas', *The Economist*, 6 March 1999, p. 65.

2. Krugman, 'The Illusion of Conflict in International Trade', p. 9.
3. Yarbrough and Yarbrough, *World Economy, Trade and Finance*, p. 33.
4. Lindert and Pugel, *International Economics*, p. 29. Furthermore, Hume argued that, in the long run, an export surplus would result in a rise in the country's price level relative to its trading partners. This would in turn reduce the competitiveness of the nation and result in the elimination of the trade surplus. Thus, it is not possible for a nation to continue to maintain a positive balance of trade indefinitely.
5. For a brief review of Adam Smith's theory of absolute advantage, see Lindert and Pugel, *International Economics*, pp. 28–33.
6. For a brief review of David Ricardo's theory of comparative advantage, see ibid. pp. 33–6.
7. For a comprehensive description of GATT and WTO, see Hoekman and Kostecki, *Political Economy of the World Trading System*, pp. 10–33.
8. A tariff is a tax placed on an imported product while a quota limits the quantity of a selected foreign product that can be imported. Both have the effect of increasing the price of the imported product and the price of domestic products faced with import competition. This results in a decrease in quantity imported, an increase in domestic production, an increase in domestic employment in the protected industry and an increase in the profits of the domestic producers.
9. von Neumann and Morgenstern, *Theory of Games and Economic Behavior*.
10. Hoeckman and Kostecki, *Political Economy of the World Trading System*, p. 57.
11. This is adapted from Krugman and Obstfeld, *International Economics*, p. 236.
12. In the language of game theory, erecting trade barriers is a 'dominant strategy'.
13. This is an example of the Prisoner's Dilemma game in the game theory literature.
14. The conclusion that non-cooperation is a dominant strategy depends on the assumption that the game is only played once or at most a small number of times. If the game is played repeatedly by the same players it is generally agreed that

players will cooperate. The reason is that non-cooperation in the long run is unrewarding since the short-run gains thereby obtained will normally be outweighed by the mutual loss that will result over the long run. For cooperation to take place, of course, future rewards must be valued; if, on the contrary, the nations do not emphasize the long run, they may prefer to protect to obtain better results in the present. Thus if nation A, by using protectionist measures, is able to reduce the imports from nation B, it will lead to a reduction in the income of nation B. This will lead to a reduction in nation B's imports from nation A, that is a reduction in nation A's exports. The reduction in nation A's exports will, in turn, lead to decline in nation A's income. Therefore, while nation A may gain in the short run, it will lead to a long-run loss. If nation B pursues the same policy, then both countries will lose in the long run. There is another strategy called tit-for-tat. According to this strategy, a nation should start cooperating and then do whatever the other nation did the last time. Here, a nation cooperates until the other nation defects; the nation then defects until the other nation cooperates again. This strategy is essentially the biblical strategy of 'an eye for an eye, a tooth for a tooth'. See Mankiw, *Principles of Economics*, p. 353.

15. Several studies estimate that owing to the recent round of trade negotiations known as the Uruguay Round, world output will rise $230 billion to $275 billion per year by the turn of the century. See Schott and Burman, *Uruguay Round* and Fieleke, 'The Uruguay Round of Trade Negotiations'.
16. Schott, *World Trading System*, p. 6.
17. Hoekman and Kostecki, *Political Economy of the World Trading System*, p. 47. Since its inception, the WTO has dealt with 163 disputes. America has brought the most cases, followed by the European Union. America and the European Union are also the most common defendants. Developing countries have used the system too, both against each other and against developed countries. To date, no government has yet defied any rulings of the WTO. Thus the United States amended gas standards when the WTO judged that they discriminated against Venezuelan products. The United States also obeyed the WTO by lifting restrictions on Costa Rican underwear. And Japan is reforming its discriminatory alcohol taxes after losing a case brought by the United States, the European Union and Canada. See *The*

Economist, 6 March 1999, p. 65.

18. This is based on the Heckscher-Ohlin theory of trade. See Lindert and Pugel, *International Economics*, pp. 57–64.
19. ibid. p. 60.
20. These results assume that labour can move across industries within the country but cannot move between countries. In the short run, however, the mobility of workers may be imperfect. For example, individuals learn skills suited for use in specific occupations. A given individual can learn new skills but the process takes time. In time, those workers that were displaced because of trade can move to the expanding industries provided they can transfer their skills to those industries. If they are unable to do so, then they have to be trained in the skills demanded by those industries, which involves costs and time. This implies that the incomes of the workers employed specifically in the comparative advantage industry rise and the incomes of the workers employed in the comparative disadvantage industry fall.
21. If labour were allowed to move freely between countries, it would flow from countries with low wages to those with high wages, thereby raising wages in the low wage countries and lowering them in the high wage countries. But in today's world, labour in many cases is not allowed to move between countries. However, under certain conditions, free trade will tend to equalize wages in all countries, even if labour is not free to move between them. When trade begins, a country increases its output of the good in which it has a comparative advantage. Since production of this good involves intensive use of its abundant factor, trade raises the price of the abundant factor and lowers the price of the scarce factor. Thus even when factors are immobile between two countries, free trade in goods tends to equalize the relative price of each factor across all countries. For example, when a labour-abundant country exports its labour-intensive good, it indirectly exports labour to a labour scarce country. Similarly, when a labour-abundant country imports a capital-intensive good, it indirectly imports capital from a capital-abundant country. In other words, trade in final goods serves as a substitute for trade in factors of production.
22. Yarbrough and Yarbrough, *World Economy*, p. 329.
23. Krugman, 'The Move Toward Free Trade Zones', p. 25.
24. 'Abdu'l-Bahá, *Selections*, p. 301. Emphasis added.

25. 'Abdu'l-Bahá, *Secret of Divine Civilization*, p. 39.
26. Shoghi Effendi, *World Order*, p. 35.
27. Bahá'u'lláh, *Tablets*, p. 167.
28. The Universal House of Justice, *Promise of World Peace*, para. 40.
29. ibid. para. 31. Emphasis added.
30. Bahá'í International Community, *Prosperity of Humankind*, p. 8.
31. Bahá'u'lláh, *Gleanings*, pp. 254–5.
32. The Golden Rule as expressed in various religions is described in Rost, *Golden Rule*.
33. Ives, *Portals to Freedom*, p. 156. Emphasis in the original.
34. ibid. Emphasis in the original.
35. Bahá'u'lláh, *Hidden Words*, Arabic no. 29.
36. Bahá'u'lláh, *Tablets*, p. 37.
37. Bahá'u'lláh, in *Compilation*, p. 335, no. 2046.
38. Bahá'í International Community, *Prosperity of Humankind*, p. 15.
39. This agreement is modelled after Bahá'u'lláh's system of collective security as a means of preventing wars. Bahá'u'lláh stated, 'The Great Being, wishing to reveal the prerequisites of the peace and tranquillity of the world and the advancement of its peoples, hath written: The time must come when the imperative necessity for the holding of a vast, an all-embracing assemblage of men will be universally realized. The rulers and kings of the earth must needs attend it, and, participating in its deliberations, must consider such ways and means as will lay the foundations of the world's Great Peace amongst men. Such a peace demandeth that the Great Powers should resolve, for the sake of the tranquillity of the peoples of the earth, to be fully reconciled among themselves. Should any king take up arms against another, all should unitedly arise and prevent him.' (Bahá'u'lláh, *Gleanings*, p. 249) 'Abdu'l-Bahá elaborated on this statement: 'True civilization will unfurl its banner in the midmost heart of the world whenever a certain number of its distinguished and high-minded sovereigns – the shining exemplars of devotion and determination – shall, for the good and happiness of all mankind, arise, with firm resolve and clear vision, to establish the Cause of Universal Peace. They must make the Cause of Peace the object of general consultation, and seek by every means in their power to establish a Union of the nations of the world. They must conclude a binding treaty and establish a covenant, the

provisions of which shall be sound, inviolable and definite. They must proclaim it to all the world and obtain for it the sanction of all the human race. This supreme and noble undertaking – the real source of peace and well-being of all the world – should be regarded as sacred by all that dwell on earth. All the forces of humanity must be mobilized to ensure the stability and permanence of this Most Great Covenant. In this all-embracing Pact the limits and frontiers of each and every nation should be clearly fixed, the principles underlying the relations of governments towards one another definitely laid down, and all international agreements and obligations ascertained . . . The fundamental principle underlying this solemn Pact should be so fixed that if any government later violate any one of its provisions, all the governments on earth should arise to reduce it to utter submission, nay the human race as a whole should resolve, with every power at its disposal, to destroy that government.' ('Abdu'l-Bahá, *Secret of Divine Civilization*, pp. 64–5)

40. An evidence of this can be seen in Europe, with the development of the European Economic Community, the Single European Market and the Euro, the new single European currency.
41. Shoghi Effendi, *World Order*, p. 203.
42. ibid. p. 204.
43. ibid.

9

Globalization and Its Conflicts[1]

Charles O. Lerche

Because of the great increase in the traffic in culture, the large-scale transfer of meaning systems and symbolic forms, the world is increasingly becoming one not only in political and economic terms . . . but in terms of its cultural construction as well; a global ecumene of persistent cultural interaction and exchange. This, however, is no egalitarian global village.[2]

The negative effects of globalization can be softened only through new and higher levels of international cooperation and consultation, filtered through a new system of moral values that puts human welfare and social justice ahead of the predominantly materialistic paradigm currently in vogue.[3]

Introduction

The pace of global change is extremely rapid and even those trained to track and analyse it have difficulty keeping up with new developments. However, trends are regularly observed and named and these new terms become 'buzz words' in the lexicons of governments, academia and the media. Such a term is 'globalization'. Though it is, admittedly, rather vague and the phenomena it is employed to describe extremely diverse, it does express a prevailing sentiment that our lives are increasingly influenced by forces that have transcended borders and which, precisely because of their scope and power, are changing irreversibly life on this planet. All levels of society are being reshaped by this process: the individual may find her/his livelihood threatened or identity thrown into question; localities and whole regions are obliged to recreate themselves or die in the face of new economic forces; and nation states themselves experience steadily decreasing freedom of action and ever closer ties to each other.

The world Bahá'í community sees in the emergence of a truly global society unmistakable signs of the fulfilment of Bahá'u-'lláh's prophecy that humankind would be united under the influence of His revelation. More precisely, the Bahá'í writings explain that the current trend towards increasing international cooperation is a sign of the emergence of what Bahá'u'lláh called the Lesser Peace:[4] a primarily political 'unity of nations',[5] involving, among other things, decreasing arms expenditures and the application of the principle of collective security to threats to international peace. At the moment, however, globalization is fully under way but existing global institutions do not yet have sufficient power, authority and scope to effectively regulate and direct this process towards beneficial ends. The result is that globalization is turbulent, often highly inequitable in its effects and all too often violent and destructive.

Many analysts have pointed to the turbulent nature of this planetary process and to the increasing frequency and variety of reactions to it. Drawing on this literature, this paper first attempts to clarify various aspects of globalization and then considers its potential for generating social conflict and unrest. Subsequently, human needs theory, as developed and applied by John Burton, is used to explore some of the roots of these conflicts and, finally, 'globalism' is put forward as a positive, and potentially corrective, dimension of globalization. Beyond this, we will argue that many social and spiritual principles necessary to moderate and channel accelerating globalization can be found in the Bahá'í teachings generally and, more specifically, in their contemporary application to global issues by the Bahá'í International Community.

Globalization: A Closer Look

Definitions

There are a variety of definitions and descriptions of globalization which, though overlapping in many respects, bring out different dimensions of the process. Robertson's is one of the first and the most general:

> Globalization as a concept refers both to the compression of the world and intensification of consciousness of the world as a whole . . . both concrete global interdependence and consciousness of the global whole in the twentieth century.[6]

Anthony Giddens adds another dimension by emphasizing the interactive, or dialectical, dimensions of the concept:

> Globalization can . . . be defined as the intensification of worldwide social relations which link distant localities in such a way that local happenings are shaped by events occurring many miles away and vice versa. This is a dialectical process because such local happenings may move in an obverse direction from the very distanciated relations that shape them. Local transformation is as much a part of globalization as the lateral extension of social connections across time and space.[7]

However, it is in regard to business and economics that the term 'globalization' is most frequently invoked. What is referred to here is 'a qualitative shift toward a global economic system that is no longer based on autonomous national economies but on a consolidated global marketplace for production, distribution, and consumption'[8] and in which 'distinct national economies are subsumed and rearticulated into the system by essentially international processes and transactions'.[9] The primary vehicles for this process have been the increasing trans-nationalization of production and the resulting rise in influence of multinational enterprises and, even more importantly, the explosion in the volume and scope of transactions on international financial markets. And one of its most often noted effects is the homogenization of consumer markets around the world, at least in certain areas – the so-called 'McDonaldization' of global consumption.

Critiques

Though often touted as representing the height of economic rationality, globalization has also been portrayed as having a very dark side. Critics repeatedly point out that the contemporary form of globalization,[10] driven by economic power, clearly promotes the hegemony of western culture and corporations, puts jobs and communities at risk in the rich countries and exploits cheap labour in the poorer countries, increases threats to the environment and undermines the foundations of democracy and social stability by subjecting national political institutions to forces of economic change beyond their control. Furthermore, as a volume of essays on the subject[11] has highlighted, globalization is *uneven* both in its processes and in its effects. It produces concentrations and deprivations which, in the aggregate, constitute an increasingly well-defined global power structure. Claude Ake, a leading African critical thinker, has argued in this regard that:

> Economic forces are constituting the world into one economy and, to a lesser extent, one political society. Nations participate in global governance according to their economic power, which is coextensive with their rights. The global order is ruled by an informal cabinet of the world's economically most powerful countries; its law is the logic of the market, and status in this new order is a function of economic performance.[12]

Critics also argue that there is a neo-liberal ideology of globalization which serves to 'normalize' the process: to make it seem natural, inevitable and beneficial. Thus while it is clearly in the particular interests of large multinational and global corporations to be free to move money, factories and goods around the planet seeking access to the cheapest factors of production, the most congenial regulatory environments and the most lucrative markets, the ideology of globalization promotes the belief that the interests of humanity and even of the earth itself will also be best served if world markets are 'left unfettered by ethical, moral, social, or environmental considerations'.[13]

In an analysis of the North American Trade Association as a case study of both the ideology and practice of globalization, economist Robert MacEwan presents data from the United States and Mexico to substantiate what he calls the 'social failures' which are produced by the trade pact: greater income inequality, environmental damage and the decline of democratic control:

> Greater income inequality is not the only social failure generated by the success of globalization generally and by NAFTA particularly. Environmental destruction is surely exacerbated with the success of globalization. The greater mobility of capital makes it more and more difficult for citizens of any one political unit to organize and use their government to impose regulations on polluting firms.[14]

Finally, he argues that globalization has a negative impact on the quality of politics and public life by placing restrictions on governments' powers to intervene in their own economies and thereby 'limiting people's power to exercise political control over their economic lives'.[15]

Though one should not necessarily take all this criticism at face value, it does indicate what can go wrong as corporations and capital have acquired the means to move and operate on a much broader scale. Furthermore, it conveys a sense of alarm that the nation state as an institutional structure cannot cope effectively with these new developments and, in fact, finds its own priorities and policies heavily influenced, if not dictated, by them.[16] The question then arises: who will articulate and defend the *public* interest against the global reach of *private* financial and commercial interests when the latter go too far? For instance, all but the most *laissez-faire* of economic thinking argues that governments must intervene to protect the public when markets fail, i.e. when they are no longer free and competitive. However, efforts to implement such a strategy at the global level, through various multilateral and international institutions, have achieved little. Consequently, world markets have become increasingly concentrated in major sectors. Furthermore, while there is a case to be made for reducing expensive and inefficient government regulatory structures, the lack of adequate regulatory standards applying across borders does provide an incentive for multinational firms to choose less-regulated operating environments and involves countries seeking foreign investment in a 'race for the bottom' – competition to see who can provide the most free, understood as the least regulated, business environment. In summary, there does appear to be at least 'a kernel of truth' in the negative characterization of globalization and this judgement becomes even more plausible when globalization is evaluated as an engine of social conflict.

Globalization and Conflict

Though the previous discussion is suggestive, the link between globalization and conflict requires further explication. Much of the literature distinguishes between conflicts which focus on issues of culture and identity and others which appear to be primarily economic; and the discussion that follows adopts this approach while acknowledging that in practice the two categories are interrelated. Conflicts of worldviews and interests should not, however, be seen as inherently threatening or negative. Indeed many of the tensions of social change are largely unavoidable and some are undoubtedly creative in their effects. At the same time, however, the analysis that follows suggests that if the human needs and rights issues involved are not adequately addressed, the incidence and intensity of conflict associated with globalization are likely to increase steadily in the years ahead.

The Pace and Scope of Change

Social change, in and of itself, has historically been associated with increasing levels of conflict. This has been explored in great depth by P. A. Sorokin in volume 3 of his classic *Social and Cultural Dynamics*, entitled *Fluctuations of Social Relationship, War and Revolution.*[17] His study of 12 European countries and empires over the period 500 BC to 1925 AD showed that the magnitude of what he called 'social strife' was at its highest during periods when a given society was undergoing a great change of worldview – for instance from a religious, other-worldly, outlook to a more secular and materialist perspective. Such periods of change are, by definition, transitional and are characterized by conflicts of values and interests, which have become widespread and violent.

One of the few points of agreement among globalization commentators as diverse as Richard Barnet[18] and Ruud Lubbers[19] is that in spreading and accelerating globalization is generating change on an unprecedented scale. Therefore, generalizing Sorokin's findings to the world as a whole, there may be grounds to conclude that the process of globalization is inherently disruptive and that an increasing incidence of conflict is an inevitable by-product of it. Following Arnold Toynbee,[20] it could be further argued that the conflicts generated by globalization represent a significant early challenge to what he himself saw as an emerging world civilization[21] whose future will be greatly influenced by how these divisive issues are approached and dealt with in the years ahead.

The Paradox of Reflexivity

Several analysts have argued that one of the characteristics of *modernity* is increased *reflexivity*, which, in turn, contributes to the incidence of social conflict. Consider this passage from Waters:

> Modern society is . . . specifically reflexive in character. Social activity is constantly informed by flows of information and analysis which subject it to continuous revision and thereby constitute and reproduce it . . . The particular difficulty faced by moderns is that this knowledge itself is constantly changing so that living in a modern society appears to be uncontrolled, like being aboard a careening juggernaut . . .[22]

Anthony Giddens states that the industrial nation state is the embodiment of 'modern' society and that it has been characterized by what he calls 'expert systems': repositories of technical knowledge that can be deployed across a wide range of social contexts. These expert systems have, for instance, given rise to a technocratic style of civil administration. However, this dimension of modernity rests on the trust which, in the face of multiple risks and uncertainty, individual people – 'citizens', 'consumers', 'clients', 'passengers' or 'patients', depending on the context – place in these rather abstract and socially distant expert systems. Growing reflexivity is undermining trust in expert systems around the globe. In regard to more and more issues there is a feeling that experts have either failed or do not have the public interest at heart. Spybey, for instance, describes how in 'late modern society' there is a 'growing refusal of people to accept expert assurances about its dangers'.[23] He goes on to state:

> If, in the nineteenth century, those people who understood it and had access to its benefits rejoiced in the bounty of modernity and its scientific-technological wonders, the people of late modernity are cultured to expect mass consumption but are increasingly sufficiently well informed to develop doubts about its benefits. This *is* self-reflexivity and it is stimulated by negative experiences shared on a global scale, like for instance the Chernobyl disaster. It is individualism, enabled by mass education and encouraged by post-1960s permissiveness and self-awareness.[24]

In a similar vein, James Rosenau has written at length about what he calls the 'global authority crisis' and his analysis provides insight into the nature and scope of political conflict in a world of globalized 'postinternational politics'. He explains that as a result of greatly increased access to information and a general impression of the diminished competence or declining effectiveness of public institutions, citizens have lost their habit of obeying. If leaders are not able to find more effective means to gather support, people 'begin to consider redirecting their loyalties and legitimacy sentiments'.[25] He goes on to illustrate how crises of this kind interact and 'cascade' around the planet:

> The world is now so interdependent that 'crisis networks' evolve, as information about a crisis in one collectivity flows to others, and as

> its consequences ramify. By virtue of the information flows and of the interaction engendered by refugees, traders, terrorists, and other boundary-spanning individuals and groups, authority crises overlap and cascade across collectivities, forming linkages among them on an issue or regional basis.[26]

Giddens and Rosenau describe a world in which people are more aware and to some extent more empowered by their access to information and their increased ability to analyse the events shaping their lives. In this picture, populations have become less compliant and more demanding at precisely the time when national political institutions, as described below, are in many cases reducing their budgets and programmes. The intersection of these trends sets the stage for intensified competition between groups who benefit from the state's protection and those who seek more freedom from state intervention.

But reflexivity, while aided and stimulated by globalized media and information technology, is also threatened by these same forces. Increasingly powerful media giants diffuse the ideology of globalization, with the effect that:

> The values of Globalization, transmitted through satellite television and the distribution of worldwide publications, permeate everyone's life. Global marketing, international stock markets, and the availability of nomadic worldwide venture capital complete the scene for the rise of a global market value system. No culture is protected by topography, tradition or just plain disinterest – essentially nobody is out of reach of the extended arm of Globalization.[27]

Thus globalization both enlightens and pacifies, both widens horizons and narrows vision. However, it does seem that the globalization narrative of the media is vulnerable to increasing cognitive dissonance as its utopian image of widening prosperity is subverted by images of deprivation and marginalization and by a rising tide of insecurity and anxiety.

Globalization and Identity

Another paradoxical effect of intensifying globalization, is that while it seeks to homogenize, it also increases awareness of social *heterogeneity*. Groups whose identity and solidarity is based on race, ethnicity, religion or language have become increasingly vocal and have used the global media to make their discontent known. This contemporary ethnic revival was to some degree unleashed by the end of the cold war. The cold war was a conflict among states and served to perpetuate the primacy of national identity in world society but in the 1990s the state, weakened by globalization, became less effective in either coercing compliance or integrating national society and minorities were able to more effectively reassert their identity in reaction to hegemonic cultural forces. These minorities often see the state as no longer a promoter and protector of domestic interests but rather as a collaborator with outside forces.[28] Thus it can be argued that the primary locus of conflict may no longer be found between and among states but between the state and sub-national groups.[29] The overall effect of these developments has been to increase the salience of cultural diversity issues, both within and across borders, for all the major participants in world politics.

Several prominent political analysts have argued variations on this theme. Samuel Huntington, for instance, put forward inter-civilizational conflict as the new 'danger' to the dominant powers in world affairs, stating that 'the efforts of the West to promote its values of democracy and liberalism as universal values, to maintain its military predominance and to advance its economic interests engender countering responses from other civilizations';[30] and he did not hesitate to take his argument to its logical conclusion, predicting that: 'The next world war, if there is one, will be a war between civilizations.'[31] The controversy and rebuttals provoked by Huntington's work are not of immediate concern here; however, his argument does provide important insights into some prominent conflicts of globalization. Globalization in its contemporary form is the carrier of values which are essentially western and liberal in character but they are being aggressively promoted internationally as universal values, the inherent worth of which should be obvious to all right-thinking people. This is the perspective behind such notions as Francis Fukuyama's (1992) 'end of history' thesis[32] or the standard package of liberal economic reforms prescribed for all struggling economies by the International Monetary Fund.[33] Huntington was explicit about debunking the globalization myth that world culture is western culture and argues further that:

> Western efforts to propagate such ideas produce instead a reaction against 'human rights imperialism' and a reaffirmation of indigenous values, as can be seen in the support for religious fundamentalism by the younger generation in non-Western cultures.[34]

Writing a few years later on a similar theme, Graham Fuller, a political scientist at the Rand Corporation, traced further the dynamics of 'culture conflict', explaining how non-western peoples are confronted with a flood of evidence that someone else's values are re-shaping their societies as:

> . . . systems of international marketing and communications create freeways for the mass import of foreign cultural materials – food, drugs, clothing, music, films, books, television programmes, even values – with the concomitant loss of control over societies, symbols and myths. Such cultural anxieties are welcome fuel to more radical political groups that call for cultural authenticity, preservation of traditional and religious values, and rejection of the alien cultural antigens. Big Macs become in-your-face symbols of American power – political, economic, and military – over weak or hesitant societies and states.[35]

Fuller also argues that, on a shrinking planet, the west cannot escape the secondary effects of these conflicts:

> Chaos and turmoil in various regions create serious ripple effects that will not leave the rest of the globe untouched: Wars, refugees, embargoes, sanctions, weapons of mass destruction, radical

> ideology, and terrorism all emerge from the crucible of the failing state order . . . The West will not be able to quarantine less-developed states and their problems indefinitely, any more than states can indefinitely quarantine the dispossessed within their own societies – on practical as well as moral grounds.[36]

Fundamentalisms of various kinds are prominent in the conflicts of 'cultural reaction'. Traditional identity groups in non-western societies were already put on the defensive during the modernization of their societies as western institutions and values were introduced through state-building. They feel even more threatened now as their national institutions are undermined by the international pressures described earlier. Both the pace and direction of change in these societies 'accelerates the search for a single, often mythologized truth that can reference all social mores and practices'[37] and fosters that kind of fundamentalist religious and ethnic movement which is a 'value-oriented, anti-modern, dedifferentiating form of collective action – a socio-cultural movement aimed at reorganizing all spheres of life in terms of a particular set of absolute values'.[38] Globalization thus sets the stage for the confrontation between what Benjamin Barber called 'McWorld' and 'Jihad'. Though covering much of the same ground in his analysis as Huntington and Fuller, Barber went further to show how neither globalizing commercialism nor parochial solidarity bodes well for democracy and he trenchantly critiques the role of religion as a contributing cause to conflict, characterizing contemporary fundamentalist movements as:

> . . . parochial rather than cosmopolitan, angry rather than loving, proselytizing rather than ecumenical, zealous rather than rationalist, sectarian rather than deistic, ethnocentric rather than universalizing . . . fractious and pulverizing, never integrating.[39]

These passages suggest that globalization is pulling virtually all identity groups on the planet out of their various degrees of isolation, pushing them into the currents of the global *ecumene* and, thereby, obliging them to redefine, or as Robertson and others put it, 'relativize' themselves in regard to global trends. Relativization, however, is a process which may involve *either* rejection *or* some form of accommodation, integration or synthesis with the hegemonic cultural and economic forces. Thus a more nuanced picture would show that instead of the steady expansion of western cultural dominance what we are really witnessing is a:

> . . . contested and undecided . . . encounter between global cultural flows and inherited local identities . . . the uneasy balance between the persistence of unique local cultural identities and the reshaping of such uniqueness by totalizing transnational cultural influences ranging from Coca-Colarization to the universalization of western ideological and political concepts.[40]

Though in some respects a more optimistic scenario for the emergence of world culture, this juxtaposition of cultural forces produces just the mix of tensions which Sorokin identified as characteristic of periods of high social strife; a situation exacerbated by changes in the global economic system.

A Changing World Economy

As mentioned earlier, the economic dimensions of globalization have attracted the most popular attention, much of which has been negative owing to the frequency and variety of conflicts for which the process is blamed. The economic realm is also an area in which it can be argued that conflict has led to some creative responses from the international community.

First, it should be acknowledged that, as Austrian economist Joseph Schumpeter argued, capitalism inevitably involves a process of 'creative destruction'.[41] Competition stimulates firms to innovate, both in products and in production, in order to outdo their rivals. However, entire industries and regions can be 'destroyed', or at least marginalized, as more innovative competitors take the lead in a given sector. This is demonstrated, for instance, by the change from the horse and cart to the automobile or from canals to railways. The liberal argument has always been that, despite the rather Darwinian way this process produces 'winners' and 'losers', society as a whole benefits from constant improvement in the quality and range of goods and services available to consumers. In this sense economic globalization is viewed as the logical extension of this process to an increasingly unified global market.

However, as MacEwan has forcefully stated:

> Losers . . . are not simply impersonal firms or abstract inefficient technologies. In the real world, losers are people, sometimes capitalists, but always workers, individually and as communities. *Creative destruction means the unemployment of real workers, the destitution of real communities, devastation of the environment, and disempowerment of the populace.*[42]

This has, in a sense, always been the case since capitalism replaced feudalism as the dominant system of production. But the contemporary period is also characterized by a reduction in both the willingness and ability of governments to keep employment high through public expenditure or to pay the unemployment and welfare benefits which, to some degree, protected workers in the industrial countries from the creative destruction of capitalism during the decades immediately after World War Two. Rather, the increasing importance of international finance capital in the world economy has compelled governments to be much more concerned about the 'investment climates' in their countries and to insure that financial markets 'approve' of their macroeconomic policies.

Put very simply, globalization has radically shifted the balance of economic power in favour of capital, which is highly mobile and thus able to move where profits are to be gained, and against labour, which is much less mobile (even in an economic community like the European Union) and whose basis of organization is still more national than international. As Ethan Kapstein has argued:

> The forces acting on today's workers inhere in the structure of today's global economy, with its open and increasingly fierce competition on the one hand and fiscally conservative units – states – on the other . . . Growing income inequality, job insecurity, and unemployment are seen as the flip side of globalization.[43]

Kapstein and MacEwan are writing primarily about the industrialized countries but the situation of those former 'Third World' countries who cannot find a place in the new world economy is even more grave, as depicted by Castells:

> . . . with the absolute costs of labour becoming less and less important as a competitive factor (versus low labour costs relative to a certain level of technological sophistication and economic integration in the world economy), many countries and regions face a process of rapid deterioration that could lead to destructive reactions. Within the framework of a new informational economy, *a significant part of the world population is shifting from a structural position of exploitation to a structural position of irrelevance.*[44]

He goes on to describe what form these 'destructive reactions' might take:

> . . . first . . . is to establish new linkages with the world economy via the criminal economy[45] . . . A second reaction is the expression of utter desperation through that widespread violence, either individual or collective, which has transformed major cities in the Fourth World (and entire regions in some countries) into savage, self-destructive battlegrounds . . . A third reaction, rapidly developing in the Fourth World . . . is the rise of ideological/religious fundamentalism, easily associated with terrorism and/or semireligious war.[46]

In his third point, Castells links the cultural reaction discussed earlier to the deteriorating economic conditions of what he calls 'Fourth World' societies. He suggests that movements of reaction – whether ethnic, fundamentalist or Marxist – have in common a wish to:

> . . . cut all bridges with the 'the Other' (i.e. the developed world and its logic in the developing world), since there is little chance that the excluded can ever become true partners in *a system that is so extraordinarily inclusive of economies and somewhat exclusive of societies.*[47]

Significantly, social deterioration and reaction are not confined to the Third/Fourth World, as Steve Hellinger, Executive Director of The Development GAP organization, pointed out:

> What has been the reality across the Third World for more than a decade is now coming home to roost. Declining incomes, growing inequalities, job insecurity, drugs, crime – these are the forces that are tearing at the social fabric of communities across the Northern hemisphere.[48]

Furthermore, both Hellinger and Kapstein argue that such conditions have been fertile ground for demagoguery in the United States, Europe (both western and eastern) and the former Soviet Union. As Kapstein puts it:

> It is hardly sensationalist to claim that in the absence of broad-based policies and programmes designed to help working people, the political debate in the United States and many other countries will soon turn sour. Populists and demagogues of various stripes will find 'solutions' to contemporary economic problems in protectionism and xenophobia.[49]

These domestic tensions also contribute to conflicts among states. Domestic manufacturers threatened by free trade frequently lobby their governments for legal protection from foreign competition. When they succeed, though some element of domestic political support is gained by the national leadership, relations with the state(s) whose exports are restricted necessarily suffers. Or states (such as the USA) which have fairly open markets for a variety of industrial imports pressure other states which are perceived as not as reciprocally open (such as Japan), for 'fairer' trading arrangements – with the threat of retaliation never very far in the background. The accelerated creation and expansion of regional trading blocs reflects the same tensions between a need to increase free trade and a concern to safeguard traditional economic activities from overseas competition by guaranteeing regional producers an expanded market.

Despite the fact that global free trade is far from an accomplished fact, there is nonetheless evidence that many governments have understood the need to avoid a return to the type of extreme economic nationalism and 'beggar thy neighbour' policies often portrayed as having contributed to the onset of World War Two. This explains why international economic relations are characterized by an institutional structure which is more comprehensive than anything yet existing in the political realm. In this regard, the International Monetary Fund and the World Bank were joined in the 1990s by the even more supranational World Trade Organization, which has a well-developed dispute settlement mechanism and the authority to impose substantial penalties on those member states which flout its decisions. These developments demonstrate that in regard to a wide range of economic matters, many of the world's political and economic elites have concluded that the benefits of submitting to these organizations outweigh the benefits of a more independent policy.

Such advances in global collective action could be seen as harbingers of similar initiatives in other areas. However, Rosenau's 'global authority crisis' should be kept in mind. The average people around the world feel they have suffered from economic globalization and they are increasingly doubtful about the wisdom and motivation behind many contemporary international 'trade deals'. It is hardly surprising, therefore, that the promotion of further free trade has become a divisive political issue. For instance, several years ago a poll by the Bank of Boston showed that 51 per cent of US citizens believed free trade pacts cost US jobs and 57 per cent opposed any new trade agreements with Latin America. Furthermore, 73 per cent wanted labour and environmental issues included in negotiations for any new trade agreements.[50]

Other events have shown that this scepticism is shared in other parts of the world. Consider the following examples:

- The Zapatista uprising in the Chiapas region of rapidly liberalizing Mexico which since January 1994 has been demanding land and social justice for the mainly Mayan, and largely disenfranchised, Indian peasants of the area[51]

- The competing agendas of governments and NGOs at every major United Nations conference
- The protests and demonstrations by a great variety of groups at almost every major, formal or informal economic summit – christened by the media the 'anti-globalization movement'.

These few examples highlight a point made by Roland Robertson when he argued that the world is already *united* but is not *integrated*.[52] On the one hand, problems and topical concerns are expressed in global terms[53] while, on the other, approaches to their solution tend to be piecemeal, halting and generally inhibited by diverging conceptions of identity and interest.[54] All of which suggests that a world society becoming more and more interconnected physically while lacking a consensus on fundamental values and priorities may well be torn by conflicts 'more intractable than the previous disputes between nations'.[55]

Analysing the Conflicts: Burton and Human Needs

As we have seen, globalization seems to be both creative and destructive but distinguishing its positive from its negative effects is a demanding and controversial exercise. One conceptual framework that provides insight into this problem is human needs theory as applied by John Burton to the study of social conflict. Burton explains that in analysing conflict one must distinguish among 'needs', 'values' and 'interests'. In trying to resolve disputes it should be understood that only interests are negotiable in the short run while values can only change over the long run in an atmosphere of security and non-discrimination, and needs cannot be negotiated away under any circumstances.[56] The implications of this formulation are far-reaching. For instance, it suggests 'that there are limits to the extent to which the human person, acting separately or within a wider ethnic or national community, can be socialized or manipulated' and 'that there are human development needs that must be satisfied and catered for by institutions, if these institutions are to be stable, and if societies are to be significantly free of conflict'.[57]

While acknowledging that there is still only limited consensus in this research area, Burton does present a plausible list of needs. First, human beings require a sense of 'security' and of 'identity'. Second, since we have a generic drive to learn, we require a 'consistent response from the environment', without which learning is impossible. Third, from their social context people require both 'recognition' and 'valued relationships', or 'bonding'. Finally, and perhaps most importantly, individuals require (some) 'control' over their environments in order to insure that their needs are fulfilled.[58]

This approach has important implications for social institutions. If, on balance, needs, whatever they are determined to be, are being met within an institution, the institution receives support and is consolidated and perpetuated. If, however, needs are not met, the institution loses support and legitimacy and confronts increasing opposition. In the latter case, authorities tend to react with repression and coercion but if an institution is 'de-legitimated' for enough people, conflict cannot be resolved this way. Rather, the institutional structures have to evolve, sooner or later, to more fully accommodate the needs of the people they affect. If a particular social order is only legitimized for a portion of the society, one would expect that, given enabling conditions, those whose needs are not met would react. Burton goes so far as to assert that this has become the general condition in modern societies, arguing that:

> Human needs are being frustrated on a large scale in all modern societies, and the more law and order is enforced to control frustration the more the frustration. There is now a widespread concern regarding the legitimacy of even the most seemingly legitimized authorities. The members of protest movements of many kinds in many different societies, and the terrorists who spring from relatively privileged classes, are demonstrating that there are features of societies, of all political types, unacceptable to a significant number of the people that comprise them.[59]

He also explains how this leads to various forms of deviant behaviour because 'deprivation frequently leads to overreaction, and the individual goes beyond the normal pursuit of needs satisfaction', an overreaction which may find an outlet in extremism of one form or another.[60]

This conceptual framework does highlight various aspects of the conflicts of globalization. First, we can see that all three types of conflict 'stakes' – i.e. needs, values and interests – come into play. However, as Burton himself explains, in any given conflict, such as a strike over better working conditions, one has to consider the possibility that it is really caused by a more general deprivation of basic needs (perhaps recognition, valued relationships or control) which will eventually have to be addressed if further disruptions of production are to be avoided. Second, as we have seen, there are signs that many of the contemporary effects of economic and cultural globalization are not considered legitimate by an increasing number and variety of populist groups all over the world. If the means to the fulfilment of basic needs are seen to be eroded by processes of globalization, reaction, rejection and increasing hostility are to be expected. Thus, in the global south, globalization has weakened the state as a barrier to western economic and cultural domination, creating an even more acute sense of vulnerability, and in the north a popular perception of economic globalization as a threat to community (i.e. valued relationships and identity) and economic security has increased receptivity to xenophobic and protectionist extremism.

In summary, Burton's work indicates that, ideology aside, globalization cannot continue indefinitely in its contemporary form. Either processes of national and global governance will evolve to better accommodate the basic needs and values of those groups now mobilizing against current patterns of change or the frequency and intensity of disruption and reaction will continue to accelerate with unpredictable, but decidedly negative, short to medium run effects. Both scenarios indicate that the only constant is change.

Making 'Sense' of Globalization

'Explanation' can be defined as putting something in a context where it makes sense[61] but specifying such a context for globalization is rather challenging. Rival explanations furnished by groups, states and institutions have been generated by the conflictual relations among them and have, in turn, contributed further to misunderstanding and a 'dialogue of the deaf'. There is, however, more common ground in this debate than is apparent at first glance. All parties (whether north or south, governmental or non-governmental, left or right) acknowledge:

- that the pace of global change is quickening
- that this change puts great stress on individuals, social institutions (like the family) and governments;
- that something must be done to help individuals and societies adjust to change

and, most importantly,

- that measures taken so far have not provided an adequate solution to the perceived problems.

These points indicate a need for new thinking about old questions and one can see that globalization issues are world order issues. As the existing institutions of international politics and society have confronted these issues, basic questions of political philosophy having to do with power, authority and distributive justice – resolved, one way or another, for the nation state in the 18th and 19th centuries – are increasingly being raised again but this time in regard to the planet as a single political, social and economic system. However, while most dispassionate analysis of the 'global agenda' calls for closer international cooperation, leadership adequate to the necessary tasks has not yet emerged. The Commission on Global Governance put the matter this way:

> As the world faces the need for enlightened responses to the challenges that arise on the eve of the new century, we are concerned at the lack of leadership over a wide spectrum of human affairs. At national, regional, and international levels,

> within communities and in international organizations, in governments and in non-governmental bodies, the world needs credible and sustained leadership.
>
> It needs leadership that is proactive, not simply reactive, that is inspired, not simply functional, that looks to the longer term and future generations for whom the present is held in trust. It needs leaders made strong by vision, sustained by ethics, and revealed by political courage that looks beyond the next election.
>
> This cannot be leadership confined within domestic walls. It must reach beyond country, race, religion, culture, language, life-style. It must embrace a wider human constituency, be infused with a sense of caring for others, a sense of responsibility to the global neighbourhood.[62]

In this regard a clarifying distinction can be made between globalization and 'globalism'. Mark Ritchie argues that since the two terms sound very similar, there is a tendency to conflate their meaning but in many respects they are opposites. He contrasts his definition of globalization, cited above, with globalism, defined as:

> . . . the belief that we share one fragile planet whose survival requires mutual respect and careful treatment of all its people and its environment. Globalism is also a set of values and ethical beliefs requiring active practice in our day-to-day lives. Active communications to foster understanding, the sharing of resources on the basis of equity and sustainability, and mutual aid in times of need are three central activities that undergird globalism.[63]

He further makes the case that: 'Globalization is both creating massive problems (ozone depletion, climate instability, mass migration, etc.) and destroying our ability to cooperate across boundaries and borders to address these very problems' and declares that:

> Globalism – the belief that the well-being of each and every neighbour, no matter how far away, affects us all – is the only way to combat the assault of globalization . . . the only weapon we still

> have for tackling the level of ecological and social dislocation caused by unbridled globalization, especially the political violence of war and the personal violence of crime, racism and xenophobia.[64]

Globalism, through a vision of the global commons and a respect for cultural diversity, can counter what Ritchie sees as globalization's unbridled exploitation of resources and 'standardization or homogenization of almost everything and everybody'.[65] He also argues that:

> In the case of inter-tribal, ethnic and religious wars a sense of globalism can reduce the xenophobia and chauvinism that bring on these wars. Globalism is also needed in order to encourage others far away from these conflicts to get involved and to share their resources to help resolve them.[66]

Finally, according to Ritchie, the longer a creative response to the negative trends of globalization is delayed, the more difficult it becomes:

> As globalization causes greater poverty and hunger, it fuels involuntary emigration, which in turn may result in racism and fear of immigrants. In this way, globalization destroys the feelings of globalism, love and concern with neighbours around the planet, while creating the economic and ecological conditions that cry out for more, not less, globalism.
>
> My fear is that if we do not challenge globalization it will not only destroy the ecology and the society but it will also engender so much resentment, greed, and violence that we will no longer have the ability as a people to work together to tackle global problems.[67]

Where does one find such an ethically grounded globalist perspective? We would suggest that though calculations based on expedience and enlightened self-interest reveal the need for a far-reaching creative response, they do not inspire leaders or citizens with the conviction necessary to actually make the changes.

Furthermore, the older religious traditions which fulfilled such a role for particular historical civilizations are now, as we have written elsewhere, 'too frequently identified with just those aspects of the past that contribute to current division and conflict';[68] rather, 'spiritual values for the present and future cannot be partisan; they must speak to the universal human need for transcendence, unity, and justice'.[69]

This is where the Bahá'í Faith makes a unique contribution. The Bahá'í teachings provide one context in which globalization can be seen to 'make sense'. Over one hundred years ago Bahá'u'lláh declared that the human race had come of age and was embarking on a new, divinely-ordained, stage in its collective evolution which would witness the gradual emergence and fruition of a fully-integrated, truly planetary civilization. He also stated unequivocally that the 'prevailing order' was 'lamentably defective',[70] that it would 'soon' be 'rolled up, and a new one spread out in its stead'.[71] Furthermore, the Bahá'í teachings reflect an unequivocally globalist perspective. These two brief citations from Bahá'u'lláh are indicative of this theme:

> The well-being of mankind, its peace and security, are unattainable unless and until its unity is firmly established.[72]

> Of old it hath been revealed: 'Love of one's country is an element of the Faith of God.' The Tongue of Grandeur hath, however, in the day of His manifestation proclaimed: 'It is not his to boast who loveth his country, but it is his who loveth the world.' Through the power released by these exalted words He hath lent a fresh impulse and set a new direction to the birds of men's hearts . . .[73]

Consider also the following distinctly cosmopolitan passage in which 'Abdu'l-Bahá critiques the origins and excesses of nationalism:

> As to the patriotic prejudice, this is also due to absolute ignorance, for the surface of the earth is one native land . . . These boundaries and outlets have been devised by man. In the creation, such boundaries and outlets were not assigned . . . God

> has set up no frontier between France and Germany; they are continuous. Yea, in the first centuries, selfish souls, for the promotion of their own interests, have assigned boundaries and outlets and have, day by day, attached more importance to these, until this led to intense enmity, bloodshed and rapacity in subsequent centuries. In the same way this will continue indefinitely, and if this conception of patriotism remains limited within a certain circle, it will be the primary cause of the world's destruction. No wise and just person will acknowledge these imaginary distinctions.[74]

Thus to Bahá'ís there really is no 'going back': the past can no longer be a guide to the future and, rather than being at the 'end of history', far-reaching vistas of scientific, technological and cultural progress stretch out before the inhabitants of this planet.[75] This vision which inspires the world Bahá'í community with optimism about the future is combined with a profound conviction that the current era, despite its crises and tragedies, is pregnant with creative potential for positive change if courageous and altruistic endeavour is made in directions that serve the true spiritual and material interests of humankind:

> The turmoil now convulsing human affairs is unprecedented, and many of its consequences enormously destructive. Dangers unimagined in all history gather around a distracted humanity. The greatest error that the world's leadership could make at this juncture, however, would be to allow the crisis to cast doubt on the ultimate outcome of the process that is occurring. *A world is passing away and a new one is struggling to be born.* The habits, attitudes and institutions that have accumulated over the centuries are being subjected to tests that are as necessary to human development as they are inescapable. What is required of the peoples of the world is a measure of faith and resolve to match the enormous energies with which the Creator of all things has endowed this spiritual springtime of the race.[76]

This passage is taken from a statement on global prosperity in the context of the Bahá'í teachings entitled *The Prosperity of Humankind.*

In this document the Bahá'í International Community (BIC) draws on relevant Bahá'í principles to analyse major contemporary economic problems and to propose solutions. One of the first points it makes is that the Bahá'í teachings on unity and justice define a very different perspective on global change than that generally prevalent today. In numerous letters and messages during his ministry Shoghi Effendi (Guardian of the Bahá'í Faith from 1921 to 1957) explained the implications of this premise for contemporary and future world affairs. For instance, writing in 1936 he argued that:

> Unification of the whole of mankind is the hall-mark of the stage which human society is now approaching. Unity of family, of tribe, of city-state, and nation have been successively attempted and fully established. World unity is the goal towards which a harassed humanity is striving. Nation-building has come to an end. The anarchy inherent in state sovereignty is moving towards a climax. A world, growing to maturity, must abandon this fetish, recognize the oneness and wholeness of human relationships, and establish once for all the machinery that can best incarnate the fundamental principle of its life.[77]

Such an outlook on world order clearly suggests, among other things, the need for a long-term pro-active approach to the issues and crises of the moment rather than one which gives priority only to short-term problem-solving. Remedies to the 'bads' of globalization – unemployment, environmental depletion, social unrest, cultural reaction – cannot be found one by one, since they are all related. Rather they should be seen as symptoms of a more profound problem which, as indicated in our discussion of Burton, calls for a far-reaching response: the reconstruction of the planet's collective life in accord with, and to promote the fulfilment of, the basic needs of all humanity. Elaborating on this idea, the BIC argues that this is, in fact the *only* approach to conflict resolution that promises lasting results:

> Laying the groundwork for global civilization calls for the creation of laws and institutions that are universal in both character and

> authority. The effort can begin only when the concept of the oneness of humanity has been wholeheartedly embraced by those in whose hands the responsibility for decision-making rests, and when the related principles are propagated through both educational systems and the media of mass communication. Once this threshold is crossed, a process will have been set in motion through which the peoples of the world can be drawn into the task of formulating common goals and committing themselves to their attainment. Only so fundamental a reorientation can protect them, too, from the age-old demons of ethnic and religious strife. *Only through the dawning consciousness that they constitute a single people will the inhabitants of the planet be enabled to turn away from the patterns of conflict that have dominated social organization in the past and begin to learn the ways of collaboration and conciliation.*[78]

From this perspective, the widespread reaction to globalization appears as an increasingly strident cry for justice and the BIC makes a number of important observations about the central role and implications of justice for social and economic change. First, observing in a vein reminiscent of Rosenau that since populations everywhere are better informed and more critical, policy proposals of all kinds will have to meet peoples' expectations for justice. It goes on to argue that justice is essential for true economic progress because, among other things, it 'protects the task of defining progress from the temptation to sacrifice the well-being of the generality of humankind – and even of the planet itself – to the advantages which technological breakthroughs can make available to privileged minorities'[79] and, because 'In design and planning, it ensures that limited resources are not diverted to the pursuit of projects extraneous to a community's essential social or economic priorities.'[80]

In analysing the question of human rights, the BIC introduces the globalist principle of 'collective trusteeship' as a basis for analysing social obligation:

> Since the body of humankind is one and indivisible, each member of the race is born into the world as a trust of the whole. This trusteeship constitutes the moral foundation of most of the other

> rights – principally economic and social – which the instruments of the United Nations are attempting similarly to define.[81]

This trusteeship involves a number of obligations of society towards its members, among which are 'employment, mental and physical health, social security, fair wages, rest and recreation'.[82] Then, in a passage bearing directly on the cultural and identity issues discussed earlier, the BIC argues that:

> The principle of collective trusteeship creates also the right of every person to expect that those cultural conditions essential to his or her identity enjoy the protection of national and international law. Much like the role played by the gene pool in the biological life of humankind and its environment, the immense wealth of cultural diversity achieved over thousands of years is vital to the social and economic development of a human race experiencing its collective coming of age. It represents a heritage that must be permitted to bear its fruit in a global civilization. On the one hand, cultural expressions need to be protected from suffocation by the materialistic influences currently holding sway. On the other, cultures must be enabled to interact with one another in ever-changing patterns of civilization, free of manipulation for partisan political ends.[83]

Furthermore, if taken seriously as a basis for new policies, principles such as these require a new paradigm which involves 'a fundamental rethinking of economic issues'.[84] In this regard the BIC declares that:

> The classical economic models of impersonal markets in which human beings act as autonomous makers of self-regarding choices will not serve the needs of a world motivated by ideals of unity and justice. Society will find itself increasingly challenged to develop new economic models shaped by insights that arise from a sympathetic understanding of shared experience, from viewing human beings in relation to others, and from a recognition of the centrality to social well-being of the role of the family and the community.[85]

These points in turn raise obvious questions about how such principles are to be put into effect and what institutional changes would be necessary for their realization. These and related issues are addressed in a subsequent BIC statement, *Turning Point for All Nations*, prepared on the occasion of the 50th anniversary of the founding of the United Nations Organization. As an introduction to its proposals for reforming and strengthening the UN, the BIC describes the great steps forward in knowledge and consciousness and the terrible upheavals and disasters of the 20th century as representing 'twin processes – the collapse of old institutions on the one hand and the blossoming of new ways of thinking on the other' which constitute 'evidence of a single trend which has been gaining momentum during the last hundred years: the trend toward ever-increasing interdependence and integration of humanity'.[86]

Our earlier discussion showed globalization to have both creative and destructive aspects and it would seem logical to suggest that both new attitudes and new institutional arrangements are necessary to address the problems without stifling the positive energies released. This is the approach adopted by the BIC. It proposes a model of governance which goes beyond contemporary concerns about democracy, accountability or transparency:

> Governance must be guided by universal values, including an ethic of service to the common good. It will need to provide for the meaningful participation of citizens in the conceptualization, design, implementation and evaluation of programmes and policies that affect them. It should seek to enhance people's ability to manage change and should offer opportunities to increase their capacities and sense of worth. It will need to provide mechanisms for equitable access to the benefits of programmes and policies, to education and information, and to opportunities for lifelong learning. Moreover, it must help to ensure that the news media are active, vibrant and truthful.[87]

It goes on to advocate federalism as a useful long-term model for global governance because it 'has proved effective in decentralizing authority and decision-making in large, complex, and heterogeneous states, while maintaining a degree of overall unity and stability'[88] but for the immediate future it suggests that:

> . . . in accordance with the principles of decentralization . . . international institutions should be given the authority to act only on issues of international concern where states cannot act on their own or to intervene for the preservation of the rights of peoples and member states. All other matters should be relegated to national and local institutions.[89]

Finally on this note, the BIC stresses that the masses of people who will be most directly affected by the process must be actively involved in setting new goals and formulating strategies of change. Acknowledging that 'international bodies have historically remained distant from the minds and hearts of the world's people' and that 'the vast majority of people have not yet developed an affinity for institutions like the United Nations', it explains further that:

> Paradoxically, international institutions cannot develop into an effective and mature level of government and fulfil their primary objective to advance human civilization, if they do not recognize and nurture their relationship of mutual dependency with the people of the world. Such recognition would set in motion a virtuous cycle of trust and support that would accelerate the transition to a new world order.[90]

In effect, to come to grips with the challenges of the 21st century, the processes of global governance must become more transparent and more participatory.

Conclusion

In this article an effort has been made to describe the various aspects of and tensions and contradictions in the contemporary process of economic and cultural globalization. In so doing, the origins of conflicts generated by the process and some possible explanations and approaches to resolution of these conflicts have been presented. In this regard, relevant commentary on contemporary events by the BIC has been drawn upon to demonstrate how the Bahá'í teachings can serve as a source of insight and inspiration to understand and come to grips with the relevant issues.

A few concluding generalizations emerge from this discussion:

- First, the new forces reshaping planetary social life cannot be contained by mindsets and institutions inherited from the past. The peoples of the world are too demanding and too well-informed to accept authority claims of elites and institutions that do not deliver just and creative policies.

- Second, the excesses of globalization highlight the fact that there is a stark choice before the world's leadership between either unity, justice and order, or chaos, conflict and social decay. The choices are hard but alternatives are available if the conviction and altruism necessary for action can be found.

- Third, a global vision and ethic which appreciates and seeks to involve the diversity of cultures and institutions in processes of governance at all levels is a prerequisite to success in channelling globalization in positive directions.

An objective assessment of the unprecedented innovations in many fields during the 20th century, combined with a basic faith in humanity's inner spiritual capacity, permits a degree of optimism that adaptive responses to the conflicts of globalization will be found. The Bahá'í writings argue forcefully, however, that the ultimate challenge of globalization is to direct the new forces it releases towards the construction of a world civilization whose 'crowning goal' is 'the unification of all the peoples of the world in one universal family'.[91]

Bibliography

'Abdu'l-Bahá. *Selections from the Writings of 'Abdu'l-Bahá.* Haifa: Bahá'í World Centre, 1978.

Ake, Claude. 'The New World Order: A View from Africa', in Holm and Sørensen (eds.). *Whose World Order: Uneven Globalization and the End of the Cold War.* Boulder: Westview, 1995.

Bahá'í International Community. *One Country: The Online Newsletter of the Bahá'í International Community*, Volume 9, Issue 2/July–September 1997 http://www.onecountry.org/oc92/oc9209as.html

— *The Prosperity of Humankind.* London: Bahá'í Publishing Trust, 1995.

— *Turning Point for All Nations: A Statement of the Bahá'í International Community on the Occasion of the 50th Anniversary of the United Nations.* New York: Bahá'í International Community United Nations Office, 1995.

— *Valuing Spirituality in Development: Initial Considerations Regarding the Creation of Spiritually Based Indicators for Development.* London: Bahá'í Publishing Trust, 1998. A concept paper presented to the 'World Faiths and Development Dialogue' hosted by the President of the World Bank and the Archbishop of Canterbury at Lambeth Palace, London, 18–19 February 1998. <http://www.bic-un.bahai.org/98-0218.htm>

Bahá'u'lláh. *Gleanings from the Writings of Bahá'u'lláh.* Wilmette, IL: Bahá'í Publishing Trust, 1983.

— *Tablets of Bahá'u'lláh.* Wilmette, IL: Bahá'í Publishing Trust, 1988.

Barber, Benjamin R. 'Jihad v. McWorld' (published originally in the March 1992 issue of *The Atlantic Monthly*). <http://www.theAtlantic.co>. 24 November 1996, p. 6.

Barnet, R. J. and J. Cavanagh. *Global Dreams: Imperial Corporations and the New World Order.* New York: Simon and Schuster, 1994.

Burton, John. *Conflict: Resolution and Provention.* New York: St Martin's Press, 1990.

Castells, Manuel. 'The International Economy and the New International Division of Labor', in Martin Carnoy, Manuel Castells, Stephen S. Cohen and Fernando Henrique Cardoso, *The New Global Economy in the Information Age: Reflections on Our Changing World.* University Park, PA: The Pennsylvania State University Press, 1993.

Commission on Global Governance. *Our Global Neighbourhood.* New York: Oxford University Press, 1995.

Cox, Robert. *Production, Power and World Order: Social Forces in the Making of History.* New York: Columbia University Press, 1987.

Fukuyama, Francis. *The End of History and the Last Man.* New York: Free Press, 1992.

Fuller, Graham. 'The Next Ideology'. *Foreign Policy*, Spring 1995.

Giddens, Anthony. *The Consequences of Modernity.* Cambridge: Polity Press, 1990.

Gurr, T. R. 'Peoples against States: Ethnopolitical Conflict and the Changing World System'. *International Studies Quarterly*, vol. 38, September 1994.

Hannerz, Ulf. 'Scenarios for Peripheral Cultures', in Anthony D. King (ed.). *Culture, Globalization and the World System.* London: Macmillan, 1991.

Hellinger, Steve. 'Fertile Ground for Demagogues'. <LABOR-L@YORKU.CA>. 3 March 1996.

Hirst, Paul and Grahame Thompson. 'The Problem of "Globalization": International Economic Relations, National Economic Management and the Formation of Trading Blocs'. *Polity and Society*, vol. 21, no. 4, 1992.

Holm, Hans-Henrik and Georg Sørensen (eds.). *Whose World Order: Uneven Globalization and the End of the Cold War.* Boulder: Westview, 1995.

Huntington, Samuel P. 'The Clash of Civilizations?' *Foreign Affairs*, vol. 72, no. 3, Summer 1993.

Institute for Agriculture and Trade Policy. 'NAFTA & Inter-American Trade Monitor'. <trade-news@igc.apc.org> 14 November 1996.

Kapstein, Ethan B. 'Workers and the World Economy'. *Foreign Affairs*, May/June 1996.

Lechner, F. 'Fundamentalism Revisited', in T. Robbins and D. Anthony, *In Gods We Trust.* New Brunswick: Transaction, 1990.

Lights of Guidance: A Bahá'í Reference File. Compiled by Helen Hornby. New Delhi: Bahá'í Publishing Trust, 5th edn. 1997.

Lubbers, Ruud. 'The Globalization of Economy and Society'. <http://www.globalize.org/globview.htm>

MacEwan, Arthur. 'Globalization and Stagnation'. *Monthly Review*, vol. 45, April 1994.

Ritchie, Mark. 'Globalization vs. Globalism: Giving Internationalism a Bad Name'. Conference 'trade-strategy'. <trade-strategy@igc.apc.org>. 26 February 1996.

Robertson, Roland. *Globalization: Social Theory and Global Culture.* London: Sage, 1992.

Rosenau, James. *Turbulence in World Politics: A Theory of Change and Continuity*. Princeton, NJ: Princeton University Press, 1990.

Sachs, Jeffrey. 'Consolidating Capitalism'. *Foreign Policy*, Spring 1995.

Said, Abdul-Aziz, Charles O. Lerche Jr. and Charles O. Lerche III. *Concepts of International Politics in Global Perspective.* Englewood Cliffs, NJ: Prentice Hall, 4th edn. 1995.

Scholte, Jan Art. 'Constructions of Collective Identity in a Time of Globalisation'. <http://nexxus.com.cwru.edu/amjdc/papers/76>

Schumpeter, Joseph. *Capitalism, Socialism and Democracy*. New York: Harper, 1942.

Shoghi Effendi. *The World Order of Bahá'u'lláh.* Wilmette, IL: Bahá'í Publishing Trust, 1991.

Sites, Paul. *Control: The Basis of Social Order*. New York: Dunellan Co., 1973.

Sorokin, P. A. *Social and Cultural Dynamics*, vol. 3, *Fluctuations of Social Relationships, War and Revolution.* New York: American Books Co., 1937.

Spybey, Tony. *Globalization and World Society*. Cambridge: Polity Press, 1996.

Steingard, David S. and Dale E. Fitzgibbons. 'Challenging the Juggernaut of Globalization: A Manifesto for Academic Practice'. <http://nexxus.com.cwru.edu/amjdc/papers/85>. 6 April 1997.

Toynbee, Arnold. 'The Dwarfing of Europe', in Arnold Toynbee, *Civilization on Trial and the World and the West.* New York: Meridian Books, 1960.

— *A Study of History*, abridgement of volumes I–VI by D. C. Somervell. New York: Oxford University Press, 1956.

The Universal House of Justice. *The Promise of World Peace.* London: Bahá'í Publishing Trust, 1985.

Waters, Malcolm. *Globalization.* London: Routledge, 1995.

Notes

1. An earlier version of the first three sections of this paper was published as 'The Conflicts of Globalization', *International Journal of Peace Studies*, January 1998, vol. 3, no. 1, pp. 47–66.
2. Hannerz, 'Scenarios for Peripheral Cultures', p. 107.
3. Bahá'í International Community, *One Country*, vol. 9, no. 2, July–September 1997.
4. In this regard, Shoghi Effendi wrote: 'that "Lesser Peace" to which the Author of our Faith has Himself alluded in His writings. "Now that ye have refused the Most Great Peace," He, admonishing the kings and rulers of the earth, has written, "hold ye fast unto this the Lesser Peace, that haply ye may in some degree better your own condition and that of your dependents." Expatiating on this Lesser Peace, He thus addresses in that same Tablet the rulers of the earth: "Be reconciled among yourselves, that ye may need no more armaments save in a measure to safeguard your territories and dominions . . . Be united, O kings of the earth, for thereby will the tempest of discord be stilled amongst you, and your peoples find rest, if ye be of them that comprehend. Should any one among you take up arms against another, rise ye all against him, for this is naught but manifest justice."' (Shoghi Effendi, *World Order*, p. 162)
5. From a letter written on behalf of the Universal House of Justice, 31 January 1985, in *Lights of Guidance*, p. 438, no. 1430.
6. Robertson, *Globalization*, p. 9.
7. Giddens, *Consequences of Modernity*, p. 64.
8. Holm and Sørensen, 'Introduction: What has Changed', in Holm and Sørensen (eds.), *Whose World Order*, p. 5.
9. Hirst and Thompson, 'The Problem of 'Globalization'.
10. Several writers have argued that globalization has been under way for a long time. Robertson, for instance, charts its evolution from the 15th century. See Robertson, *Globalization*.
11. Holm and Sørensen, 'Introduction: What has Changed,' in Holm and Sørensen (eds.), *Whose World Order*.
12. Ake, 'The New World Order: A View from Africa', p. 26.
13. Ritchie, 'Globalization vs. Globalism: Giving Internationalism a Bad Name'.
14. MacEwan, 'Globalization and Stagnation', p. 2.
15. ibid.

16. This is what political economist Robert Cox has called the 'internationalizing of the state'. See Cox, *Production, Power and World Order*, pp. 253–65.
17. Sorokin, *Social and Cultural Dynamics*, vol. 3, *Fluctuations of Social Relationships, War and Revolution*, pp. 409–75.
18. Barnet and Cavanagh, *Global Dreams: Imperial Corporations and the New World Order.*
19. Lubbers, 'The Globalization of Economy and Society'.
20. Toynbee, *A Study of History*. Toynbee argued that the progress, stagnation or disappearance of civilizations has been a function of the sort of challenges they have faced and how they have dealt with them.
21. Toynbee, 'The Dwarfing of Europe', p. 107.
22. Waters, *Globalization*, p. 51. Emphasis added. The juggernaut image is from Giddens.
23. Spybey, *Globalization and World Society*, p. 153.
24. ibid. Emphasis in original.
25. Rosenau, *Turbulence in World Politics: A Theory of Change and Continuity*, p. 389.
26. ibid. p. 390.
27. Steingard and Fitzgibbons, 'Challenging the Juggernaut of Globalization: A Manifesto for Academic Practice'.
28. Scholte, 'Constructions of Collective Identity in a Time of Globalisation'.
29. Gurr, 'Peoples against States: Ethnopolitical Conflict and the Changing World System'.
30. Huntington, 'The Clash of Civilizations?', p. 29.
31. ibid. p. 39.
32. Fukuyama, *End of History and the Last Man*. Fukuyama argues that the spread of liberal democracy and free-market economics represents the culmination of social evolution – i.e. the end of history.
33. Jeffrey Sachs has provided the following list of 'core reforms': 1) open international trade, 2) currency convertibility, 3) private ownership as the main engine of economic growth, 4) corporate ownership as the dominant organizational form for large enterprises, 5) openness to foreign investment and 6) membership in key international economic institutions, including the International Monetary Fund (IMF), the World Bank and the new World Trade Organization (WTO). See Sachs, 'Consolidating Capitalism', p. 51.

34. Huntington, 'The Clash of Civilizations', pp. 40–1.
35. Fuller, 'The Next Ideology', p. 152.
36. ibid. p. 154.
37. Waters, *Globalization*, p. 130.
38. F. Lechner, 'Fundamentalism Revisited' in Robbins and Anthony, *In Gods We Trust,* p. 79, cited in ibid.
39. Barber, 'Jihad v. McWorld', p. 6.
40. Waters, *Globalization*, p. 130.
41. Schumpeter, *Capitalism, Socialism and Democracy*, p. 84.
42. MacEwan, 'Globalization and Stagnation', p. 3. Emphasis added.
43. Kapstein, 'Workers and the World Economy', p. 17.
44. Castells, 'The International Economy and the New International Division of Labor', in Carnoy, Castells, Cohen and Cardoso, *The New Global Economy in the Information Age*, p. 37. The declining importance of labour costs has been confirmed by the UN.
45. The types of crimes referred to include drug production and trafficking, illegal arms deals, smuggling and commerce in human beings (women and children in particular) or even in human organs for transplants in the private clinics of the north.
46. Castells, 'The International Economy and the New International Division of Labor', in Carnoy, Castells, Cohen and Cardoso, *The New Global Economy in the Information Age*, p. 38.
47. ibid. p. 39. Emphasis added.
48. Hellinger, 'Fertile Ground for Demagogues'.
49. Kapstein, 'Workers and the World Economy', p. 17.
50. Institute for Agriculture and Trade Policy, 'NAFTA & Inter-American Trade Monitor'.
51. In its early stages this confrontation was also 'globalized' by the fact that the Zapatista leader 'Commandante Martí' made extensive use of the Internet to communicate his group's views and demands.
52. Robertson, *Globalization*, referred to in Waters, *Globalization*, p. 42.
53. Waters expresses it this way: '. . . we define military-political issues in terms of a "world order"; or economic issues in terms of an "international recession"; or marketing issues in terms of "world products" (e.g. the "world-car"); or religious issues in terms of ecumenism; or citizenship issues in terms of "human rights"; or issues of pollution and purification in terms of "saving the planet".' (Waters, *Globalization*, p. 42)

54. In this regard, one often hears national leaders justifying their hesitation to take far-reaching and comprehensive action in terms of fears about 'losing sovereignty'. Strictly speaking, 'national sovereignty' is really a legal concept referring to a given national political unit's constitutional independence. In that sense it cannot be 'given up' in pieces – a political unit is either sovereign or it is not. Thus the contemporary controversy over 'loss of sovereignty' is really about control, identity and preserving political and economic advantage in the face of globalization and other challenges.
55. Waters, *Globalization*, p. 46.
56. Burton, *Conflict*, pp. 36–41.
57. ibid. p. 23.
58. ibid. pp. 47 and 95. Burton also presents a list of eight needs from Paul Sites, another leading theorist in this field: security, recognition, stimulation, distributive justice, meaning, rationality and control (p. 95). See, in this regard, Sites, *Control.* Others add such terms as 'development', 'self-realization', 'growth', 'meaning' or 'fulfilment'.
59. ibid. p. 98.
60. ibid. p. 99.
61. The author first heard this definition from the late Professor Claude Ake.
62. Commission on Global Governance, *Our Global Neighborhood*, p. 353.
63. Ritchie, 'Globalization vs. Globalism', pp. 1–2.
64. ibid. p. 2.
65. ibid.
66. ibid.
67. ibid.
68. Said, Lerche Jr. and Lerche III, *Concepts of International Politics in Global Perspective*, p. 292.
69. ibid.
70. Bahá'u'lláh, Lawḥ-i-Maqṣúd, in *Tablets,* p. 171.
71. Bahá'u'lláh, *Gleanings*, p. 7.
72. ibid. p. 286.
73. Bahá'u'lláh, *Tablets*, pp. 87–8.
74. 'Abdu'l-Bahá, *Selections*, p. 300.
75. In fact, it could be argued that the Bahá'í writings present a perspective in which humanity should be seen as currently nearer to the 'beginning' than to the 'end' of its collective history.

76. Bahá'í International Community, *Prosperity of Humankind*, pp. 33–4. Emphasis added.
77. Shoghi Effendi, letter dated 11 March 1936 addressed 'To the beloved of God and the handmaids of the Merciful throughout the West' and entitled 'The Unfoldment of Civilization', in *World Order*, p. 202.
78. Bahá'í International Community, *The Prosperity of Humankind*, p. 8. Emphasis added.
79. ibid. p. 10.
80. ibid.
81. ibid. p. 12.
82. ibid.
83. ibid. pp. 12–13.
84. ibid. p. 26.
85. ibid. pp. 26–7.
86. Bahá'í International Community, *Turning Point for All Nations*, p. 1. Predictions of the arrival and intensification of these twin processes occur frequently in the major writings of Bahá'u'lláh, 'Abdu'l-Bahá and Shoghi Effendi.
87. Bahá'í International Community, *Valuing Spirituality in Development*, p. 24.
88. Bahá'í International Community, *Turing Point for All Nations*, p. 6. In this regard the BIC cites one of Shoghi Effendi's several statements on this theme: 'Some form of a world super-state must needs be evolved, in whose favour all the nations of the world will have willingly ceded every claim to make war, certain rights to impose taxation and all rights to maintain armaments, except for purposes of maintaining internal order with their respective dominions. Such a state will have to include within its orbit an international executive adequate to enforce supreme and unchallengeable authority on every recalcitrant member of the commonwealth; a world parliament whose members shall be elected by the people in their respective countries and whose election shall be confirmed by their respective governments; and a supreme tribunal whose judgement will have a binding effect even in such cases where the parties concerned did not voluntarily agree to submit their case to its consideration.' (Letter of 28 November 1931 addressed to 'Fellow-believers in the Faith of Bahá'u'lláh' and entitled 'The Goal of a New World Order', in *World Order*, pp. 40–1)

89. ibid. p. 5.
90. ibid. pp. 13–14.
91. The Universal House of Justice, *The Promise of World Peace*, p. 23.